Shavetails
and
Bell Sharps

The History of the U.S. Army Mule

Emmett M. Essin

University of Nebraska Press

Lincoln and London

⊗

First Bison Books printing: 2000

Most recent printing indicated

by the last digit below:

10 9 8 7 6 5 4 3 2 1

Library of Congress

Cataloging-in-Publication Data

Essin, Emmett M., 1940–

Shavetails and bell sharps /

Emmett M. Essin.

p. cm.

Includes bibliographical

references (p.   ) and index.

ISBN 0-8032-1819-2 (cl: alk. paper)

ISBN 0-8032-6740-1 (pa: alk. paper)

1. Mules—United States—History.

2. United States. Army—

Transportation—History. I. Title.

UC603.E84   1997

358'.25'0973—dc21   96-45626

CIP

For Donald E. Worcester
Valued Mentor and Friend

Contents

Illustrations

Acknowledgments

In the research and writing of this book I am indebted to a host of people. Donald E. Worcester, to whom the book is dedicated, tirelessly read each chapter, offering expert advise and wise council. Robert M. Utley also encouraged me in this undertaking and read a version of the manuscript before it was submitted to the University of Nebraska Press. The chairman of the History Department at East Tennessee State University, Ronnie Day, continually made me feel a member of the department even while I have been occupied with other duties outside of history. Charles E. Rankin, editor of *Montana: The Magazine of Western History*, was most instrumental in having me pursue "my" mules. My colleagues Colin F. Baxter and Stephen G. Fritz listened to my ideas and offered worthwhile suggestions. I also value the comments and support given by history professor John R. Finger at the University of Tennessee.

Several librarians and archivists have aided me. The staff at the National Archives and the Still Picture Reference Section at Archives II have gone out of their way to provide expert assistance. The late Sara Jackson initially expedited my research at the National Archives and later referred me to Michael P. Music; both have been extremely helpful in pointing me toward important files. At East Tennessee State University by far the most important assistance came from Beth Hogan, formerly interlibrary loan and reference librarian at the Sherrod Library. She could find a needle in a haystack and did so pleasantly on numerous occasions. Also supportive were Rolly M. Harwell, Ric LaRue, and Claudette B. York. I also owe special thanks to the editorial staff at the University of Nebraska Press.

The final chapters would have been incomplete without the assistance of Eve Iversen, a one-time member of the Mule Committee, who supplied me with much needed information on the possibility of reinstituting mules into the United States Army.

Men from the World War II era who worked with and depended on mules have given me additional significant insights into the value the animals were in all land theaters of the conflict. In a telephone interview in May 1995, Donald J. Willems cheerfully answered questions and honed some of my initial conclusions. His papers found in the Fort Carson archives were most valuable. More important was the interview with Willems conducted by Dr. Melvin Bradley, professor emeritus of animal science at the University of Missouri. Bradley answered my numerous questions on mule care and anatomy and also provided me with copies of written transcripts of his valuable interviews with World War II mule skinners Frank Graham, Donald J. Willems, Maurice Ryan, William Bennett "Woody" Woodruff, Douglas F. Watson, and Delbert E. Long. His two-volume book aided my research tremendously.

Members of the staff in the Division of Developmental Studies gave me tremendous support. Executive Aide Janet Pickel taught me some of the finer points of WordPerfect and anticipated ways to help in preparing the manuscript. She and secretary Debbie Buckles came to my support in numerous ways and made life easier during hectic times. The chief counselor for the division, Ramona Williams, willingly attended meetings for me while I was away from campus and assisted me in many thoughtful ways.

I need also to thank a number of people who were not directly involved in the research process but made my work more agreeable through friendship. Jim Hunter read several chapters and commented on his likes and dislikes. Calvin Morgan kept me from being consumed with the project by adding levity and by allowing me to visit on occasion his rustic mountain cabin. Betsy and Paul Hutchins, editors of *The Brayer*, invited me into their home, left me alone to use their library, and introduced me to a host of mule fanciers. Their friendship and hospitality are appreciated.

Finally, I owe much to my family. My grown children, Matthew and Christin, have often humored their "mulish" father and listened to his mule stories. My wife, Sally, has supported me on this and all my projects. She gave me needed encouragement and convinced me that in spite of administrative and teaching duties, I needed to write this book.

Introduction

The first time I remember reading about army mules was as a teenager when I discovered Fairfax Downey's *Indian Fighting Army* in my father's library. After rereading it I made the mistake of loaning the book to a friend. My father lost a lot of good books that way.

Years later as an assistant professor of history at East Tennessee State University I was doing research at the National Archives for my dissertation on cavalry horses. I kept running across interesting documents about mules while working my way through several record boxes from the Office of the Quartermaster General. The animals seemed important enough for me to include a chapter in the study "Mules, Packs, and Packtrains." My dissertation director and major professor, Donald E. Worcester, not only agreed but hinted that I might have some misplaced values between cavalry mounts and mules. He was right, of course.

The next year I read a paper based on my mule chapter at the Southwest Social Science meeting in Houston and was asked to submit it for publication to the *Southwestern Historical Quarterly*. The article was published in July 1970 and to my complete surprise was well received. I have been haphazardly collecting material and publishing articles on these logistical marvels ever since. In 1993–94, as I was writing "Army Mule" for *Montana, The Magazine of Western History*, I knew that the time had come to begin writing this volume in earnest. Partial chapters were here and there in a semiabandoned state with incomplete footnotes and facts concerning the army and its most useful and dependable animal. Even before the article appeared I had discarded most of the earlier manuscript and so began at the beginning.

The reception of "Army Mule" helped me along with my research and writing. The more I got into the subject the more I appreciated these superior animals. From their introduction into the army until after the Korean conflict, they played an important role in all American conflicts. They proved themselves to be indispensable even after the army became "modernized and mechanized," and even today devocalized mules could be used to advantage in some guerrilla-style operations.

A word about the title *Shavetails and Bell Sharps.* Shavetails were new and untrained mules sent to a packtrain. A packer shaved the new arrivals' tails and roached their manes to distinguish them from the bell sharps, who knew to follow the sound of the bell on the mare's neck and to line up before their own packsaddles at the sound of the bell each morning. Shavetails tended to wander around and get into trouble. The analogy is so typical of the U.S. Army's use of mules. New "shavetail" officers experimented with these animals and eventually became "bell sharps." They used mules mainly to pull wagons and then also discovered how effective they could be as packers of supplies and artillery.

Pack mules gave horse cavalry, infantry, and artillery units almost unlimited mobility. The officer who was recognized as first using packtrains to full advantage was George Crook. He took such pains to organize his civilian trains with efficient packers, well-bred, barrel-bellied mules, and properly fitted Mexican packsaddles that other commands initially scoffed at his efforts. Only after his troops performed so well in subduing the Paiutes and Apaches and he was promoted over some forty senior-ranked officers of the line to become a department commander did other envious officers take notice and begin organizing trains of their own based on the Crook model. Until then some had ridiculed him with a little ditty about his mule packers.

> I'd like to be a packer,
> And pack with George F. Crook,

And dressed up in my canvass suit.
And be for him mistook.
I'd braid my beard in two long tails,
And idle all the day
In whittling sticks and wondering
What the New York papers say.

Downey, *Indian Fighting Army,* 163

No matter what the papers said, the army employed, at least in part, the methods used by Crook's packers until the mule was retired in 1956.

The history of the mule and the army are so intertwined that even during World War II it would be difficult to discuss logistics without including the use of mules in every land theater of war. Mules were still the work animals of the army.

Shavetails and Bell Sharps

CHAPTER I

The Army Mule

On 15 December 1956 at Fort Carson, Colorado, the U.S. Army deactivated the last two operational mule units—the Thirty-fifth Quartermaster Pack Company and Battery A of the Fourth Field Artillery Pack Battalion. The ceremony in the high plains country, witnessed by an estimated three thousand people, was a somber one for old cavalrymen and artillerymen as men and mules under full pack passed in review for the last time. Several veteran sergeants from World War II and earlier participated in the review. For them especially, it was a moving event.

Next to the reviewing stand stood army mules 583R and 9YLL, known as Trotter and Hambone, both of whom were oblivious of the honor. After the guidons and colors were lowered and cased, symbolizing deactivation, Maj. Gen. Henry P. Storke added a bit of wry humor to the otherwise solemn occasion by presenting certificates of special recognition to each mule. Trotter was acknowledged as "one out of thousands" of mules that had "mastered four gaits: the walk, trot, gallop and pace." The certificate further affirmed that in retirement as a combat veteran, Trotter would not be "plagued with those horrors" that had caused him to "unburden" himself "of riders and other equipment—a glimpse of either of those hideous devices, the umbrella or the bicycle." Depending on one's point of view, Trotter's retirement years were as distinguished as his active career, for he served as a mascot for cadets at the U.S. Military Academy at West Point, New York.[1]

Hambone was acknowledged as having served in the army since 4 January 1943 and with the Fourth Field Pack Artillery since May 1948. He was an extraordinary jumping mule, as General Storke pointed out.

> Special commendation is due to you for your extraordinary abilities displayed in jumping events, and for the record of having never lost a mule jumping contest, as well as your phenomenal success in bettering all except the first place winner in a competition with horses at Fort Carson in 1950.
>
> In addition, your exhibition jumping at the international Stock Show in Chicago in 1950, at Pikes Peak Rodeo in 1954, and other equestrian functions has been a credit both to yourself and the United States Army.
>
> In view of these outstanding achievements, your refusal to perform such menial tasks as carrying a pack and your refraining from associating with other mules are hereby recognized as privileges specially accorded to you.[2]

After Storke had completed reading the citations, the mules were led back to their positions in the reviewing stand. Next, an army helicopter that had been hovering in the background flew in front of the stand and gave a salute to the two mules by dipping its fuselage, thereby paying homage to the mules and accepting responsibility for their work.

The remaining 136 army mules were not treated as regally as Hambone and Trotter. They were quietly sold off to anyone interested for from ten to forty dollars. Seventy-seven orders were placed by forty-seven Rocky Mountain farmers, mule fanciers, and ranchers, in person and by mail. Individuals could purchase no more than three animals and must move them off Fort Carson by 4 P.M. on 13 February 1957. The mules were sold for $3,320.00, an average of only $24.41 per animal.[3]

Two weeks before the 1956 deactivation, an army spokesman announced that the Fourth Field Pack Artillery would be replaced by the Experimental Fourth Amphibious Field Artillery Firing Unit. This new unit was equipped with helicopters and assigned to the

Artillery and Guided Missile Center at Fort Sill, Oklahoma. The spokesman explained that this experimental unit would be superior in every way. It would be equipped with howitzers and rocket launchers and would rely on thirty-eight helicopters. Its "speed and flexibility of operations through the use of helicopters" would "be superior to similar units using ground transport means." It would also be "particularly suited for use in special operations in the mountains, Arctic, and the jungle, and it could normally occupy positions not readily occupied, or may be inaccessible to units with ground [transportation] including areas surrounded by the enemy."[4]

Not all army men were as sanguine as the writer of the army's release. Helicopters of the 1950s (as with those of today) were even more temperamental than mules. Mules with vocal cords cut surely made less noise than helicopters, and in damp, cold, overcast weather, as well as during sandstorms and in arctic conditions, mules were as reliable, if not more reliable, than sophisticated whirlybirds that depended on access to huge amounts of fuel. Mules could operate in all types of weather and live off the land if necessary. "Amphibious!" roared an old sergeant. "What in the hell did they think those mules were?" But remember, "it's only an experiment."[5]

It was not, however, "only an experiment." The army, after having had mules on the payroll for 125 years, had finally succumbed to complete mechanization. It now needed to find a suitable substitute for the simile "tough as a government mule."

Since before the Mexican War the army had maintained a special relationship with these hybrids as they became the principal beasts of burden and replaced oxen and horses. Many soldiers were, therefore, closely acquainted with mules, and most looked upon them with scorn. To them this hybrid cross of the ass and noble mare was an outrage upon nature, a monstrosity, unapproachable in devilment, fathomless in cunning, and the originator of a distinct and uninterrupted series of tricks. The mule showed little dexterity except for the accurate flinging of its hooves or its ability to step on the nearest soldier's feet or gear.[6]

Army quartermasters would surely have jumped at the chance to replace the mule if a better animal had been available. Such was not the case, for in spite of their supposedly unlovely characteristics, mules were the most important four-legged animals in the army. Even though they claimed to abhor the creatures, most soldiers would not dispute the statement that the mule was an indispensable animal. Although many cavalrymen would disclaim such a blasphemy, they might secretly admit that the pack mule was almost as important as their mounts. This admission showed a misplaced loyalty and was untrue, for if any horse was as important as a pack mule, it was not the cavalryman's mount but the pack mules' bell mare, which they followed as if they were her foals.[7]

Several attributes made the mule an indispensable military adjunct. It showed the head, ears, and bone structure of the jack, and the height and body of the mare. It exhibited the patience, endurance, and "surefootedness of the jack and the vigour, strength, and courage" of the mare. Mules needed less grain than horses and in most cases could live on the vegetation available. When given a steady diet of grain and hay, they were truly superior to other work animals. More agile and stronger than either parent, they could haul or carry heavier loads longer distances over more difficult terrain than any other beast of burden; in addition, they also were fast walkers. They displayed remarkable recuperative powers and were "long livers." Mules were also sensitive, intelligent animals, more so than parent stock. They quickly recognized approaching danger and knew by instinct how to avoid it.[8]

Mules were the ideal work animals for the U.S. Army, and the army set exacting standards for harness and pack mules. These standards, with surprisingly few exceptions, endured until bureaucrats and others decided that the army no longer needed mules. Except for emergency requisitions and purchases that officers had to make in the field without good knowledge of mule flesh, animals that did not meet the specifications were rejected. When quartermasters began purchasing wagon mules during the 1830s, they followed brief but specific guidelines. Harness mules had to be of dark color, strong, stout, compact, "sound in all particulars," in good condition, well broken to the harness, not under 14 hands high (hh) but preferably 15 to 16 hands, not less than four nor more than nine years of age, and "suitable in every respect for the transportation service of the Army." In 1873 quartermasters were given guidelines for purchasing acceptable pack mules. In addition to observing the general orders for harness mules, officers were to concentrate on purchasing the "heavily-bodied, compactly-built mule, from 13½ to 14 hands high, but when suitable in all respects," they could accept the Mexican mule between 13 and 14 hh.[9]

By the time the United States entered World War I, requirements for purchasing mules had become even more exacting. According to general orders that QMG J. B. Aleshire issued:

The draft mule must be sound, well bred, and of a superior class; of a kind disposition, free from vicious habits, gentle, and well broken to harness, with free and springy action at the walk and trot; without material blemish or defect, and otherwise to conform to the following description:

A mare or gelding of uniform and hardy color, in good condition; from three to eight years old; weight and height to be as follows:

Three-year-old mules will be purchased only when exceptionally fine individuals.

Wheel mules to weigh from 1,150 to 1,250 pounds, depending on height, which should be from 15¾ to 16¼ hands high.

Lead mules to weigh from 1,000 to 1,150 pounds, depending on height, which should be from 15 to 15¾ hands high.

Head.—Well formed and of medium size, with ears long, tapering and erect; forehead broad and full; eyes large, clear, prominent, and mild, with well-developed brow and fine eyelid; vision perfect in every respect; teeth sound and meeting vertically; tongue free from blemishes; muzzle well rounded and firm, with large nostrils.

Neck.—Medium length and smoothly joined to the shoulders and withers, with crest firm, full, and inclined to arch.

Shoulders.—Long, oblique, well and smoothly muscled, and so formed as to provide proper support for the collar.

Chest.—High, wide, very deep and full.

Back.—Short, straight, well and smoothly muscled.

Loins.—Broad, straight, very short and muscular.

Barrel.—Large, with ribs well arched and definitely separated from each other,

Fore legs.—Vertical from both front and side view and properly placed; with elbow large, long, and clear of chest; forearm large, very long, heavily muscled, and vertical.

Knees.—Large, wide in front, well placed, and free from blemishes.

Hind quarters.—Wide, thick, very long, full, heavily muscled, rounded externally, and well directed.

Hocks.—Neatly outlined, lean, free from puffs, large, wide from front to rear, and well directed. Gaskins well developed.

Limbs.—From knees and hocks downward vertical, short, flat, wide laterally, with tendons and ligaments standing well out from bone and distinctly defined.

Pasterns.—Strong, medium length, not too oblique, and well directed.

Feet.—Medium size and round, with horn smooth and of fine texture; frog well developed, elastic, and healthy.

Each mule will be subjected to a rigid inspection, and any animal that does not meet the above requirements should be rejected.[10]

The specifications for riding and pack mules conformed to those for draft mules with certain exceptions. Basically, pack and riding mules were smaller, more compact animals, standing from 14½ to 15½ hh and weighing from 950 to 1,150 pounds. Stipulations for pack and riding mules for use in the Panama Canal Zone allowed quartermasters to purchase smaller animals standing only 13 to 14 hh and weighing from 700 to 850 pounds.

Within these exacting specifications purchasers had a certain amount of discretion. They sought wagon or harness mules that weighed at least 1,150 pounds and stood 15¾ hh. Mules weighing 1,000 pounds and standing 15 hh were occasionally purchased and branded as lead mules. Pack mules also tended to be smaller than the regulations prescribed. No doubt purchasers believed that all pack mules could be sent to the Canal Zone, where a 15 to 15½-hh pack mule was the exception rather than the rule. Most pack mules tended to weigh 950 to 1,000 pounds and to stand 13¾ to 14½ hh. The same was true of riding mules that could be used in pack-trains when needed.[11]

Henry W. Daly, chief packer of the army from 1903 to 1917, and a civilian packer for the army for more than thirty years, remained even more adamant than army bureaucrats on specifications and conformation of pack mules. Reiterating the official specifications in his 1917 *Manual of Pack Transportation,* Daly was even more specific. For example, he wanted animals purchased for packing only to be from four to six years old and from 14.1 to 15 hh, and purchasers were to seek animals that were intelligent looking. (For Daly's list of specifications, see the appendix.)

More interesting perhaps were some of Daly's admonitions regarding what quartermasters should avoid in selecting pack mules. Those mules whose heads were dish-faced, long, and large, with Roman noses, "narrow between the eyes," and "lip hanging down" were suspect. If they were "chicken-breasted," "pigeon-toed," knees small and out of line, with hocks standing close together, "swaybacked indicating weakness over kidneys," and hips prominent and angular, they were to be rejected.[12]

Six months after the United States's entry into World War II, requisition officers were given more discretion in purchasing animals. "In times of emergency, when large numbers of animals are required," read Army Regulations 30-440, which superseded those of 2 January 1929 and 30 August 1935, "the specifications may be modified when so directed by The Quartermaster General." Included in these new regulations was the admonition that mules purchased should "conform to average." That meant that the weight and height of "any class" of mules purchased under one contract "must conform closely to the average between the maximum and minimum specifications."[13]

Also as a part of these regulations, purchasers of mules were to use the "general specifications" for horses, yet "consideration" was to be "given to the natural differences in conformation between the horse and the mule." The advice about conforming to the average and natural differences between the horse and the mule was army bureaucratic double talk meaning to go back to previous general orders that contained specific requirements for mules. The same official advice appeared in the subsequent army regulations of the immediate post-war years and in pamphlet AR 880-5, *Public Animals Horses, Mules, and Dogs* of 1 September 1953.[14]

In the specialization of mule production, breeders developed a semiscientific approach. At first they paid attention only to the mule jack (male ass). Many initially believed that the contribution of the mare to the offspring was unimportant, and poor quality (even diseased) mares were quite acceptable as dams for mules. Likewise, the mule jacks were not as fine a quality as the jennet jacks that were to be bred exclusively for producing jacks and jennets (female asses) rather than mules. So the hybrid mule was often the product of a common mare at best and a better quality, although not the best quality, jack. Breeders believed that the best way to ruin a good mule jack was to let him service a jennet, for then he was no longer interested in covering a mare. Often breeders had to tease a mare in heat with a stallion to prepare her for receiving the jack.

Despite such characteristic beliefs in male dominance, gradually even the most chauvinistic breeders realized that both parents were almost equally important and chose the best quality mares, sometimes even using jennet jacks. Very desirable mule mares were those of about one-fourth draft blood and three-fourths "lighthorse" blood. By the mid-nineteenth century, breeding for mules in the state of Kentucky had reached such proportions that one man complained that "the sport of racing is in collapse and good horses have been somewhat scarce, for pedigreed mares are now prostituted to jacks while stallions are slenderly patronized."[15]

Breeders also quickly discovered that individuals preferred mare mules and would pay up to fifteen dollars more for them than for male mules. Many perceived mare mules as more manageable, of a sweeter disposition, and easier to train. Mare mules also tended to keep their shape better then gelded males. All males were gelded. A stud mule usually behaved worse than a stallion, was difficult to control, was considered dangerous, and was unreliable unless continuously worked. The army accepted no male mules not already gelded.

Size of the mule depended on the size and conformation of the parents. Mule jacks under 12 hh serviced 14- to 15-hh mares—sometimes with difficulty—to produce mules 13 to 14½ hh. Mules could be larger than either parent. To aid the small jacks in mounting, mares were sometimes "pitted," or placed in a pit so the jacks could service them more easily. Mares 15 to 16 hh, that were covered by jacks of 15 hh usually produced mules of at least 16 hh, and often larger. To protect the jack and to make his job easier, mares were usually hobbled.[16]

The use of mules in American agriculture and by the military had become so important in this country that after World War I the U.S. Department of Agriculture issued Farmers' Bulletin No. 1341, *Mule Production*. Written and issued in 1923 by J. O. Williams of the Bureau of Animal Industry and revised in 1938 by S. R. Speelman, this pamphlet explained the attributes of mules and how to breed them successfully for good stock. It contained the collected wisdom of the mule-breeding business of the last century and became a firm basis for breeding practices after World War II.

Bureaucratic procedures for the procurement of acceptable mules and other public animals had become a fairly standardized process by the twentieth century. Beginning in 1818 QMG Thomas Sidney Jesup, in coordination with Maj. Gen. Winfield Scott, had drafted rules and regulations for the quartermaster's department that were approved by then Secretary of War John C. Calhoun. In general these rules made the quartermaster general and quartermasters in the various departments totally accountable for purchasing for the army. Except under most unusual circumstances, officers were not allowed to take matters into their own hands and purchase animals or supplies. This system worked adequately except during wartime, when the quartermasters were overwhelmed with requests and greedy suppliers inflated prices. But when the department was expanded by training additional quartermasters and when the officers could offer more money for goods and animals received, the quartermasters department served the military operations satisfactorily.[17]

The mule had become the most important four-legged animal in the U.S. Army, and packers and quartermasters readily rejected animals that did not meet standards. For years they had procured animals under contract after advertising for bids. This procedure often resulted in delays at the worst possible times, and quartermasters often did not have a good opportunity to judge the qualities and dispositions of the animals before sending them to cavalry troops or infantry and artillery companies. Beginning in 1908 the army established depots where breeders could present animals for sale. These depots initially proved to be more successful in obtaining draft horses and mules than cavalry mounts because breeders were able to produce more suitable draft animals than cavalry horses with acceptable conformations. When breeders were unable to offer enough mules for sale at a depot, quartermasters could either advertise for additional animals or enlist the help of officers at other depots in purchasing additional stock.[18]

Despite both the popularity of mules among civilians and a system designed for the quartermasters to acquire the animals, the army turned only reluctantly to using mules. Major problems faced by the army in the western theater were supplying its remote posts and provisioning soldiers on long campaigns. During the 1820s and most of the 1830s, it used wagons drawn by either oxen or horses; only rarely were wagons drawn by mules. Even though Santa Fe traders were herding mules, jacks, and jennets back to Missouri on each trip, and more mules and breeding stock were available throughout the South, mules were still fairly expensive. Many quartermasters were not familiar with the attributes of the mule. Those who did know how to judge mules were forbidden to pay the going rate, sometimes as high as $175 an animal. When four companies of Maj. Bennet Riley's Sixth Infantry Regiment escorted the 1829 Santa Fe caravan, it used oxen to pull its wagons because the army had no mules available.[19]

Another problem was the lack of funds in the army's operating budget to maintain animals that were with companies after campaigns had been completed. The army almost starved to death on the appropriations given by cost-conscious congressmen who quoted (but did not necessarily believe) the over-used axiom that large standing armies are a menace to democratic institutions and that volunteer militia could successfully meet any threat. Even if that were true, mules menaced only those who got in their way or mistreated them. Nevertheless, no mules were put out to pasture and kept in reserve for future use. It took time to train mules and volunteer militiamen during any crisis, and sometimes commanders had reason to question the effectiveness of both.

By the 1830s quartermasters had acquired a small number of mules to be used at various posts. Not only did they recognize the worth of mules for military purposes, they could now afford to purchase the animals. Ever larger mule populations finally meant lower prices—mules were sometimes less expensive than harness horses. Increasingly, breeders tried to satisfy a new, stable, and sometimes localized market. The conformation for army mules set standards that guided both large breeders and individual farmers and ranchers who bred mules as a sideline business. Many breeders near the areas where troops were stationed probably reasoned that satisfying quartermasters was easier than meeting the demands of individual farmers and freighters, and when the army no longer needed the mules, traders could repurchase them at considerable savings. No doubt some mules joined the army more than once. A Kentuckian wrote of the "mad competition to buy asses because mules, which would sell for forty or sixty dollars at eight to ten months of age, furnished one fine prospect of prosperity." Although referring only to the local market, this Kentuckian had expressed the sentiments of many. He was selling his foals to a mule grazier who raised them for future resale.[20] In two or three years the grazier could sell the three- and four-year-olds for a substantial profit. Perhaps he could receive a contract from the army for those animals not sold to individuals.

Mule raising had become an important business. As more mules were bred, more were bred especially for the army. Selling to the government was less trouble and more profitable than selling to farmers, for the army purchased thousands of mules each year, especially after the Civil War. And purchasing inspected and condemned (IC) mules from the army was even more profitable. Many IC mules served as faithful plow and draft animals for farmers and their families years after the army had discarded them.[21]

Army mules had become a fixture on almost all installations and army bases during the post–Civil War years. They had become so visible that they became almost invisible. Even their unmelodious neighing had become too familiar a sound to excite indignation. Although they had earned an excellent reputation, they remained the butt of many army jokes, and men spoke of sergeants who demon-strated stubborn, mulish behavior. Some even claimed that the mules had inoculated far too many army officers with their own stubborn characteristics. Mules were definitely an enduring symbol for the army.

CHAPTER 2

Army Mule Power in Florida and Mexico

The actual use of mules by the army before the mid-1830s is difficult to document. In all probability, however, quartermasters purchased few if any of these expensive work animals to accompany infantry expeditions. These early forays, mainly to explore and to resettle eastern Indian tribes, depended on steamboats, oxcarts, and wagons for hauling their supplies, and most of the wagons were pulled by oxen or draft horses. When augmented by volunteer state militia, army troops might have become acquainted with mules.

During the Black Hawk War of 1832, for example, some of the Illinois state militia's supplies could have been hauled by mules. For that matter some of the mounted militiamen might have ridden mules, but it is highly unlikely that volunteers would have risked such valuable animals in an Indian conflict. Mules no doubt did haul supplies for the army but only when military agents hired civilian wagon masters to deliver yearly supplies to posts and installations. Some wagon masters realized the superior attributes of large, heavily built wagon mules and used six- and eight-mule teams for wagons transporting "40 hundred" to "50 hundred" pounds of cargo. From the end of the War of 1812 to the 1830s when short eastern railroad lines began operation, the army sent the bulk of its overland supplies in civilian wagon trains.[1]

The U.S. Army first used mules in significant numbers during the Second Seminole War, 1835–42. During this expensive, grueling, and desultory war in which the army could take little pride, the only participants to come out of the fray with undamaged reputations were the pack animals—horses and mules. Even the hero of Okeechobee, Col. Zachary Taylor, could not escape criticism from the Floridians. In both conventional and guerrilla warfare, the pack animals played a decisive role but died by the hundreds. If the commanders had not persisted in European strategies of war and had instead protected their trains, animals and supplies would not have been needlessly sacrificed. The army used almost an equal number of horses and mules to pack company supplies through the inhospitable countryside. With few roads and swampy undergrowth conditions, wagon transportation was of limited effectiveness. Even forage masters used pack mules and horses wherever possible. In the fall of 1840, 1,008 wagon and riding horses and 1,133 mules were used to supply forage to 1,337 horses and 1,260 mules. The equal use of horses and mules actually made mules the preferred pack animals since they were usually more expensive to purchase than horses and quartermasters usually purchased the less expensive animals to save funds for food and forage.[2]

During this conflict the U.S. Army for the first time also hired many civilians as auxiliaries. Earlier soldiers had been detailed to serve as teamsters, blacksmiths, wheelwrights, carpenters, and common laborers. The scope of the operations in Florida, however, was too large, and more skilled technicians were required. The army now needed teamsters who were well "acquainted with the nature of mules" and "muleteers," or packers. Quartermasters in St. Louis were ordered to recruit "muleteers or packhorse drivers" from the yearly caravans of fur traders returning from the Rocky Mountains.[3] Although it would be an exaggeration to claim pack animals were effectively used at all times, mules and horses did provide increased supplies for soldiers and give them more mobility in a seek-and-destroy sort of war.

The Second Seminole War is important in American military history for several reasons. It developed guerrilla- or partisan-style warfare to a higher degree; it showed duplicity by both the Indians and army commanders; it was not a complete victory for the U.S. Army, for several thousand Indians could not be removed from the

Everglades; and it was a costly war both in finances and loss of life considering its limited accomplishments. Ten thousand regulars and thirty thousand volunteers fought in Florida at one time or another during this conflict. A total male population of not more than a thousand Seminoles killed more than fourteen hundred soldiers, and the U.S. Army spent between $30 million and $40 million in just over seven years. More important than these factors, the military had learned valuable lessons on how to supply troops in the field, and they had found a workhorse for the army—the mule.

For all the lessons learned, however, the U.S. Army was unable to preserve its gains. Retrenchment followed as quartermasters were obliged to break up wagon trains, sell all mules and horses, and discharge teamsters, packers, mechanics, and laborers. In 1842 the U.S. Congress reduced the size of the army by more than 30 percent, from 12,539 to 8,613 officers and men. Within three years the army establishment would begin the same process of preparing for war all over again. In the meantime, the army had lost a chance to experiment with its mule transportation system during peacetime.[4]

The army would, however, depend heavily on mules in all theaters during the Mexican War. Mule power played a vital, prominent role in Brig. Gen. Zachary Taylor's army in northern Mexico. Mules transported supplies for Brig. Gen. Stephen Watts Kearny's force from Independence, Missouri, to Santa Fe and played an even more direct role in moving the dragoons from Santa Fe to California. They accompanied Col. Alexander W. Doniphan's Missouri volunteers. Space was even saved for mules on naval transports to make sure they were available when the troops landed at Vera Cruz. Maj. Gen. Winfield Scott's expeditionary force on the march from Vera Cruz to Mexico City made heavy use of mules.

When Taylor's infantry began landing near Corpus Christi, Texas, late in July 1845, they had no transportation available except twenty four-mule wagons minus the mules. Dragoons coming overland had some fifty wagons drawn by horses and mules, and quartermasters had ordered an additional thirty wagons built and shipped. One of Taylor's highest priorities was to obtain animals and additional wagons to support his army in the field, for he would soon march his assembling army to the east bank of the Rio Grande near Matamoras.[5]

In purchasing horses and mules for the army, quartermasters in Texas asked few questions. American traders obtained mules from Mexican smugglers for not more than five dollars apiece and sold them to quartermasters for eight to eleven dollars each, a tidy profit of between 45 and 63 percent. Mexican vaqueros captured large numbers of range horses and sold them individually to officers for between eight and eleven dollars. Quartermasters, however, purchased them for only thirty-six dollars a dozen. Second Lt. Ullyses S. Grant, who would later act as quartermaster for his regiment, both with Taylor's and Scott's armies, commented that he saw nothing wrong with these purchases and suspected that some of the smugglers were paid only for their time and not for the mules. But as he explained, "Such is trade; such is war." Grant himself would ride a five-dollar mustang all through the war.[6]

Not enough draft mules, however, could be purchased in this manner, and quartermasters began purchasing oxen wherever they could find them. By January 1846 quartermasters had purchased 592 oxen. Two hundred and forty of these were used daily to haul forage for the other animals and firewood for the soldiers. They were used for general duties as well.[7]

Breaking wild range mules to the harness, according to Grant, was a slow but amusing process. First, a number of mules were driven into a large corral to be branded. Mexican vaqueros, all expert ropers; soldiers detailed as teamsters with ropes to serve as halters; and blacksmiths with branding irons all entered the corral. Then the fun began. A mounted vaquero lassoed a mule; the mule ran to the end of his lariat, and while he was "plunging and gyrating," another vaquero threw his lasso over the mule's forefeet and threw the mule to the ground. Then it was seized and held by several teamsters while a blacksmith branded it on the shoulder with the initials us. Snubbing ropes were then placed around its neck. With a teamster on each side holding these ropes, the mule was "released from his other bindings and allowed to rise. With more or less difficulty he would be conducted to a picket rope outside [the corral] and fastened there."[8]

The method of breaking mules to the harness was "less cruel and much more amusing." Each teamster selected five mules according to color and size for his team. "With a full corps of assistants" he then proceeded to "get his mules together." In twos, declared Grant, the teamsters approached each animal selected, "avoiding as far as possible its heels," and placed two snubbing ropes around its neck. Each mule was then led from the picket line, "harnessed by force and hitched to the wagon in the position [it] would keep ever after."[9]

When all five mules were hitched, two men were placed on each side of the lead mule, with lassos around its neck. Other teamsters were assigned to each of the other four mules. They too had lassos around their mule's neck. "All being ready," the hold was slackened and the team started. "The first motion was generally five mules in the air at one time, backs bowed, hind feet extended to the rear." Eventually the leader started to run, which would "bring the breaching tight against the mules at the wheels." This movement was regarded by the wheel mules as a "most unwarrantable attempt at coercion," and they resisted "by taking a seat, sometimes going so far as to lie down." Finally, the team worked as a team, "but there never was a time during the war when it was safe to let a Mexican mule get entirely loose."[10]

On receiving orders on 4 February 1846 to advance from Corpus Christi to the east bank of the Rio Grande, Taylor faced endless transportation difficulties. Supplies that went by ship to Point Isabel had to be transferred from Corpus Christi to Saint Joseph's Island to await shipment. Organizing the land shipment was a major problem. Not until 8 March was the first of four columns of Taylor's army able to move out of Corpus Christi. When the last column, including the entire wagon train, finally left, the quartermaster in charge, Col. Trueman Cross, observed that "the organized trains" were using the "crudest materials" imaginable. There were "1,000 wild mules, drawn by stealth from Mexico" and "600 half-broke oxen from the interior of Texas, and drivers from all parts of the civilized world."[11]

Only enough mules and oxen were available for each company to take a single wagonload of fifteen hundred pounds. The wagon train was barely large enough to move the garrison's equipage, officers' baggage, rations, and grain for artillery horses and the mules that had transported supplies for the dragoons marching from Louisiana. Mules accustomed to being grain fed did not last living on grass and having to pull even lightly loaded wagons. The small Mexican mules, however, thrived on grass and mesquite. The entire wagon train consisted of only 307 wagons, with 223 of them pulled by approximately 1,115 mules and 84 by oxen.[12]

The overloaded wagon column traveled at a snail's pace even over fairly level terrain. The first 125 miles of the march were agonizing for men and animals, for the only ponds of drinkable water were sometimes separated by an entire day's march. It took a full ten days to reach the steep banks of the salty Rio Colorado and catch up with the other three columns that were waiting for supplies. But the small Mexican wagon mules had performed above anyone's expectations.[13]

Reaching the river, officers and men knowledgeable of the habits and prejudices of mules concerning water were able to maneuver the mules and their wagons across with only minimum difficulty. Nevertheless, the process consumed several days. As Grant described the crossing, the teams of mules and their wagons were moved across at the same time "by attaching a long rope to the end of the wagon tongue" and passing the rope "between the two swing mules" and by the side of the lead mule, "hitching his bridle as well as the bridles of the mules in rear" to the rope. A teamster then took this lead rope across the river. Another long rope was attached to the rear axle of the wagon, and teamsters behind held this rope to prevent the wagon from beating the mules down the banks of the Colorado into the water. The rear rope also served the purpose of bringing the end of the forward rope back to be used again. Grant observed that the water was deep enough toward the middle of the river to force the "little Mexican mules" to swim, "but they and the wagons were pulled through so fast" by the teamsters across the river that "no time was left them to show their obstinacy."[14]

After the last of the wagons had crossed, Taylor's army, no longer in single-file columns but four abreast, headed for the Rio Grande. When close to Matamoras, Taylor rode with an escort to Point Isabel, a town on the left bank of the mouth of the Rio Grande. There he made certain that other supplies had arrived by water. His army, halting only ten miles from its objective, impatiently awaited the general's return. On 28 March it set up camp on the east bank of the Rio Grande just opposite the Mexican town of Matamoras. Taylor's troops began building a bastion that he called Fort Texas. The wagon mules now spent almost a month hauling building materials for the fort and fattening up on the grass of South Texas, or Northern Mexico, depending on one's point of view before the war began. While the participants waited for hostilities to begin, Colonel Cross, the assistant quartermaster general responsible for organizing the wagon trains, was killed. He did not return the evening of 10 April from a pleasure ride. Whether he was killed by members of the Mexican army or by rancheros loosely connected with the army was never known. His loss hurt Taylor's forces because no one with his ability would replace him, and in the subsequent march to Monterrey the quartermasters had more than the usual trouble building a large train.[15]

On 25 April 1846 hostilities began. A large Mexican cavalry force crossed the Rio Grande and surrounded a reconnoitering detachment of Second Dragoons commanded by Capt. Seth Barton Thornton. They killed eleven of Thorton's men and captured Thornton and the rest, many of whom were wounded. Taylor immediately sent dispatches to President Polk that hostilities had commenced, and only then seems to have become concerned about his supply base at Point Isabel.

On 1 May, after leaving an artillery detachment to guard Fort Texas, Taylor's army marched to Point Isabel to collect his supplies. Accompanying the army were two hundred five-mule supply wagons hauled by a thousand mules. After strengthening fortifications on the coast, which required almost a week, troops loaded the wagons for the return to Fort Texas on 7 May. Taylor led the army in a Jersey Wagon of ponderous materials and questionable shape. Also accompanying the force of twenty-three hundred men were two new siege eighteen-pounders drawn by oxen.

In the meantime the Mexican army under Gen. Mariano Arista had not been able to attack the Americans before they reached their supply base. Instead, he awaited to intercept them on their return. At noon on 8 May at a spot called Palo Alto, the Americans saw across the open prairie a force of more than four thousand Mexican soldiers under Arista barring their way to Fort Texas. Taylor, who had detailed part of his soldiers to the rear to guard the supply train, was outnumbered more than two to one, and the Mexican cavalry greatly outnumbered the dragoons. Taylor's advantage, however, was vastly superior artillery. The advancing Mexicans were blasted with canister from the two eighteen-pounder siege guns, and the American flying artillery six-pounders firing solid shot, and the twelve-pounder howitzers firing shell forced the Mexicans to fall back rapidly. By contrast Arista's artillery was mostly ineffective. According to Grant, as the infantry got nearer "the cannon balls commenced going through the ranks. They hurt no one, however, during the advance, because they would strike the ground long before they reached our line, and ricocheted through the tall grass so slowly that the men would see them and open ranks and let them pass." Another soldier claimed that "the balls were constantly hissing over our heads or mowing their way through the tall grass, and it was astonishing how few struck our ranks." By nightfall, when both armies bivouacked, Mexican casualties numbered about 320 killed and 380 wounded. The American army suffered 9 killed and 47 wounded.[16]

The next morning the Americans saw the Mexicans in retreat. Taylor followed but in a leisurely manner. The morning was spent erecting defenses around the supply train, which would logically remain behind. In the meantime Arista deployed his army in a new position. Beyond the Palo Alto battlefield the gently rolling prairie became a dense tangle of chaparral and trees. The terrain was also cut by long, meandering depressions sometimes containing occasional stagnant pools of water (*resacas*) that represented the course of the Rio Grande at some time in the past. At one of these, called Resaca de la Guerrera by the Mexicans and Resaca de la Palma by the Americans, Arista took his stand. He chose a strong position, for the dense chaparral and trees prevented the Americans from effectively using their flying artillery or the dragoons. The battle was basically one of small groups of infantry in hand-to-hand combat. Many of the Mexicans were already demoralized by the fighting the day before, and after putting up some determined opposition they gave up the fight and fled to Matamoras. Gen. Rómulo Díaz de la Vega was amazed at the outcome and admitted, "If I had had with me yesterday $100,000 in silver, I would have bet the whole of it that no 10,000 men on earth could drive us from our position." Taylor had probably engaged no more than seventeen hundred soldiers, for the rest were protecting his precious mule train.[17]

The American victories at Palo Alto and Resaca de la Palma could have been more impressive if Taylor's regulars had pursued the Mexicans across the Rio Grande. Unlike Corpus Christi where he had requested pontoon bridges, Taylor had made no provisions for boats or barges after reaching the river. On 18 May the navy sailed some small craft up from Point Isabel and began ferrying the army to Matamoras. Whether the mules were ferried across or forced to swim with wagons is not known. Probably most were crossed as teamsters had crossed them at the Rio Colorado.

The battle of Resaca de la Palma was significant in spite of Taylor's hesitancy. The Mexican army was demoralized, and according to Grant there was an enormous amount of captured spoils including "over four hundred mules and pack saddles or harness."[18]

With war now officially declared, Taylor needed those captured mules and more besides. Within six weeks his army had more than doubled as volunteer units flocked to the camp. His plan was to capture Monterrey, located in a pass of the Sierra Madres leading to the city of Saltillo, by first setting up a base camp at Camargo, a small town on the San Juan River, a tributary of the Rio Grande. Camargo, 130 miles upriver from the gulf, could be reached by land or by vessels. Troops with some supplies marched overland to Camargo while others with most of the supplies were sent by steamboats.

The army desperately needed shallow-draft steamboats, wagons, and mules. By July, ten steamboat crews were learning the whims of the river and transporting terrified infantrymen and supplies to Camargo.[19] Through attrition and by scavenging parts of one wagon to fix another, the army's train was reduced from 307 to 175 fairly sturdy wagons, not nearly enough for a large-scale operation. New wagons did not arrive, and although Taylor fumed over the lack of them with an army "five-fold" larger, Jesup was not concerned. He knew that Taylor was in a country abounding in mules and that he must avail himself of "the only means of transportation used by the enemy."[20]

Still, Jesup initially worried about providing enough mules for Taylor's army. For example, in a letter to deputy QMG Lt. Col. Thomas F. Hunt, who was operating out of New Orleans, he stressed the importance of purchasing in Texas "all the wagons, mules, and drought horses that can be obtained." Those animals, Jesup knew, would be better "acclimated and accustomed to graze" and less in need of the forage required by other government animals moving into Mexico. But Hunt must not rely on Texas alone. Buy "well broke" mules readily available in Louisiana, he also urged Hunt, and "send agents to the Mississippi to purchase all that can be taken across by land, or sent by water, as you may think best. Send all the wagons and harness you can purchase." Jesup felt "so much anxiety" in obtaining enough animals that he sent Hunt "a duplicate of this letter by an express."[21]

Assistant quartermasters hired or purchased pack mules along with conductors and *arrieros*, paying them by the mule load of three hundred pounds. They purchased hundreds of pack mules for as little as eighteen to twenty dollars each and hired more than fifteen hundred. With pack and driver, each pack mule cost only fifty cents a day. They also bought ox teams and mule-drawn Mexican carts. Part of Taylor's animal woes was caused by Maj. Gen. John E. Wool's army in Texas; it had taken nineteen hundred horses and mules meant for Taylor's army.[22]

Few ranking officers yet recognized all the advantages of pack transportation. Pack mules with experienced packers using Spanish packsaddles were plentiful in Taylor's army. Under different conditions with less confusion, pack mules could have made a bigger impact. The assistant quartermaster, Lt. Col. Henry Whiting, wrote Jesup that pack mules might answer every purpose if the American force "makes war as the enemy makes it." He did not, however, feel Americans making war like Mexicans was likely to be the case, for "we have customs which neither the officers nor the soldiers [would] forego" under normal conditions. "Our camp equipage, so comfortable and yet so cumbrous, our rations, so full and bulky, all must be transported." In a message to Col. Henry Stanton, Whiting admitted that it was expensive and time-consuming to remodel nearly every package to be carried on pack mules.[23]

By August there was a force of fifteen thousand in Camargo, and Taylor began to move his army to a supply depot at Cerralvo. The hired pack mules had been increased to nineteen hundred, and the army was also using 180 five-mule wagons. To increase volume, the pack mules and wagons shuttled back and forth between Camargo and Cerralvo. One result of shuttling the mules was another limitation on baggage. One pack mule was allowed for every eight soldiers, three mules for company officers, and four to regimental headquarters. Each brigade and each division headquarters was assigned a five-mule wagon, "while three wagons were assigned to each regime—one to transport water and two to carry such articles that could not be packed on mules." Fifty-three wagons carried ammunition; four were reserved for the medical department and one for the engineers.[24]

Regimental officers in Taylor's army assigned junior officers to coordinate the wagons and pack mules. Lieutenant Grant of the Fourth Infantry Regiment was given the unofficial rank of "regimental quartermaster." Years later he well remembered his mule experiences. He admitted that there were not enough men in the army to manage a mule train without the help of Mexicans "who learned how. As it was the difficulty was great enough." Each day Grant was responsible for getting "his" mules ready to follow the regiment. Tents and cooking gear were made into packages "so that they could be lashed to the backs of mules. Sheet-iron kettles, tent-poles and mess kits were inconvenient articles to transport in that way." Grant wrote that it took several hours each day to get the train ready, and by that time some of the mules that had been packed first would be tired of waiting with loads on their backs. "Sometimes one would start to run, bowing his back and kicking up until he scattered his load." Others, Grant related, would "lie down and try to disarrange their loads by attempting to get on the top of them by rolling on them." Some with tent poles "would manage to run the tent pole on one side of a sapling while they would take the other." He summed up his experiences with the observation that he had never used a "profane expletive in [his] life; but I would have the charity to excuse those who may have done so, if they were in charge of a train of Mexican pack mules at the time."[25]

Evidently, Grant had the right job with the Fourth. From all accounts he was a natural horseman and knew the nature of animals and how to take care of them. He no doubt checked "his" mules for abrasions or nicks to the skin, for without treatment (calomel) wounds would attract screw worms that would bore into the flesh and within days produce a large hole in the mule. He also displayed the patience needed with tired, overworked animals, and probably with the assistance of a packer was able to judge replacement mules for his trains. He prided himself on making sure that the regimental train arrived at bivouac with the regiment, if not earlier.[26]

By 19 September Taylor's army reached the outskirts of Monterrey, the capital of Nuevo León. That evening Taylor sent a group of officers and engineers to reconnoiter the heavily fortified city and estimate the number of defenders. The officers quickly discovered that the city was well suited to resist attack and that Mexican soldiers had materially strengthened its defenses. On 21 September the American army attacked the city from two directions in a pincher movement, the bulk of the army from the northeast and a smaller force from the west. By 23 September, despite several hundred dead and wounded, the American troops had penetrated only to the eastern edge of the city and were fighting from street to street. Victory was still elusive at best. Early on the morning of 24 September, however, the Mexican commander, Maj. Gen. Pedro de Ampudia, offered to surrender the city on condition that the defenders be allowed to withdraw with their weapons unimpeded and that an eight-week armistice be declared. Taylor accepted. He had lost more than five hundred men killed or wounded; the army was 125 miles from a tenuous supply base; and he later claimed that he believed magnanimity would advance peace negotiations. Col. Jefferson Davis, who had helped negotiate the armistice, claimed triumphantly that "they were whipped, and we could afford to be generous."[27]

Upon learning of the armistice, President Polk condemned Taylor for letting the Mexican army escape and ordered him to terminate the armistice and to halt his movement southward. Taylor ignored Polk's order and sent a thousand men to occupy Saltillo, an important juncture on the road to Mexico City. He then moved the majority of his troops near the hacienda of Agua Nueva, eighteen miles south of Saltillo. Suspicious of Polk's motives, and knowing that most of his regular troops would now join Scott's expeditionary force destined for Vera Cruz, he could not move south to attack the Mexican army at San Luis Potosí as another step toward the Mexican capital. He was probably now much more interested in capturing the capital city of the United States.[28]

Although Taylor himself continued to complain about transportation problems, at least his army had partially solved the problems, mainly through inactivity. With most of his regulars marching to Tampico and the rest relatively inactive, the animals left with him got a well-deserved rest. Those who traveled between the supply stations and the army did so at a leisurely pace. John E. Wool's one-thousand-man army with more than adequate mule transportation also had arrived in time to enter Saltillo. By December there were some twelve hundred serviceable five-mule wagons on the way from Brazos de Santiago. The wagons would have been sent sooner, but the army could not find enough men with the skills necessary to drive five-mule wagons.

The problems involved in transporting supplies by mule wagons and pack trains convinced all that more good mule men were needed in the U.S. Army. Quartermasters in Mexico wanted soldiers from the ranks assigned to wagon duty, but Taylor and his commanders objected on the grounds that there was no way to insure that the ordinary soldier would make a capable teamster. Their solution was to hire American civilians and Mexicans to drive the wagons and eventually to enlarge the regiments with teamsters and hostlers paid at the same rate as artificers. When not needed in their special capacity, these men could serve as ordinary soldiers. Jesup favored the suggestion and urged congressional action. On 3 March 1847 Congress passed a bill that provided one principal teamster for each regiment at the rank and pay of quartermaster sergeant and two teamsters at the pay of artificer for each company of infantry, dragoons, mounted riflemen, and artillery. The bill was not as beneficial as army officials wanted, and it came too late to help in Mexico, but it did, in time, place more good mule men in the ranks.[29]

In his position Taylor felt secure from attack. He reasoned that a Mexican army of twenty thousand could not march across the barren desert between San Luis Potosí and his position, and that Gen. Antonio López de Santa Anna's first responsibility was to match wits with Scott. But Santa Anna had learned of the depletion of Taylor's force and without hesitation led his army across the two-hundred-mile terrain, anticipating a quick victory. A comparison of the two generals' approaches to logistics is interesting. Taylor believed that he had too many transportation difficulties to move his small army two hundred miles. Santa Anna, however, evidently did not flinch from moving a force five times larger than Taylor's. The basic difference in style between the two generals was in the amount of supplies each believed necessary to sustain troops, and whether they should be well or marginally fed; it made a huge difference. Another difference was how the Mexican and American armies moved supplies—by fast-moving pack mules or by slow-moving wagons. Packtrains simplified the line of march and made distances shorter because they could traverse difficult terrain and keep rations closer to the troops they served than wagons could. If indeed the Mexican army was slowed down in any way, it was by Santa Anna's carriage drawn by six mouse-colored mules.[30]

By 19 February 1847 Santa Anna's army of twenty thousand was only thirty-five miles from Agua Nueva. On 21 February Taylor learned that the Mexicans were swinging east to block the road between his army and Saltillo. He withdrew to Angostura, closer to Saltillo and a mile from Hacienda San Juan de la Buena Vista. At Angostura the road to Saltillo passed through a narrow valley that was an ideal location for making a defensive stand.

The hardest fought battle of the Mexican War soon began. Late in the morning of 21 February, Santa Anna sent a note to Taylor stating that the American army was surrounded by twenty thousand men, but because Taylor "deserved consideration and particular esteem," Santa Anna was willing to give him an hour to surrender and save himself from a catastrophe. Taylor was said to have exclaimed after getting the drift of the message, "Tell Santa Anna to go to Hell." He told his chief of staff "to put that in Spanish and send it back." What Maj. William Bliss politely wrote, however, was that the general declined "acceding to your request."[31]

In the three-day Battle of Buena Vista both armies performed well. Despite inadequate food supplies and not enough ammunition, to say nothing of the many untrained soldiers, the Mexicans bravely forced the fighting. On 23 February they initially attacked along the mountainside on the American left and made some headway while other Mexican troops probed the American right without success.

The fighting was fierce. When Gen. John E. Wool saw the assault to the right unfolding, he ordered the commander of the two Indiana regiments, Gen. Joseph Lane, to hold his position if at all possible. The Indiana volunteers, anxious to prove themselves in their first battle, surged forward to meet the enemy, but confusion stopped them. When an artillery battery shifted to a more advantageous position, a regimental colonel thought the battery was abandoning his men and ordered a retreat that quickly became a rout involving not only the Indianians but four companies of Arkansas volunteers.

Mexican success in that part of the battlefield left the way open for cavalry to attack both the supply base in the rear and Taylor's vulnerable mules and wagons. Dragoons and volunteer American cavalry fought off this attack. While many of the American volunteer cavalrymen fled, dragoons and those who remained, with help from the Second Indiana Regiment that had recovered from its earlier panic, split the Mexican force in two and saved the supplies. Unable to meet their original objective, the Mexican cavalry attacked positions held by Mississippi troops and the Third Indiana Regiment volunteers. They were beaten back and forced into a ravine, and they escaped only under cover of a flag of truce. The deadly fire of both groups had cut them to pieces.

Encouraged by his army's progress, late that afternoon Santa Anna combined several brigades for another assault. The Mexicans were met head-on by Illinois and Kentucky volunteers. Bitter hand-to-hand fighting ensued, and effective American artillery tore large holes in the Mexican line, but the Mexicans kept coming. "No troops in the world," wrote dragoon private Chamberlain, "showed more reckless valor." They were making significant inroads on the American position until Capt. Braxton Bragg arrived with another artillery battery. This new battery threw down a murderous fire that effectively stopped the Mexican advance. At one point during the advance Taylor had been ready to retreat toward Monterrey and regroup, but General Wool had dissuaded him. A heavy rainstorm finally put the finishing touches on the day's fighting. Santa Anna's army was as close to victory as Taylor's and still maintained strong positions on the field, but that evening Santa Anna ordered an ill-advised retreat to Agua Nueva, abandoning the field to Taylor. The victory mainly by American volunteers almost assured Taylor's election as president of the United States.[32]

Taylor's army had relied heavily on mules. The same was true for

Col. Stephen W. Kearny's Army of the West in its nine-hundred-mile trek from Fort Leavenworth to Santa Fe and for the dragoons' march from Santa Fe to California. Kearny's force of fewer than 1,700 men, containing some 300 First Dragoons, 860 members of the First Missouri Mounted Volunteers, and various volunteer artillery, irregular cavalry, and infantry companies, left Fort Leavenworth during June 1846. In August reinforcements of some 1,200 mounted volunteers commanded by Col. Sterling Price followed to Santa Fe. Transportation for the Army of the West, including the reinforcements, consisted of 459 horses, 3,658 mules, 14,904 oxen, 1,556 wagons, and 516 packsaddles.[33]

The march to Santa Fe by way of the Santa Fe Trail to the Upper Crossing of the Arkansas River and the subsequent trek along the Bent's Fort route took a heavy toll of both men and animals. The same journey could have been made with fewer hardships at a slower pace and following a different route, but Kearny's orders were to proceed as rapidly as possible. Until all the units rendezvoused at Bent's Fort, the troops covered a minimum of sixteen to twenty miles each day and on many occasions as many as thirty to thirty-five miles. There would be no relief in the rapid march after leaving the fort, even when they reached the Raton mountains and negotiated Raton Pass.

At this rapid pace problems constantly arose. Some of the provision wagons moved well ahead or lagged far behind the columns. Inexperienced men had packed most of the wagons, many of which were old and in poor condition. Many volunteers were assigned as teamsters without the necessary experience or skill to keep the wagons moving with the army, even at a much slower pace than Kearny's. The supply wagons fell far behind; both animals and wagons were abused, "inevitably leading to the death of large numbers of oxen and mules and the breakdown or abandonment of many wagons." One volunteer wrote that "our animals perish daily." It soon became a march of hardships. Rations had to be shortened. Then a measles epidemic broke out. Carrying the sick men, the wagons, now even more heavily loaded, fell even farther behind, but the march did not slacken. One of the volunteers wrote that the colonel was at one point of the trip still traveling with his company, or rather they were still traveling with Kearny, since he was "fond of rapid march."

Fewer than three weeks from Fort Leavenworth, Doniphan sent a dispatch to a battalion, which was a day behind Doniphan's men; he requested supplies immediately because 220 of the men in his command were on the verge of starvation. The problem of inadequate transportation and supplies haunted the Army of the West all the way to Bent's Fort and beyond to Santa Fe. Its only relief was a short reprieve at Bent's Fort. There mules and horses with missing shoes were shod, and the wagons that continued with the expedition were repacked. Once reaching Bent's Fort, most of the teamsters refused to go farther, having contracted only to haul supplies from Fort Leavenworth to Bent's Fort. So few wagons remained with the expedition that from August until the end of September none of the men marching with Kearny had coffee and existed basically on half-rations.

Also at Bent's Fort some of Doniphan's troopers lost their mounts. "Day before yesterday under the order of Col. Doniphan," reported Richard Smith Ellis for the *St. Louis Daily Reveille*, "about 300 horses . . . were turned loose to graze." Evidently something spooked the animals for they "raised a furious *stampede*" and a large number of them escaped. Some were recovered but "from 40 to 60 are still gone, and it is feared, forever." Mules and horses, related Ellis, were now in great demand.

Negotiating the trail through Raton Pass proved dangerous and difficult. Many of the wagons had to be abandoned; yet only two weeks after leaving Bent's Fort, Kearny's Army of the West reached the outskirts of Santa Fe. The first troops of the army entered Santa Fe on 18 August without opposition. Kearny's army had marched nine hundred difficult miles in fewer than fifty days, a remarkable feat for both the men and animals.[34]

At Santa Fe Kearny split his army into three separate forces, and with the three hundred dragoons he set out for California. Doniphan and the Missouri volunteers were ordered to wait in Santa Fe until the reinforcements arrived; then they were to subdue the Navajo Indians before marching to Chihuahua to join General Wool. Price and his reinforcements were to hold Santa Fe.

On 25 September Kearny and his travel-weary dragoons and engineers began their wilderness march to California. Instead of horses they rode mules, described as half-starved and half-broken-down even at the beginning of the march. Better mules were available, and fine specimens were publicly sold in Santa Fe but at a higher price than quartermasters were allowed to pay. Kearny knew, however, that these poor specimens were better than any of the horses available in the army. Jaded mules of the same size had more stamina than stallions or geldings in the same condition. Kearny no doubt intended to purchase or trade for more stock on his way to California. Several wagons pulled by eight mules each accompanied the expedition.[35]

Throughout the entire march transportation remained the major problem; riding and harness mules collapsed and died or were shot by sympathetic troopers. Kearny purchased horses and mules whenever possible and did not worry about the appearance of the animals. Almost any beast of burden found was in better condition than the troopers' mounts. Kearny also bought mules from the Indians he encountered but admitted that those mules were poor, half-starved animals of slight value. At some point on the thousand-mile trek, every dragoon was marching as infantry. In a letter to his wife, Kearny wrote of this stark, barren land in which for days he had not seen a blade of grass. The mules, he said, were living off the thorns and branches of mesquite trees to keep alive. A diet of mesquite branches would not sustain mules for long, especially as Kearny's troopers worked them long hours.

Even after 6 October when he learned from Kit Carson of the surrender of California, Kearny pushed on as rapidly as possible. He sent two hundred dragoons back to Santa Fe on the weakest of the mounts or on foot, abandoned his wagons, and packed the mules. The remaining men were still forced to walk much of the way because their mounts were still too weak to carry them. At the Colorado River the expedition encountered horse traders bound for Sonora with a herd of five hundred animals, and Kearny was able to purchase remounts. But even the new horses and mules soon gave out, and more than half the men were on foot when they walked across the Mojave Desert.[36]

When Kearny's depleted, badly mounted, and half-starved force reached California, Kearny learned that Comdr. Robert F. Stockton held the port of San Diego, which was not too far from where his weary dragoons were resting from their ordeal. He sent word, therefore, to the commodore of his whereabouts and asked for an escort to San Diego. On 3 December Stockton sent Capt. Archibald H. Gillespie with a brass four-pounder and thirty-nine men to join Kearny. Gillespie also brought word from the commodore that Kearny might want to attack a group of California lancers in the vicinity of San Diego.

On 5 December the combined force discovered that Capt. André Pico with a large group of lancers watched over the road to San Diego at the small village of San Pascual. Kearny decided to attack the lancers at daybreak on 6 December despite the fact that a large majority of his weary men were mounted on very jaded mules. He probably reached his decision after Kit Carson convinced him that the Californians would not stand against the American force and after observing once again the pitiful animals his men were using. It would be an excellent opportunity, he no doubt reasoned, to capture badly needed remounts.

On 6 December a twelve-man advance guard, riding the best of the animals, began a charge about three-quarters of a mile from the lancers. Pico's men easily forced the outnumbered Americans to withdraw. Meanwhile, Kearny's main force meandered toward the lancers in a ragged order because of the rickety conditions of their mounts. Pico leisurely withdrew his mounted force toward more even terrain to give his lancers an even greater advantage. When the dragoons reached the desired location, Pico ordered a counterattack. The Americans did not know how to fight lancers, and their worn-out mules were vastly inferior to the California horses. One thing the dragoons quickly discovered was that mules were reluctant to wheel around to avoid lance thrusts. Kearny later wrote that the lancers were "admirably mounted and the best riders in the world; hardly one that is not fit for the circus." After about fifteen minutes Gillespie and the artillery finally arrived, saving the dragoons from an even greater disaster. Pico, unwilling to confront artillery, withdrew. As the Californians left, they accentuated their success by taking one of the dragoon's howitzers with them. Its mule team had earlier bolted into the lancers' line.[37]

The details of Kearny's march have been well chronicled. Kearny must have learned, as did Gen. George Crook and others later, that sturdy, well-proportioned mounts and mules and an extra remuda were required for any extended expedition through the Spanish Borderlands. During much of the year, some forage, or at times even grain, was needed to supplement the horses' and the mules' diets. This was especially true when troops made extended march through mountainous regions. Although the dragoons' role was insignificant in taking California, the fact that they were even able to reach their destination makes their expedition significant. Others would learn the lessons needed to avoid or alleviate some of the suffering of both men and animals.

When the Second Regiment of Missouri Mounted Volunteers under Col. Sterling Price arrived in Santa Fe after experiencing many of the same hardships as Kearny's troops, Doniphan's First Missourians began a journey that would form one of the most enduring sagas of the Mexican War. On 25 November Doniphan's force, 856 strong, left the city. They had been ordered to subdue the Navajo Indians and then proceed to Chihuahua to join Wool's command, which supposedly had already occupied Chihuahua City. Wool's command, unknown either to Kearny or Doniphan, would not reach its objective.

Like most volunteers, the Missourians complained about conditions in the army. They showed complete disdain for the regular army and believed that they had received nothing but leftovers for supplies. These included wagons and mules. As one of Doniphan's men complained, "The volunteer troops were furnished with very sorry and indifferent wagons and teams, wholly inadequate for such an expedition, whilst the regulars were furnished in the very best manner." He added that the mules and other animals were mostly unused to the harness and often "became refractory and balky." Wagons "daily broke down. Time was required to make repairs. Hence the march [to Santa Fe] was of necessity, both slow and tedious."[38]

The march to Chihuahua was neither slow nor tedious. After brief skirmishes with the Navajo Indians, the Missourians marched toward El Paso del Norte. The terrain had been so difficult on the expedition against the Indians that Doniphan had abandoned wagon transportation and ordered all supplies packed on mules. The Missourians also "threw away their tents, that being light armed and unembarrassed, they might make their marches with greater expedition amongst the rocks, ravines, and steeps of the mountains." Now Doniphan again used wagons to transport supplies.[39]

In traveling toward El Paso the Missourians passed over terrain known as Jornada del Muerto (Journey of the Dead Man), a ninety-mile stretch of desert that challenged men and mules. The weather was extremely cold. There was no water to drink or wood for fires. The soldiers straggled along day and night, "fatigued with marching, faint with hunger, and benumbed by the piercing winds." The teamsters labored "incessantly night and day with their trains to keep pace." On 22 December the men wandered into the town of Doña Ana, where they found grain and forage for their animals, water and food for themselves. By Christmas Day they were camping at Brazito when a Mexican army of twelve hundred attacked them. The Battle of Brazito lasted thirty minutes. Only seven or eight Missourians were wounded; the next day the victorious volunteers entered El Paso without further opposition.[40]

On 11 February 1847, after appropriating additional supplies and horses, mules, and oxen, the Missourians marched toward Chihuahua. They had learned of the Taos Revolt and knew that they would have to live off the land, but this was neither a new nor frightening experience for them. The days were hot while the nights were bitterly cold, but no hardship seemed to discourage this hardy band. Most of the supplies were finally left behind after the supply wagons almost continually bogged down in sand. Initially, teamsters quadrupled the teams to move wagons through the sand to firmer ground. But they were killing the animals that were already dying of fatigue and thirst. Many soldiers walked as their horses were too weak to carry them; others killed their mounts for food. The mules and horses were continually "neighing and crying piteously for water. Some were too weak to proceed further. They were abandoned."[41] Despite the suffering, the Missourians did not falter. They sacrificed their horses and mules in their hasty advance, knowing more animals would be available the farther they advanced into Mexico. They had only to capture them from the Mexicans. As frontiersmen many of them had little concern for the lives of animals, which were expendable. By 27 February they had covered 225 miles and were within a short day's march of Chihuahua City.

On Sunday, 28 February, Doniphan's army attacked twenty-seven hundred Mexican infantry and some eight hundred mounted *rancheros* armed with machetes. By five o'clock that afternoon the Missourians had won a complete victory, as the Mexican forces abandoned the field leaving three hundred dead. The Missourians' losses were one man killed and eleven wounded. Although well trained, most Mexican soldiers had vastly inferior weapons. Not all of them, in fact, even possessed muskets. They had a full complement of artillery, but the powder used in the cannons was of extremely poor quality, and during the engagement the Missourians claimed they were able to see the cannonballs coming and to dodge them. With better equipment the Mexicans undoubtedly would have put up a much more effective fight.

In Chihuahua the Missourians found themselves isolated, for no other American troops were within several hundred miles. Late in April, nearly two months after their arrival, they were ordered to join Taylor at Saltillo, which meant another hard march and a disappointment at the end, for Taylor had already left. After a halfhearted attempt to join the American force at Monterrey, the Missourians returned to Saltillo. Their one-year enlistments were about to expire, and they declined to reenlist. They had campaigned enough. At Reynosa on the Rio Grande they boarded transports for New Orleans and left behind what few animals they still possessed.

The exploits of the First Missouri Mounted Volunteers were amazing in the military history of the United States. In a little more than a year's time they had marched more than thirty-five hundred miles and experienced more than their share of hardships. They had subdued Pueblo and Navajo Indians and defeated two Mexican armies. They were untrained, undisciplined, irregular troops operating with few supplies, their pay always in arrears, and literally no instructions. When they finally arrived at New Orleans, it must have been difficult for the crowds that met them to believe that these men had been part of an organized army. In a sense it was a moot point.[42]

The Army of the West's march to Santa Fe, its further adventures, and the replacement regiments of the one-year enlistment soldiers sent from Missouri and Illinois to Santa Fe increased travel along the Santa Fe Trail. Quartermasters sent large supply trains of wagons pulled by both oxen and mules to meet the increased demand for supplies and rations. Santa Fe traders, sensing even larger markets for their goods, joined these trains. No longer needing to follow the treacherous Raton Pass route, huge caravans followed the Cimarron route of the Santa Fe Trail. As with the initial expedition, the army sent no military escorts to protect the wagon trains. The army had ignored the need for protection, expecting the teamsters to take care of their wagons and themselves.

The lack of mounted troops was an invitation for Comanches and Pawnees to attack the trains. The Indians "infested" the trail, wrote John T. Hughes, a member of Doniphan's regiment, and "committed repeated depredations on the government trains." They "killed and drove off great numbers of horses, mules, and oxen" and killed or captured many of the teamsters. On 22 June "a large body of Indians" attacked a returning government train near the Arkansas River, "drove off eighty yoke of oxen, and in sight of the teamsters, whose force was too weak" to resist, "wantonly and cruelly slaughtered them for amusement." In October 1846 Indians attacked twenty-four government wagons and drove off 280 mules, "leaving only twelve behind." Unless "an imposing mounted force be employed against" the Indians and "they be severely chastised," exclaimed Quartermaster General Jesup in his annual report, "it will be impossible to send supplies on that route."[43]

To protect the government and civilian caravans, the army at first countered with a defensive measure. In the spring of 1847 quartermasters established a small station (later called Fort Mann) just east of Cimarron Crossing. Initially not meant as a station for troops, it was to serve as a depot where wagons could be repaired, mules reshod, and supplies cached. It was later abandoned but within the same year was reoccupied as a base for troops.

More importantly President Polk and his military advisers concluded that previous events, as well as Jesup's warning, warranted establishing a substantial police force along the trail. With no troops readily available Secretary of War Marcy requested five additional companies of one-year volunteers (two dragoon companies, one of foot artillery, and two of infantry) from Missouri to control the Indians. Gov. John Edwards hoped that Colonel Doniphan, recently returned from his year's service, would agree to head the new command. Doniphan declined, however, but Edwards persuaded William Gilpin, the major of the First Missouri Volunteers, to accept command of what became known as the Indian Battalion. The new lieutenant colonel faced a difficult task in recruiting the type of men needed for his new command. Most of the men of his previous regiment followed Doniphan's example and refused to reenlist. The men of the Indian Battalion were mainly recent German immigrants and "green city boys" who had been lured to enlist by the promise of a 160-acre land bounty after a year's service. The supply officer at Fort Leavenworth gave out only the most meager equipment to state volunteers, whom he believed would totally fail in their stated mission. In such circumstances it was a tribute to the men of the Indian Battalion that they accomplished any of their objectives.

During the coming year the Indian Battalion actively attempted to provide much-needed protection along the Santa Fe Trail but with only limited success. In March 1848, a month after the Treaty of Guadalupe Hidalgo, Gilpin obtained mounts from William Bent and commenced an expedition against the Comanches. With few horses available, Bent furnished mules not only for the dragoons but also for the artillery battery, infantry companies, and a small supply train. From Bent's Fort the mule-mounted command marched west at a leisurely pace, taking two weeks to cross through Raton Pass and move south to the Mora River. They rode west along the river and camped about twenty miles below the town of Mora. Gilpin then sent the wagon train to the town to obtain additional mules and supplies. His plan was to attack Comanche and Plains Apache camps along the main or south fork of the Canadian River while the Indians were still in winter camps and their ponies still weak from lack of adequate grazing.

As was so often the case the Indians knew of the battalion's movement well in advance and took effective measures to stop it. They burned off the grass on both sides of the river, which effectively delayed the march. The large grain-fed mules and horses still required from two to four hours of grazing each day to stay in good condition and not break down on a march. Although the parched earth tactics did not stop the Indian Battalion, they slowed it down so much that it took forty days to reach the vacated camps, about the same time it took for an ox-pulled wagon caravan to reach Santa Fe from Independence. The expiration of the Indian Battalion's enlistments and the end of the war meant that protection along the Santa Fe Trail was thereafter the task of the regular army, which would face many of the same obstacles as those of the Indian Battalion.[44]

The last campaign of the war was to capture Mexico City. To win the war, Polk and members of his cabinet believed that American troops must capture the Mexican capital. Always the politician, Polk needed a general for this campaign who would not be a Whig candidate for the presidency, but there were no Democratic generals high enough in service or experience. As a way out of his political dilemma Polk even considered appointing the chairman of the Senate Committee on Military Affairs, sixty-four-year-old Sen. Thomas H. Benton of Missouri, lieutenant general of the U.S. Army. Unfortunately for Mexico, Congress refused to create the new rank. On 19 November 1846 Polk, with the approval of a majority of his cabinet, finally named Scott to the command and ordered him to employ his own plan of using an amphibious force to capture the port of Vera Cruz and then to march on Mexico City.

The logistics to carry out such an amphibious operation were tremendous and, as Jesup phrased it, were enough to try the patience of mere men. The army and navy designated three ports of debarkation—New Orleans, Santiago de Brazos, and Tampico. At these ports the supplies (repackaged for easier transportation by pack mules,) wagons, men, and horses and mules were loaded for the final destination of Vera Cruz.[45]

On 9 March at 5:40 P.M., the first American troops landed on Collado Beach south of Vera Cruz. Sixty-five surfboats commanded by naval officers and manned by sailors discharged soldiers, returned to the transports, embarked another load, landed it, and returned for more troops. The entire assault force of eighty-six hundred soldiers had been landed by 11:00 P.M. without the loss of a man, a feat without parallel in amphibious landings even in the twentieth century. During the next few days, whenever the tides and weather permitted, surfboats also unloaded field artillery and supplies. Horses and mules evidently received a low unloading priority. By 12 March only a few carts and one hundred horses—no doubt officers' mounts—were on shore.[46]

Most mules and horses were apparently the last to reach the beach. If the animals had been brought to Vera Cruz in small vessels having light draught, "they were thrown overboard as near the beach as the vessels could safely get." If transported in a larger ship, they were first loaded on board the steamer *Petrita*, then taken in as far as possible, pushed overboard, and made to swim to shore in tow of the surfboats. Nearly five hundred animals were "got ashore in one day." Several of the horses and mules were lost as high winds interrupted the operations and drove as many as forty vessels ashore.[47]

The accounts of the unloading of the horses and mules do not mention any problem of sailors pushing or throwing overboard animals that are usually afraid of water unless trained, which was not likely the case. Perhaps the horses and mules were so weary of ship life that they willingly boarded a noisy steamer that was belching smoke and then allowed sailors to push them into the water—though this seems highly unlikely. That five hundred animals could be landed in this way in a day's time was remarkable.

On 27 March the American force captured Vera Cruz and the supposedly impregnable castle of San Juan de Ulua. Scott now faced a substantial problem of logistics in getting his ten-thousand-man army moving on the road to Mexico City. He had earlier written the quartermaster at Brazos de Santiago that for the landing at Vera Cruz he initially needed one hundred wagons and five hundred mules. If he was successful, "say in three weeks," Scott would require "a much more considerable train of wagons" and pack mules for the army, and he hoped to obtain "a large portion of the mules by capturing them from the Mexican army or purchasing them from Mexican civilians."[48] Scott later informed Jesup that he needed from eight hundred to a thousand wagons, five thousand harness mules, two to three thousand pack mules, and from three hundred to five hundred draft animals for the siege train. Before all plans for the expeditionary force had been finalized, Jesup had calculated that an army of 25,000 would require 9,303 wagons pulled by 46,515 mules and some 17,413 pack mules. Since Scott's force consisted of only 10,000 men, 40 percent of Jesup's estimate meant that Scott needed 3,721 wagons, 18,606 wagon mules, and 6,965 pack mules. Jesup's estimates proved to be more reliable than Scott's.[49]

While Jesup was calculating needs and ordering wagons and mules and Scott was fuming over delays in getting his army to higher ground to escape a possible yellow fever epidemic, President Polk was becoming exasperated at the cost of transportation. To the acting quartermaster general in Washington DC, Col. Henry Stanton, Polk emphatically stated that he "condemned the purchase and employment of thousands of wagons" requested for Scott's army and thought that "long trains of miles of wagons" would retard the progress of the army and require too many men to guard it. He believed that pack mules were the answer to the transportation dilemma and that both horses and mules needed by the army could and should be purchased in Mexico instead of the United States for one-fourth the cost.[50]

Jesup agreed with the president. In a letter to Secretary of War William L. Marcy he wrote that except for artillery the armies should not have used "a single wheel" in Mexico. The quartermasters should have supplied their troops like the Mexicans did. "To make our operations effective," he claimed, "we must do as he does."[51]

Still, Jesup went on approving the purchase of wagons. Transportation needs remained so critical that quartermasters continued to purchase expensive American horses and mules for shipment to Mexico, a country famous for its saddle horses and pack animals. In fact, Scott's army was not able to obtain substantial numbers of mules until after the Battle of Cerro Gordo.[52]

Not until 8 April did officers collect enough pack mules and wagons for the advance toward Jalapa. By 12 April there were 500 wagons and 250 pack mules on the road with the advancing army. At the narrow pass of Cerro Gordo the Mexicans chose to resist the American invaders. In a two-pronged assault on 17 April, Scott's soldiers captured the ground above Cerro Gordo and also the artillery positions commanding the road. By noon the next day the American troops had won a decisive but costly victory. The fighting at times was hand-to-hand and fierce. One soldier described it as the kind of combat he hoped "never to see again. It seemed like murder to see men running bayonets into each other's breasts." American casualties were 63 killed and 368 wounded, but Scott's soldiers had taken more than 3,000 Mexican prisoners including 200 officers. The Battle of Cerro Gordo was a severe defeat from which Santa Anna's army never really recovered. Many Mexicans had lost all faith in Santa Anna and his army to keep the Americans out of the Mexican capital. On 19 April the Americans entered Jalapa. They were now only 170 miles from their objective—Mexico City.

At Jalapa Scott faced a serious loss in manpower. Seven of the volunteer regiments' enlistments were about to end, and not many of the men agreed to reenlist. When they left to board transports at Vera Cruz, Scott had fewer than six thousand soldiers, some of whom were sick or wounded. In May he cautiously marched his depleted army to Puebla, having been unable to increase substantially his mule supply.

Scott's army was in desperate need of more troopers' mounts and wagon and pack mules. When Col. Jack Hays's Texas Rangers entered Puebla, for example, "they rode, some sideways, some standing upright, some by the reverse flank, some faced to the rear, some on horses, some on asses, some on mustangs, and some on mules." The army waited at Puebla until August for additional supplies and reinforcements and collected as many horses and mules as possible to replenish its diminished stock.[53] On 15 August, with new reinforcements arriving daily, Scott's army left Puebla and marched toward the Valley of Mexico. It was on its own, having cut itself off from a supply base. On 20 August a portion of the army overwhelmed a larger Mexican force, capturing more than seven hundred prisoners and liberating several hundred pack mules and twenty-two cannons, including two American guns the Mexicans had captured at Buena Vista. The Battle of Contreras (or Padierna) was another costly Mexican defeat.[54]

Scott's army inflicted an even more serious defeat on them the same day. A larger force of Santa Anna's army, eighteen hundred soldiers, had concentrated at Churubusco in a fortified convent. Three other regiments guarded the bridge across the Churubusco River. The Mexicans at the bridge beat back several attacks before retreating. The army then concentrated on the convent where two companies of the defenders were American deserters, the San Patricios. After a determined resistance, the Mexican force saw that further opposition was useless and they surrendered. The army had captured more than twelve hundred additional prisoners including eighty-five San Patricios and seven additional cannons. In both battles, it had lost 12 percent of its force in dead and wounded, or almost one thousand men in all.

After the Battle at Churubusco, Scott offered a truce so that negotiations for a peace treaty could begin between an agent of the State Department, Nicholas Trist, and Mexican officials. These talks made no progress and on 6 September Scott renounced them. Two days later the American army again attacked the Mexicans, this time at El Molino del Rey. Again the Mexican army resisted valiantly; the Americans lost in excess of a hundred men but took the objective.

The last battle in the American advance on Mexico City was at Chapúltepec Heights and at Belé Garita. Scott's diversionary ploys had worked against Santa Anna, and on 13 September the Americans again gained their objective as an American flag flew over Chapúltepec Castle. Santa Anna supposedly exclaimed, "I believe that if we were to plant our batteries in Hell the damned Yankees would take them from us." One of his subordinates shook his head and replied, "God is a Yankee." By late afternoon American soldiers were fighting inside Mexico City. Santa Anna still had an army of twelve thousand to defend the capital but civilian authorities, convinced that the general would again fail, persuaded Santa Anna to take his army elsewhere. At night the Mexican army slipped away to Guadalupe Hidalgo. Early on the morning of 14 September 1847 American forces took possession of Mexico City. For the first time an American flag flew over a foreign capital. The shooting war in Mexico was over.[55]

Throughout the entire campaign Scott had faced many of the same problems in mule supply that had plagued Taylor. After entering Puebla his officers had been able to purchase most of the necessary mules, equipment, and supplies needed. Like Taylor's supply trains Scott's were plagued by attacks from guerrillas and bandits. Both generals responded in much the same way. Taylor let a force of Texas Rangers extract retribution from the areas where the attacks occurred, which was harsh but had a beneficial effect for the trains. The names of Texas Rangers "'Old Reid,' Captain Bayley, Harry Love, Ben McCulloch and, more terrible than all, 'Mustang' Gray," wrote Private Chamberlain, "will always remain fresh in the memory of Mexicans, as the fearful atrocities committed by them now form part of the Nursery Legends of the country." Scott used details to guard the trains and also sent squads to "investigate" suspected bandits. Both armies experienced trouble keeping qualified teamsters with the wagon trains. Scott's trains were maintained by hiring volunteers at premium prices whose year's service was about to expire and by using dragoons and infantrymen from the ranks. According to one officer, not one in ten of these replacements was capable of driving a wagon correctly. This meant that wagons and mules broke down and that wagons, harnesses, and mules had to be replaced every four months. In the end both generals ordered knowledgeable officers to deal with the difficult matter of supplies. These officers were able to confiscate enough mules from the enemy, or purchase them from civilians, to keep the armies on the march. Toward the end of Scott's campaign to capture Mexico City, American quartermasters had been unable to use all the mules captured from the Mexican army.[56]

At the conclusion of the war Quartermaster General Jesup directed that while surplus property could be sold, that property did not include serviceable mules or wagons. All sound, well-broken mules in Mexico City and along the route were to be shipped from Vera Cruz to the United States. Some Mexican mules therefore learned the joys of being cooped up aboard steamers. Those in Monterrey and surrounding areas were to be sent to the coast for shipment. The quartermaster in the Monterrey area, however, detailed men to drive four thousand mules, four hundred wagons, and seven hundred horses overland to western Louisiana. There the best of the mules were sent to the southwestern posts and the others auctioned off. At Santa Fe all serviceable mules were kept for use in the newly acquired American Southwest.[57]

In all four major campaigns in the Mexican War pack and wagon mules had proved themselves superior beasts of burden. And the small, well-proportioned Mexican mules had proved to be as capable as the larger ones bred in the United States. A fitting tribute to the Mexican mules used during the war was a story told by Ulysses S. Grant. While waiting passage home, Grant and several other young officers went on an excursion to visit Popocatépetl, the highest volcano in Mexico. At a village near the base of the mountain the party hired guides with two pack mules to carry forage for the officers' mounts. While climbing near the edge of a steep drop-off, one of the mules loaded with two huge sacks of barley struck his load against the mountainside and fell over the precipice. "The descent was steep but not perpendicular." The mule rolled over and over to the bottom and all thought that it had been killed. "What was our surprise, not long after we had gone into bivouac, to see the lost mule, cargo, and owner coming up the ascent." All agreed that the sacks of barley had protected the animal, but they also surely agreed that it was one tough little mule.[58]

CHAPTER 3

Mule Power in the Army, 1848–1861

During the Mexican War the military achieved a number of significant firsts. The army and navy cooperated and completed an overseas expedition and amphibious operation that included transporting and landing thousands of mules and horses. The army waged its first war of aggression and indirectly acquired more territory for the United States than the country gained in the Louisiana Purchase. Army expeditions made the longest marches in American military history to that time, proving especially the durability of mules. And despite complaints from a host of officers, including Zachary Taylor and Winfield Scott, transportation and supply were never seriously delayed; the lack of supplies or transport never cost American soldiers a major battle. The use of thousands of wagon and pack mules to supply troops on the march was in no small measure a reason for the army's success.

Mules remained major players because distance became as great a concern to the small peacetime army as it had been during the war. With the acquisition of the Mexican Cession and all of the Oregon country, the United States could rightly claim the army faced a herculean task of policing the entire Department of the West; yet it must operate on a yearly peacetime budget that was further restricted by congressmen who were never enamored of a professional army and were especially wary of mounted troops. By 1850,

59 percent of 10,763 actual army personnel were scattered over the Department of the West. A decade later more than 80 percent of the actual strength of 19,006 men was stationed in the states of Texas and California and the territories of New Mexico, Utah, and Oregon.[1] Soldiers in the West became quite reliant on army mules. Despite the fact that actual army strength in personnel increased by only 5,933 men, during the decade, the army's use of mules continued to expand dramatically. On most expeditions soldiers depended on pack and wagon mules to haul supplies and ammunition and even to serve as stretcher carriers for the wounded. The five army railroad surveys between 1854 and 1855 depended on mule-drawn wagons to carry supplies. Sometimes most-reluctant infantrymen mounted even more disinclined army mules to perform dragoon duties. In these and other ways mules proved themselves to be indispensable and superior to oxen, camels, and horses. If given a fair chance, they might have performed even better than horses did for dragoons and later cavalry troopers. Percival G. Lowe, who served with the First Dragoons for five years, left the regiment as a sergeant and then served as a civilian wagon master for the quartermaster's department at both Forts Leavenworth and Riley, never admitted that mules would make desirable mounts for dragoons. But on occasion he observed that mules were more reliable than cavalry mounts. This was especially true during stampedes, which he referred to as the "terror of terrors" for army expeditions. "Mules tone down after a short run," Lowe remarked after being caught up in one stampede, "whereas frightened horses never know when to stop and run until exhausted. A herd of mules without horses to lead them in a stampede will hardly ever run more than two miles, circle around a little and then either stop to graze or strike a trail at a moderate gait."[2]

Every year following the war army officials campaigned for additional regiments of mounted troops—dragoons, cavalry, or mounted riflemen—arguing that only mounted troops could successfully combat mounted Plains Indians. Congress did not initially respond to these requests but in June of 1850 passed an "Act to increase the Rank and File of the Army, and to encourage Enlistments." One of stipulations in the act increased the number of privates from sixty to seventy-four in companies of any regiment serving at remote stations. It also allowed such companies serving on foot to be properly equipped and mounted whenever the need arose. The only animals available, except officers' mounts, were mules. Dragoons never had remudas from which to draw extra horses; they had to struggle to maintain one reasonably good mount. So Congress effectually approved of mounting infantry on wagon and pack mules rather than increasing the number of arrogant dragoons.

The act did not go unchallenged. "Employing foot regiments in this way," warned Scott in his report to the secretary of war, would "result in disorganizing them as infantry and converting them into extremely indifferent horsemen." The "wear and tear" on animals and equipment "would be enormous—probably three-fold greater than with regular cavalry . . . thus making this nondescript force the most expensive and the least efficient ever known" to the army. Corroborating Scott's remarks, Gen. George M. Brook wrote from San Antonio that mounted infantry were miserable riders, that most of them had never been astride an animal and were "utterly incapable of using their arms when in the saddle." Several other observers echoed this sentiment.[3]

Teresa Griffin Viele, an army wife stationed in South Texas during the late 1850s, however, wrote that mounted infantry could be effective. The "soldiers of our garrison belonged to that horse marine class 'mounted infantry,' so that drilling them into dragoons was by no means a pleasant task." They had no knowledge of drill, she claimed, sat on their mounts like a "parcel of clothes-pins, and it was not an unusual thing to see a dozen dismounted at once. In spite of their mishaps," the soldiers "seemed to enjoy it very much, and after a few months' perseverance became quite a presentable cavalry company."[4]

While army brass bridled against using mounted infantry, the army was using mules effectively as both draft animals and mounts in actual expeditions sent to chastise Plains Indians for treaty violations. In 1855, for example, Secretary of War Jefferson Davis sent Bvt. Brig. Gen. William S. Harney with a six-hundred-man force to seek vengeance against the Sioux for the so-called Grattan Massacre and subsequent plundering of civilian trains along the California-Oregon trail during the previous year. Harney's army contained portions of his own regiment of Second Dragoons, the Sixth and Tenth Infantry (some of which were mule-mounted), and the Fourth Artillery. Lt. Col. Philip St. George Cooke, the army's foremost authority on cavalry, commanded the dragoons and mounted infantry.

On 4 August the Sioux Expedition left Fort Laramie and followed the emigrant trail, accompanied by a large array of mule-drawn wagons. Harney was looking for a fight. Two weeks later he reached Fort Kearny where the wagons were resupplied and the animals allowed to rest. Four days later the expedition left the fort, and on 2 September it crossed from the South Platte River to the North Platte and camped at Ash Hollow. Days before, scouts had discovered the peaceful camp of Little Thunder not far away on Blue Water Creek. Little Thunder had no reason to expect trouble.

Harney ordered a surprise attack the next morning. Mounted troops and infantry rode on the camp from different directions. The fight was more pursuit and killing than a battle. The Sioux lost eighty-five killed, and more than seventy women and children were taken prisoner. Less than half the people in the village escaped. The Battle on Blue Creek effectively ended resistance and convinced the other Sioux to abide by the demands of Harney. His harsh treatment would keep the Sioux at peace for almost a decade.[5]

With the Sioux now subdued, army troops faced the Cheyennes. Both sides deserved blame for the troubles that erupted in 1856 along the emigrant trail, but the new commander of the Department of the West, Gen. Persifor Smith, decided that the Cheyennes were at fault and must be severely punished. He planned for a spring offensive in 1857 under Col. Edwin Vose Sumner and the recently established First Cavalry Regiment.

The Cheyennes faced a worthy opponent. Sumner had been in uniform since 1819 and had become captain of the First Dragoons in 1833. In 1855 he, then lieutenant colonel of the First Dragoons, had won the coveted colonelcy of the First Cavalry. Known to his men as "Bull o' the Woods" because of his booming voice, he was a hardened old dragoon who loved a fight.[6]

At Fort Leavenworth Sumner was preparing an offensive that would employ three formidable columns, including the impressive mule-drawn supply trains. Late in May Lt. Col. Joseph E. Johnston led off with a column consisting of four companies of the First Cavalry and two of the Sixth Infantry. This force had the impossible mission of surveying the southern boundary of Kansas while cooperating with Sumner. On 18 May Maj. John Sedgwick left the fort with four companies of the First Cavalry and proceeded west along the Santa Fe Trail and then up the Arkansas River. The command was to meet Sumner's columns on 4 July at the site of Fort St. Vrain near the South Platte River. Sumner's command, consisting of the other two companies of the First Cavalry, left Fort Leavenworth on 20 May and followed the emigrant trail to Fort Laramie. There he was supposed to be joined by two companies of the Second Dragoons, and both were then to follow up the Platte in search of Cheyennes. At Fort Laramie, Sumner learned that the two companies of dragoons had been ordered to join the punitive expedition to Utah. He picked up three companies of the Sixth Infantry to replace the dragoons. Each of the three columns had two prairie howitzers hauled by four-mule teams, and each company was provided with two six-mule wagons. Transportation for Sumner's column consisted of fifty six-mule team wagons, a four-mule ambulance, and twenty replacement mules. In addition, a remuda of mounts and a beef herd followed the column. Including extra riding mules for the teamsters, the three columns were probably supplied with more than five hundred mules, quite a sizable number for an army command of the 1850s.[7]

Lowe served as head wagon master for Sumner's transportation. Almost fifty years later he wrote an account of the advance into Indian country. On the march from Leavenworth to Laramie the command had to cross the South Platte at Beauvais' or Lower Crossing. The river was dangerous to cross, even when the water level remained fairly low, for the bottom was uneven and changes were sudden, "sometimes a foot deep, suddenly becoming two, three, and in a few places four feet deep." After determining a route that avoided quicksand and as many deep holes as possible, Lowe stationed teamsters on saddle mules across the route to assist any wagon needing help. A teamster tied a strap to the bridle of each lead mule in the team and led the wagon across the river while two or three others "rode on the lower side to whip up the mules and keep them from drifting down." When one wagon was safely across, the teamsters recrossed to assist another.[8]

Only the most lightly loaded wagon containing the medical supplies was lost at Beauvais' Crossing. Half of the wagons had already forded the river, wrote Lowe, "when the oldest wagonmaster started in with a wagon for the first time. . . . In the middle of the stream, the team tangled up, the leaders swung around and the saddle-mule sank in the sand and got under the tongue, the lower (off) wheels sank, and the wagon rolled over in the deepest water." The young driver was attempting "to extricate himself from his saddle mule and crying for help. The man on the lower side could not reach him and the wagonmaster sat on his horse like a wooden man." Lowe was fifty yards away from the incident, "but put spurs to my horse and reached the boy in time to keep him from going under the tongue with the saddle-mule, which drowned." Others saved the rest of the wagon's mules by cutting the harness, and Lowe swung the driver on behind him and reached shore.[9]

The wagon mules were well trained for the expedition. Each evening when the wagon master circled the wagons and made a corral within the circle, the mules were allowed to graze. To corral the mules before dusk or whenever Indians appeared, one of the herders who always led a horse with a bell on his neck rattled the bell violently and galloped for the corral. The mules quickly learned to respond to the bell and could not be kept from the corral when the bell was rung. In time, packers and wagon masters learned that mules responded more readily to mares than to horses.[10]

When the Sumner and Sedgwick commands rendezvoused, they cut loose from the supply train to search the heart of the Cheyenne hunting grounds. To furnish the basic supplies needed for the combined command, Lowe formed a packtrain, carefully selecting mules that could be packed and using any that were broken to ride. Teamsters were busy meanwhile breaking other mules. As important as the selection of mules was to the makeup of the packtrain, Lowe realized that he also needed competent packers. "Except a few Mexicans," he wrote, "I have not a man who is a practical packer; among the soldiers there are none." With the Mexicans who knew how to pack, Lowe established a training school, but the Mexicans had difficulty imparting to others what they themselves knew well. The teachers were, however, able to instruct a few men in the basics. Sumner's command would be supported by 180 pack and riding mules with "Big Nick" Beery, who had been in charge of Sedgwick's wagons, in command of the train and novice packers.[11]

On the morning of 29 July scouts discovered a large force of Cheyennes. Leaving his infantry and howitzers to follow as quickly as possible, Sumner pushed ahead with the cavalry and the pack-train, hoping to overtake the Cheyennes before they scattered in the presence of such a large force. But the Indians had no intention of scattering. They had washed their hands in a magic lake whose waters would make the soldiers' firearms harmless, and some three hundred were waiting for the horse soldiers near the Solomon River. The cavalry formed in a line of three squadron columns and began to trot its mounts toward the Cheyenne warriors; the packers halted the train to await further developments. The Cheyenne line also moved forward. As the gap narrowed between the opposing forces, the bugler sounded the call "gallop-march." Moments later Bull o' the Woods bellowed "Sling carbines, draw sabers," quickly followed by the command, "CHARGE!"[12]

Almost immediately the Indians reined in their mounts. The long knives worried them, for their medicine men had said nothing about being protected against sabers. Their will to fight now broken, most splashed across the Solomon in hope of escaping. For seven miles the long knives chased them but killed only nine warriors. Eleven cavalrymen, including Lt. J. E. B. Stuart, were wounded and two killed, but the Cheyennes had suffered a major setback. When the First Cavalry pursued them two days later, they broke up into small groups and scattered. Only in September, when most of the command was ordered to join the Utah expedition, did Sumner suspend operations. By then the packers knew how to pack their mules, and the mules had become accustomed to being packed instead of ridden or harnessed.[13]

Providing supplies, horses, and mule-drawn wagons for large and small expeditions tried the ingenuity of quartermasters throughout the West. The quartermaster's department faced a far greater logistical headache, however, that of providing transportation for supplies and actually transporting soldiers to their various posts. Costs escalated and expenditures so frequently exceeded appropriations that deficiency appropriations were often necessary. Jesup calculated that during the five-year period, 1852–57, the average number of soldiers was 13,600 rank and file, whose transportation had cost more than $2 million a year. During the five-year period preceding the Mexican War, the average numbers were 9,900 rank and file and $156,000 a year. Prior to the war most of the garrisons and forts were fairly accessible to navigable rivers, and the cost of transportation by barge and steamer was fairly reasonable. Overland transportation costs were also usually minimal. By 1848–50, however, soldiers were scattered in posts on the plains and in mountain regions hundreds of miles from navigable rivers, and the cost of transportation had increased substantially. In addition, the quartermasters were having to provide transportation for more supplies than in the past—supplies that they or post commanders had previously purchased locally.

Many posts required building materials, fuel, and forage for horses and mules. At Fort Quitman, Texas, for example, lumber was so scarce that there was not enough wood to make coffins. Contract freighters were called to supply the fort with lumber in addition to normal supplies. In West Texas and much of the New Mexico Territory where mounted troops were stationed, quartermasters were required to send forage shipments at least once a year either to keep down costs or because of scarcity of grain in the region. In California, during some years forage grain came by ship from other countries. Army forage contractors no doubt kept the price of grain at a steady rate throughout the West and in midwestern states and territories. This steady market greatly enhanced farmers' buying power and helped produce a healthy regional economy. Quartermasters spent almost $1 million annually for forage to feed army animals. Including transporting supplies and soldiers to the Pacific Coast by ships, the cost of army transportation had increased by 1,500 percent from 1844 to 1850, while the army had expanded by only 50 percent. Prior to the war with Mexico, the annual cost of transporting the entire military was less than $120,000. During the war the annual cost rose to $5 million, and between 1848 and 1860 it averaged about $2 million.[14]

In 1848 the quartermaster's department established a number of major depots to supply army posts throughout the West. Fort Leavenworth, near the Missouri River 411 miles from St. Louis, became the chief depot for all posts on both the Oregon and Santa Fe Trails.

From Leavenworth wagons hauled supplies 310 miles to Fort Kearny, 637 miles to Fort Laramie, 728 miles to Fort Union, and 821 miles to Santa Fe. To service most of the forts in Texas, quartermasters sent supplies by ship from New Orleans to Indianola, Texas, at Matagorda Bay. Indianola supported the interior depots at San Antonio some 200 miles away and at El Paso 820 miles from Matagorda Bay.[15]

By 1855 the quartermaster department supplied more than fifty posts scattered over two million square miles of territory. Jesup, well aware that using civilian teamsters and packers during the war had at times been unsatisfactory, still turned partially to private contractors to supply these posts. Civilians working for the army had usually proven to be less than desirable personnel because quartermasters were unable to pay teamsters a competitive salary. If quartermasters considered high forage costs, possible wagon repairs, and the cost of feeding inactive animals during the winter months when freighting was suspended, private contractors were no more expensive than army trains. The deciding factor was the ability to supply the army installations efficiently. A report by the assistant quartermaster at San Antonio, Edwin B. Babbitt, shows one example of comparable costs and services between government trains and contract freighters. During the fiscal year 1851 Babbitt sent out 752 six-mule wagons and engaged the services of 99 two-team ox-drawn wagons owned by contractors to supply Texas forts. The mule-drawn government wagons carried 1,930,207 pounds of supplies, while the contract freight wagons carried 255,085 pounds. On this occasion the contract freighter was an economical alternative.[16]

Yet another comparison taken over a three-year period is a little more favorable to army supply trains. In 1849 Capt. Samuel G. French conducted a train of 275 wagons and 2,500 mules, oxen, and beef cattle from San Antonio to El Paso. The long, grueling trip cost the army at least $20 per 100 pounds to haul the needed supplies. The next year the quartermaster hired a contract freighter to make the long haul. The freighter was required to transport 865,000 pounds of military supplies at $12 per 100 pounds. Since the civilian train required an army mounted escort and the army paid the contractor to carry rations and forage for the horses, the actual cost was more like $22 per 100 pounds. The next year El Paso received its yearly supplies by army supply train, again under French. The cost came to $19 per 100 pounds.[17]

Two years after the Mexican War, quartermasters were using contract freighting to supply army installations almost five times as often as they were using government trains. It was easier for a quartermaster to hire a contractor ready to haul supplies than to find suitable wagons and mules and hire competent civilian personnel. By the mid-1850s the freight firm of Russell, Majors, and Waddell had almost monopolized the freight business for the army along the Santa Fe and Oregon Trails. Instead of using mules, the private contractor employed ox teams and used J. Murphy wagons capable of carrying three or four tons over rough roads. By operating on a gigantic scale and offering other services to the army at no increase in cost, the firm was able to help itself and the army at the same time. One way to keep the army supplied and make larger profits was hauling for other businesses at the same time the company was freighting for the army.[18]

The U.S. Army, however, did maintain a supply system that depended mainly on mule-drawn wagons. Despite the problems involved with underpaid, inexperienced teamsters, wheelwrights, and other necessary civilian personnel, the army did not leave the entire transportation business to freighting companies. Although expensive, Scott, Jesup, and numerous other high-ranking army officers knew the importance, through the prior experience of the Seminole and Mexican Wars, of keeping an army supply system in operation. In 1848 and 1849, for example, troops sent to Oregon, Santa Fe, and El Paso required the logistical support of more than eight hundred army wagons, thirty-five hundred horses and mules, and thirty-seven hundred oxen.[19]

Supply caravans employing tremendous numbers of mules increased the army's dependence on and familiarity with the animals. An official train consisted of 28 four-mule "escort" wagons, 112 harness mules, 5 or 6 saddle mules that also served as replacements for unserviceable harness mules, a wagonmaster, a farrier, a cook, and an animal watchman. On many occasions heavier six-mule jerk-line wagons were substituted for the escort wagons, which changed the makeup of the train. Indeed there seemed to be few official trains, for many times quartermasters combined trains and portions of trains to ship the required supplies. In 1854 and 1855, for example, 450 mules pulled 70 wagons from Fort Leavenworth to California. According to an assistant quartermaster, Capt. Rufus G. Ingalls, he "neither lost or abandoned anything," and the mules were in "fine condition" at the conclusion of the journey.[20]

By now the army set high standards for harness mules. Mules had to be of dark color, strong, stout, and compact animals, sound in all particulars, in good condition, not under 14 hh, not fewer than four nor more than nine years of age, and "suitable in every respect for the transportation service of the Army." Sometimes smaller, compactly built Mexican mules could be used to advantage. Although quartermasters accepted responsibility for the mules they purchased, they were often no match for mule traders who took advantage of every opportunity.[21]

Despite the fact that private contractors continued to use stout oxen and large wagons to haul supplies for the army, not only throughout the 1850s but during and after the Civil War, overall army personnel began to prefer mule power to ox power. Quartermasters and many other officers came to the same conclusion—that the hybrid mule was best suited for army services. They made their separate decisions after employing both ox and mule teams during the same expeditions.

Assistant quartermaster Captain French, for example, seemed to make up his mind during the expedition from San Antonio to El Paso, Texas. In an extensive report to Quartermaster General Jesup, French favored using mules—even "wild Mexican mules"—over oxen. A mule was faster than an ox, he stated, and with a load could travel "two and a half miles per hour and gain in that time on the ox 900 yards." Mules were more "gregarious" than oxen and easier to herd at night. Oxen, French claimed, would "stray off singly from the herd and lie down in the bushes" and were often lost. Mules tended to remain with the herd. "Mules will subsist where oxen cannot, and in mountainous country they can always feed on the hill sides." French added that mules could endure more fatigue, hunger, and thirst, and that on marches during the heat of the day they needed only one-fourth as much water as the oxen. Oxen were also more finicky than mules and would not drink the water mules would drink. French realized that mules were the more trackable animals and that although oxen could haul heavier loads, for general service mules were clearly preferable.[22]

In making his choice known to Jesup, French did not minimize some of his perceptions of the less desirable attributes of mules, and he gave specific examples. Mules were easily stampeded. French had seen a "drove of 300 stampeded in the daytime from such a slight cause as one of their number with a saddle on joining the herd at a run." Mules, he wrote, could be stampeded by an Indian, a wolf, or a horse running into the herd. They were therefore less reliable in Indian country. He also knew from experience that once stolen by Indians, mules could not be overtaken by a hasty pursuit, whereas oxen could be. French warned that horses should not be permitted to graze with mules, for the mules would invariably follow the horses. He added that the best way to stop mules from fleeing with a horse was to shoot the horse.[23]

During the march to El Paso, agents purchasing mules in Mexico kept the expedition supplied with replacement stock. French, always in need of fresh stock, anxiously waited to be resupplied. Probably not realizing at the time he wrote his report that he was praising mules over horses, he acknowledged that the experience he had gained from being in charge of the train had taught him, among other things, that herdsmen needed two animals to ride—one during the day and the other at night. "I have never seen any service harder for animals than herding a large drove of cattle," French wrote, "and so severe was it on the saddle horses that many of them died before we could get mules to replace them."[24]

While the army preferred mules over oxen, it continued to use both mules and oxen. Although either could often be purchased for from forty to eighty dollars depending on conformation and market conditions, their initial cost often was not as great as the cost of feeding them. In many of the arid portions of the West, working animals could not always forage for themselves and needed subsistence. Few animals ever received the full daily ration of fourteen pounds of hay and twelve pounds of corn or oats except during the bitter winter months when grazing was impossible. Even then, only animals that were worked daily ever approached that amount of rations, and mules probably never received that much corn or oats.

Officers usually performed a juggling act in making limited corn and hay supplies last. Nevertheless, the cost of forage, hovering at $1 million a year, was staggering to the peacetime army.

Although concerned over the cost of animals and of forage to feed them, army personnel were not able to take care of the animals properly. In 1853 Jesup recommended appropriations to establish a veterinary corps under the direction of the surgeon general. More money was lost every year by the sacrifice of horses and mules for want of proper veterinary aid, Jesup asserted, than would support the expense of such a corps for two or three years. Jesup's plea fell on deaf ears. The army finally established a mere semblance of a veterinary corps in 1916. Before then quartermasters had hired veterinarians when necessary by using funds appropriated for incidental expenses. Without an effective system to care for public animals, the army unnecessarily lost large numbers of horses and mules each year.[25]

In an attempt to reduce transportation expenses, including the cost of forage in the arid regions of the Southwest, in 1855 the army began experimenting with camels as pack animals. Several people had considered using these animals to replace oxen and mules in the Great American Desert as early as the 1830s. After the Mexican War the United States possessed a large area seemingly appropriate for using these beasts of the desert. The cost of contract freighters and army transportation's using mules and oxen was increasing dramatically, and with this knowledge camel advocates, including assistant quartermasters Maj. George H. Crosman and Maj. Henry C. Wayne, made their ideas known. Wayne influenced then Mississippi senator Jefferson Davis, chairman of the Senate Committee on Military Affairs, and Davis attempted unsuccessfully to amend the annual army appropriation bill in 1850 to provide funds to purchase fifty camels.[26]

After becoming President Franklin Pierce's secretary of war in 1853, Davis renewed his efforts. For his annual report of 1853 he asked Wayne to draft a statement on camels and dromedaries. Writing with enthusiasm, Wayne described the geography of the West and argued that communication "with the interior of our continent and throughout its center is rare, and carried on slowly, and expensively by means of wagons drawn by horses, mules, or oxen, averag-

ing on long journeys not more than twelve miles a day." Added to
the cost of the teams, harness, and wagons was the continuous
expense for teamsters, forage, shoes, and repairs. Camels, Wayne
claimed, needed no wagons or harness, few teamsters, and required
almost nothing for forage, yet they could double the average of a
day's journey by mules or oxen. He also noted that camels lived to a
considerable age and possessed "great strength, and astonishing
powers of abstinence from food and drink." One draught of water
would "last it for several days—say three or four—whilst a few
beans, a little meal, or dry herbage and plants by the wayside, served
it for food." Wayne claimed that camels could each carry seven hundred to twelve hundred pounds of supplies, day after day for from
thirty to forty miles. Wayne also asserted that camels would not
suffer from tender feet and could be used for other purposes as well.
Dromedaries would allow rapid communication and "give power of
controlling the Indians by checking and promptly punishing their
aggressions." What Wayne did not say, of course, was that mules
could travel forty to fifty miles a day, required little grain during
forced marches, were much easier to load, and were familiar to all
engaged in army transportation.[27]

In his annual message Davis requested extra funds for a camel experiment and generally followed Wayne's arguments. He concluded
that for military purposes such as expresses and reconnaissances
the dromedary would "supply a want now seriously felt in our service; and for transportation with troops rapidly moving across the
country, the camel, it is believed, would remove an obstacle which
now serves greatly to diminish the value and efficiency of our
troops on the western frontier." Yet no congressman or senator
came forward to present a bill for such an experiment.[28]

That same year John Russell Bartlett, having earlier returned
from his misadventures in the Southwest as director of the Mexican
boundary survey, published his rambling *Personal Narratives*. In
the concluding chapter of volume 2, he blatantly entered the fray on
the camel advocates' side. His chapter concerning camels and
dromedaries and the various positive statements of others kept the
idea before the public and convinced Davis to ask Congress again
for an appropriation. In 1855 Congress finally appropriated thirty

thousand dollars for bringing camels and dromedaries to the United States.[29]

Over the next two years the army imported some seventy-five camels and dromedaries into Texas. The camels quickly demonstrated what everybody acquainted with them already knew, that they were powerful animals that could carry heavier loads longer distances than either horses or mules. They required little water or food en route for five or six days and thrived on brush, mesquite bushes, and plants the other animals would usually not eat. In trips from their headquarters at Camp Verde to San Antonio, a distance of eighty miles, the camels required only two days to complete it, while three-mule teams and wagons took three days for the same journey. Edward Fitzgerald Beale's successful survey from Fort Defiance to the Colorado River brought these beasts of the desert new acclaim, as did other successful expeditions using camels.

Despite their overall success in transporting supplies, most soldiers and packers despised camels. Mules had been roundly cursed by the very men who depended on them, but camels made many conventional soldiers pause. Their odor was overpowering and totally unlike the sweet musky smell of horses or mules. When packed, they groaned, bleated, snarled, and wheezed in a noisy manner. By comparison mules' neighs were like fine music. When full of water, camels tended to spit without provocation. After partially digesting whatever they had eaten, they regurgitated their food into their mouths for further chewing or spitting. The cud was a foul-smelling, sticky mass that soldiers were sure caused terrible sores. Mules might be noisy eaters but they did not rechew. Camels were hard to pack, and they loaded differently than mules and horses. When they began shedding their winter coats in the spring, they appeared to have a dreadful skin disease. Camels could be much more dangerous than mules. Mule kicks and bites could sober a drunk but were usually not life threatening. Camel bites were dangerous, however, for their sharp teeth and strong jaws could cut a person's arm or leg to the bone. Worse still, the appearance of camels on roads and trails stampeded wagon- and packtrains, cavalry detachments, and civilian riders. Mules and horses literally ran away from camels. They could sense their presence before they actually saw them, and they became nervous and unmanageable. Even animals that had been on expeditions with the camels kept a respectable distance from them. Teamsters and packers hated and feared them. In comparing the habits of camels to mules, these men no doubt spoke of even the most ornery mules in reverent tones. The camel experiment was an interesting failure.

For the camel experiment to have been successful, all the principals needed to agree on its feasibility and necessity. Davis approved of the experiment, but Scott had not been consulted in advance and Jesup wanted to leave the experiment to private enterprise. Most of the older officers were only lukewarm at best to the idea of experimenting with camels. Quartermasters could have purchased a lot of mules for that thirty thousand.[30]

In retrospect, army officials, including the secretary of war, should have given more attention to the Mexican method of packing mules and less attention to packing foreign humped dromedaries and camels, even if they did carry more supplies per animal than mules. Mules were plentiful and known for what they were and what they were thought to be. They were respected from a distance and sometimes even up close. Their teamsters and packers were mule men and mule-minded. If used correctly mules could take care of most of the transportation needs of the army.

The army was actually using mules correctly as the experiments with using camels continued. Far to the west mules were demonstrating proficiency in supplying troops by methods that hired Mexicans packers had used during the Mexican War. During the Rouge River and Yakima Indian disturbances in the Oregon country in the 1850s, commanders contracted civilian packtrains. Their use met with limited success. A few of the young officers in the Oregon Territory, such as then Lt. George Crook, perhaps saw future possibilities. If commanding officers could direct the civilian trains instead of contracting them merely to move supplies from one location to another, packtrains employing the Mexican method of packing and the Mexican packsaddle, the *aparejo*, could be used on expeditions much more effectively than cumbersome escort wagons.[31]

During the 1850s army officers in Florida were also experimenting with pack mules, using modified cross-tree packsaddles. In 1857 Capt. Winfield Scott Hancock, assistant quartermaster, reported to Jesup that the packsaddles used in his command were totally unsuitable. The saddles lacerated mules' backs, rendering them unfit for service for weeks, and the belly bands were so narrow that saddles could not be properly secured. Hancock and Lt. Samuel Archer, Hancock claimed, improved the saddles by replacing the belly straps with wide leather girths similar to those used for saddle horses in Mexico and by making the crosstrees on the saddles more vertical and reinforcing them with iron plates at each end. The saddles could then use either panniers made from cattle hides or sacks to pack supplies. They possessed the additional advantage: in case of emergency all of the pack mules having these types of saddles could be used for mounting soldiers.

Evidently Jesup did not encourage Hancock and Archer to continue the experiment with new packsaddles. He no doubt knew pack mules did not take kindly to riders, especially infantrymen. More to the point, Jesup probably was not convinced by Hancock's report and Archer's sketches that new types of pack transportation were needed in Florida, in spite of the fact that he had once served as commander of operations during the Second Seminole War. The quartermaster department's budget was already too extended to experiment with another type of mule packsaddle. What was important was that the Florida command depended on pack mules for much of its transportation, and Hancock and Archer realized that established methods of packing were unsuitable.[32]

During the last half of the 1850s, army commands not only had to contend with policing the Indians but also with civilian problems in the Kansas and Utah territories. A most unpleasant episode developed in Utah that was costly to the army in more ways than money. Within three months after taking the oath of office on 4 March 1857, President James Buchanan removed Brigham Young as governor of Utah Territory and ordered the army to suppress what he irrationally believed to be Mormon lawlessness and rebellion. Scott and others warned Buchanan that it was too late in the season to move troops to Utah and that likely the troops would have to spend a harsh winter on the plains. Buchanan and John B. Floyd, the anti-Mormon secretary of war, ignored these warnings. Consequently, toward the end of May Scott issued orders to assemble a force of twenty-five hundred men at Fort Leavenworth as soon as possible. Included in the Utah command would be eight companies of the Second Dragoons, a battery of the Fourth Artillery, and the Fifth and Tenth Infantry regiments. Many of the troops, especially those of the Fifth Infantry whose last assignment had been in the swamps of Florida, were reluctant participants in a trek to Utah. More than two hundred men deserted, and several officers submitted letters of resignation.

Time itself worked against the army. Advance units did not leave Fort Leavenworth until 18 July. Most knew that beginning a march toward the high plains and mountains so late in the year would invite all types of problems for the participants. Seven companies of the Second Dragoons under Lt. Col. Philip St. George Cooke did not leave until mid-September. They had been ordered first to restore peace in Lawrence, Kansas. Surely at least some of the dragoons must have known that during a substantial portion of their march they would be on foot since supply wagons could carry only so much grain or corn and there would be little green grass left on the plains. The Utah expedition also faced leadership problems. General Harney, now known to the Sioux as "Squaw Killer," wanted to escape the assignment altogether and became extremely cautious. In September senior colonel of the Tenth, Edmund Alexander, became temporary commander and made the unwise decision to send the expedition on an alternate route. It was a decision, later reversed, that caused delay and unnecessary strain on the already overworked wagon mules. Not until Gen. Albert Sidney Johnston reached his new command in October did the expedition have a strong leader.

Earlier quartermasters at Fort Leavenworth had hurriedly assembled the necessary equipment for such a large force, found enough transportation, and attempted to make other needed provisions. No previous expedition dispatched by the army was better equipped and provisioned. Quartermasters quickly purchased five hundred wagon mules and three hundred mounts for the dragoons. Escort wagons pulled by three-mule teams would accompany and supply all the needs of the Utah command. Two thousand head of beef cattle were sent ahead of the expedition. Army contractors Majors and Russell would haul all other materials and subsistence stores that the expedition would consume in three months on the march. The firm had at first resisted the demands placed upon it, but Floyd illegally assured the partners that they would not suffer in any government transactions associated with the expedition. To secure desperately needed additional forage for the animals of the expedition and other supplies including lumber to build winter quarters, Capt. Stewart Van Vliet, an assistant quartermaster who was known to the Mormons as a friend, arrived at Salt Lake City in September 1857.[33]

The Van Vliet mission produced no supplies or forage for the horses and mules and gave Young the opportunity to warn Van Vliet that the Mormons would resist a hostile force—an armed mercenary mob. Whether or not the victim of a bluff, the quartermaster evidently believed Young. He left Utah Territory and reported to the senior officers of the expedition that the Mormons occupied all strategic positions and likely would forcibly resist the army entering Utah Territory. Initially, however, they confined their campaign to burning the grass and other acts of harassment without actually confronting the troops.

Young's resistance strategy was sound. Without adequate weapons, and being well aware of the probable consequences of starting a shooting war, he ordered the Mormons to begin a campaign of economic attrition. On 4 October a small Mormon force skirted companies of the Tenth Infantry, destroyed two Majors and Russell wagon trains, and ran off the oxen. The next day the Mormons burned another supply train. In all they destroyed seventy-two wagons containing three hundred thousand pounds of bacon and flour, enough food to feed the entire army for several months. They also torched thousands of acres of much needed grazing lands, Fort Bridger, and their own Fort Supply near South Pass, and they kept all associated with the expedition agitated and awake at night by fake raids. Actually, the Mormons could have destroyed several other supply trains that were spread out over twenty miles and beyond army protection. This scorched-earth policy combined with early blizzards seriously weakened the expedition. It was impossible for the army to reach Utah that year. It would be forced to winter near Fort Bridger.[34]

Hundreds of army mules as well as horses and contractor oxen died during the winter of 1857–58. While detouring up Hams' Fork, the army witnessed the first real signs of trouble with the animals.

By 14 October the wagon mules were receiving only half-allowances of corn. By now, hard frosts had destroyed much of the grass that the Mormons had not already burned. Young wagon mules were becoming lethargic; sixty-six were taken from harness and exchanged. The next day three to four inches of snow fell, and twenty-three additional exhausted three-year-old mules were released from harness. Horses now began to die. Mormon horsemen still harassed the command, but they easily stayed out of range of the dragoons because of the pitiful condition of their mounts. On 17 October the first bad snowstorm of the season began. On 24 October fifty-three mules were reported unfit for service, and further movement was impossible without forage. On 26 October enough grain arrived for half-allowances for eighteen days.

The worst was yet to come. The temperature had earlier dropped to 44 degrees below zero and generally hovered between 10 above and 16 degrees below. On 6 November the army marched for Fort Bridger and the sheltered valley thirty-five miles away before the horses and mules failed completely. So bad was the weather that it took the command fifteen days to reach its destination. Johnston called it a "tedious operation." The animals were rested several days, then marched a short distance and rested again. "A more rapid advance," he claimed, "would be attended with immense loss." The only thing for the army to do was "to press forward perseveringly [sic], though, slowly, marking our route by the frozen horses, mules and oxen." On 10 November a quartermaster reported that the command had lost fifty mules in the last thirty-six hours. The mules were hungry enough to eat almost anything. They were finally tied at the wagons. Some "gnawed and destroyed four wagon tongues, a number of wagon covers, ate their ropes, and getting loose, ate the sage fuel collected at the tents; some of these they also attacked; nine died."[35]

In a letter to his wife Capt. Jesse Gove vividly described the horror of the animals "dying rapidly. They are seen fallen in such attitudes," he wrote, "as could only result from the last possible effort of remaining strength to resist the effects of starvation and cold— bent crushed down in every variety of posture by the stern cold hand of death." He also said that in death the horses, mules, and oxen often all lay together.[36]

Cooke also depicted the animals' suffering in what the men now called "Buchanan's Blunder." Two-thirds of the Second Dragoons were now dismounted. The mounts had either died of starvation, had frozen to death, or were abandoned when they became too weak to keep up the extremely slow pace. Of the original 144 horses in Cooke's command, 130 lay dead. Cooke's men at one location found grass for some of the horses and mules, but they could not eat it because it was in an area not protected from the furious blasts of the storm. The mules huddled together and moaned piteously. Later the dragoons found a more protected location with grazing for the animals. When herders attempted to move the mules, they would not budge from the grassland and were left to perish. Revealing his utter disgust with the badly planned expedition, Cooke wrote that the earth contained "scarcely a wolf to glut itself on the hundreds of dead and frozen animals which for thirty miles nearly block the road."[37]

By the time the command struggled in to Camp Scott near Fort Bridger, it had lost almost a thousand animals. Of 2,400 mules sent with the army, about 588 had died and nine-tenths of them in the last month. Two-thirds of the dragoons' mounts were dead, as were one-half of the horses of the two batteries. The animals remaining were "leg weary and without life," wrote Capt. John J. Dickenson, command quartermaster, "and many of them must die during the winter." Johnston should not count on even having five hundred serviceable mules and forty battery horses by 1 May.[38]

To save as many animals as possible, they were moved from the immediate area around Camp Scott. As Dickenson lamented, there was not enough grass within ten miles to last the animals for six weeks and they had already eaten off one-and-a-half miles of grass in every direction. Johnston ordered some 2,400 animals, including beef cattle, driven to Henry's Fork to graze during the winter. The six companies of Cooke's Second Dragoons guarded the stock and herders. Only 172 mules were kept at Camp Scott for daily duty, and these animals, which could realistically work only one day in three, were exchanged with others at Henry's Fork at the end of each month.[39]

To resupply the command for those animals already dead and others that would not last the winter, Dickenson recommended purchasing in New Mexico an additional four hundred battery horses and mounts and eight hundred mules. Including two months' labor for packmasters and packers to load grain and other supplies on the animals, he estimated the cost at $138,800. Although the command needed a thousand mules, he thought that the quartermasters department could furnish the additional two hundred. In his estimates Dickenson showed a sound knowledge of animal costs and how to purchase the best animals for the money. One hundred and fifty American horses at $175 a head would cost $26,250, while 250 large Mexican horses at $85 each would cost only $21,250. For mules he suggested only two hundred American mules at $125 a head or $25,000, and six hundred Mexican mules at $80 each or $48,000. Within these prices quartermasters could purchase some animals for more and some for less than the maximum. Dickenson hired 10 packmasters for two months at $75 a month, or $1,500, and 280 packers for two months at $30 a month, or $16,800. The cost of horses averaged $118.75 and the mules only $91.25. In both cases costs were easily within the maximums of $125.00 and $100.00 that quartermasters could pay for horses and mules.[40]

Johnston sought the replacements quickly in order to mount an early spring campaign. On 24 November he ordered Capt. Randolph B. Marcy of the Fifth Infantry to lead a small detail of volunteers to Fort Union near Taos, New Mexico. Three days later Marcy, forty enlisted men, and twenty-four civilian scouts and packers riding mules and carrying enough rations for thirty days left camp. Bridger's prediction that Marcy's volunteers would not make it almost came true. After a grueling trip in which they were finally forced to eat their surviving, bony, almost starved mules, and through the heroic efforts of a civilian scout, Marcy's men finally reached Fort Union late in January.

Marcy's return trip with more than a thousand mules, 160 horses, and some sheep was not in time for Johnston's expected early campaign. Although taking a better return route, the now enlarged expedition faced unexpected delays. At one point Marcy was ordered to wait for additional soldiers to join his command. In another incident he faced delay caused by a stampede of the horses and mules. On the evening of 29 April a sudden snowstorm accompanied by violent north winds that raged continuously for sixty hours caught everyone by surprise. Men and animals fled to the nearest grove of trees to keep from being blown away. One herd of some three hundred mules and horses stampeded in spite of the herdsmen's efforts and ran with the wind for fifty miles. More than one hundred mules died during the storm, and it took five days to round up the runaways.

Marcy's expedition reached Camp Scott on 11 June. By then the Utah command had obtained other reinforcements as well. The War Department had ordered three thousand additional men to the scene, and Lt. Col. William Hoffman arrived from Fort Laramie with a large mule train loaded with supplies.[41]

By June 1858 the Mormon conflict had reached a climax. President Buchanan had issued a proclamation of pardon for all Mormons willing to obey federal laws, and Young and a delegation of church officials had accepted the president's terms. On 23 June, Johnston in a final act of insensitivity led a column of five thousand soldiers down the main street of Salt Lake City. The war was over. Later the War Department stationed troops throughout the territory and at other locations in the West.

In the aftermath of the conflict the army sold surplus equipment and animals for ridiculously low prices, many times in order to meet monthly army payrolls. At one sale, quartermasters sold thirty-five hundred oversized freight wagons that originally cost the army at least $150 apiece for only $10 each. In July 1859 quartermasters sold mules originally costing $175 for from $60 to $140. Leather harnesses sold for $3 a set. Buyers who purchased a whole team were given harnesses, double trees, and fifth chains. One man claimed that he purchased a wagon, three spans of mules, "harness and everything for $210, about the worth of one span of mules." In November 1860 Cooke auctioned off bacon purchased for $5.00 per hundred weight at $1.34. Flour purchased at $28.00 per hundred also sold for $1.34. Altogether the Mormons and others purchased goods valued at $4 million for only $100,000.[42]

Not all the sales concerning mules were conducted fairly. On one occasion the quartermaster detailed Alexander Toponce to match up mules into spans and place numbers on their headstalls. Toponce noticed that whenever Ben Holiday purchased a span of scrub mules, someone took the numbers from their headstalls and changed them for the numbers on two big Missouri mules. Toponce bought some of the scrub mules, but no one changed their numbers for those of better mules for him. Finally he blatantly exchanged the numbers himself. No one dared to object because he knew too much.[43]

Some mule auctions benefited both the army and civilians. In June 1860 Capt. H. D. Wallen, Fourth Infantry, reported to Secretary of War John B. Floyd that both immigrants preparing their wagons for the trip to California and Mormon farmers purchased mules at fair prices—some at nearly the army's cost. "Out of thousands of mules," wrote Wallen, "some twenty-six or twenty-eight hundred of the smallest and poorest were selected for sale." Auctioneers sold "small lots to suit the condition of the bidders." All the mules were sold to the highest bidder "and *all* was done for the best interests of the service."[44]

With the further dispersal of troops throughout the West after the Mormon conflict, the U.S. Army awaited its next challenge. During the years between the end of the Mexican War and the beginning of the Civil War, it had redefined its role in the nation and especially in the western domain. It was protecting the emigrant trails, organizing an almost permanent defense system, establishing usually amicable yet ambiguous relations with the native populations, and performing as a policeman in Kansas and Utah. It had unsuccessfully struggled with the hostile conditions of climate and geography and experimented with using camels as beasts of burden in the more inhospitable regions of the Southwest and West. More importantly the army was in the process of establishing a transportation system that relied primarily on mules. All soldiers from privates to colonels and even generals were more closely associated with these tough, surefooted beasts of burden than with any other animal. Mule-wagon transportation during this period had become almost a science, and men were now using pack mules in a limited way. By the eve of the Civil War the army would have been totally incapacitated without the dependable mule.

CHAPTER 4

Mules and the Civil War

American Civil War soldiers depended a great deal on animal power, and mules were prominent in the mix of cavalry mounts and artillery horses. During the conflict Union quartermasters purchased a conservative estimate of one million mules for use of armies in the field. All together these mules required massive amounts of forage and equipment to care for them. For example, in 1864 the chief quartermaster of the Mississippi Valley, Bvt. Maj. Gen. Robert Allen, was responsible for supplying the forces at Chattanooga and later the consolidated columns under Maj. Gen. William T. Sherman in the Atlanta campaign. To accomplish this enormous task, Allen ordered the principal stores gathered at the Nashville depot. He accurately noted that it was a "herculean task to collect, transfer and concentrate at one point horses and mules by the hundreds of thousands, corn and oats by the millions of bushels, hay by the tens of thousands of tons, wagons and ambulances by the tens of thousands, fitted out with harness, subsistence stores by the hundreds of thousands of tons, and miscellaneous articles, in the aggregate, proportionably [sic] large." Under Allen's leadership, between 1 October 1861 and 30 June 1865, quartermasters had purchased in that theater 75,329 mules, 100,364 horses, 8,864,173 bushels of corn, 26,234,423 bushels of oats, 377,518 tons of hay, 6,638 wagons, 1,269 ambulances, and 60,854 sets of harness.[1]

In fact, that one year, 1864, Union armies numbering 426,000 men depended on 221,000 animals, more than one for every two Union soldiers. This number included 113,864 artillery and cavalry horses and 87,791 wagon mules. The remaining 19,345 animals were several hundred oxen and unserviceable horses and mules. The numbers of animals, however, could be misleading. Since cavalry and artillery depended every bit as much on mule power as did the infantry, these 426,000 men depended on those 87,791 mules, one for almost every five men. Those numbers could be interpreted as a six-mule wagon serving every thirty or so soldiers.[2]

The numbers of men per mule-drawn wagon stayed approximately the same or decreased as the war continued. After Antietam the trains to support the Army of the Potomac, now 130,000 men, increased to 3,798 wagons drawn by 19,588 mules. At Harrison's Landing the ratio of wagons to men was 26 to 1,000; during the Maryland Campaign, 29 to 1,000. Just before Gettysburg George T. Stevens, a surgeon in the Sixth Corps, wrote that the wagon trains of the army had "crowded by" all day long, sometimes four and five wagons abreast, "their drivers shouting and lashing their beasts to their greatest speed. No one who has not seen the train of an army in motion," he observed, could "form any just conception of its magnitude, and of the difficulties attending its movements. It was said that the train of the Army of the Potomac, including artillery, if placed in a single line, the teams at the distance necessary for the march, would extend over 70 miles." At the beginning of Grant and Meade's 1864 campaign, 4,300 wagons drawn by 258,000 mules gave the Army of the Potomac a ratio of mule-drawn wagons to men up to 33 per 1,000. Probably few men, even experienced quartermasters, could have conceived of such numbers of mules in the U.S. Army in 1861.[3]

With such numbers certain tales about mules became famous during the war. After Grant was elevated to lieutenant general of the army, his past accomplishments as a quartermaster and a keen judge of animals during the Mexican War became a proper subject for the evening campfires, and his abilities were enhanced with each telling of another tale. As a second lieutenant, one story went, Grant came upon a soldier attempting to move his pack mule in line for the day's march. In spite of tugging, whipping, and cursing the animal, the handler had not accomplished his objective. Grant dismounted, faced the mule, and quietly cast unfavorable aspersions on the mule's paternity and chances of posterity. The animal shook himself and walked off.[4]

QMG Montgomery C. Meigs thought American soldiers were lavishly supplied by a four-horse or six-mule wagon for every twenty-six to thirty-three men. He compared how quartermasters supplied Union troops with wagons and supplies during the Civil War to what was advocated by Napoleon Bonaparte some sixty years before. Napoleon stated that during campaigns twelve wagons should be reserved for every thousand soldiers or one wagon for every eighty-three men. Meigs believed that on campaign Napoleon's estimates were workable and asserted that for an army of forty thousand, a train of 480 wagons could carry a month's provisions. He qualified his estimate to an army in motion, however, noting that an army remaining in one place for any length of time consumed the vicinity's forage and that trains must be increased to supply all the animals of the expedition. Late in the fall of 1863 Meigs, no doubt exasperated, protested about the inactivity of the Army of the Potomac. It had drawn nothing from the countryside it occupied during the last five months, Meigs complained, except wood.

Meigs could have further qualified his estimate by defining the location of the army expedition and telling whether it was moving south. If so wagons would need to carry adequate forage. Throughout the war forage supplies in most of the battle areas were so minimal that advancing armies had to supply with their wagons most of the feed for the wagon mules as well as artillery and cavalry horses. Since horses each required a combined twenty-six pounds of hay and grain daily and mules twenty-three pounds, and because each soldier's ration weighed three-and-a-half pounds, the number of wagons for forage quickly multiplied. Too often, many of the wagons could serve only their own animals. During Gen. George B. McClellan's Peninsula Campaign of 1862, for example, 150 wagons hauled a daily ration for 114,000 men while it took 300 wagons each day to furnish grain for the animals. Even then cavalry mounts sometimes went without grain for days at a time.[5]

Meigs understood the ramifications of the forage-mule dilemma. The larger the army, he knew, the more supplies it required, and ad-

ditional supplies meant more wagons and more mules and more forage wagons for the additional mules. The problem was never ending. An army on the move could usually find additional forage, and
the animals were generally healthier. But if the brigades were
massed together, teamsters were hard pressed to find adequate forage for their teams. If commanders spread out brigade trains to facil-
itate finding additional forage, the trains and men guarding them
became vulnerable to Confederate cavalry and partisan attacks.
Commanders and their quartermasters had to be very careful in the
makeup of the different segments of their forces. Portions of the
army traveling together must be large enough to resist cavalry raids
and yet small enough to find forage for the mules and horses. Meigs,
though stating that he clearly understood commanders' dilemmas,
still leaned somewhat toward the French standard, while field commanders faced unpleasant realities.[6]

To complicate matters, horses' and mules' daily rations were insufficient for the work performed in the field and excessive when
animals were relatively inactive in camp. During campaigns, draft,
artillery, and cavalry horses received as little as 60 percent of the
necessary daily forage allotment. Mules were a little better off, receiving 80 to 90 percent of grain and hay needed to sustain them.
Each horse required fourteen pounds of hay and twelve pounds of
grain, while mules needed the same amount of hay and nine pounds
of oats, corn, or barley. The consequences of the lack of adequate
nutrition coupled with insufficient transportation contributed to
the large loss, especially of horses but also of mules, throughout the
war.[7]

During the war, Union quartermasters used more horses and
mules than ever before, and the demand for them became as critical
as the demand for soldiers. At the beginning of the war quartermasters had attempted to adhere strictly to standards for purchasing
wagon mules for the army, as outlined in chapter 1. More times than
not they had been able to purchase satisfactory animals with only
an occasional misfit slipping into a remuda. Purchasing conditions
soon changed, and they were obliged to purchase increasing numbers of less than desirable animals. Even though they were not always able to purchase the totally qualified animals, they constantly

sent replacements from the huge supply depots to wherever they were needed, by railroads, river barges, side- and stern-wheel steamers, and even by ocean vessels. Large numbers of mules—regardless of what could be termed proper conformation—when used effectively to support brigades in the field kept soldiers supplied with rations and ammunition. In May 1863 Gen. William S. Rosecrans complained of the low quality of horses and mules that the Army of the Cumberland had received. Meigs replied that Rosecrans' urgent demand for twelve thousand animals had the "natural effect of inducing officers and inspectors to be less nice than when acting under less urgent orders."[8]

The availability of replacement mules became most important, despite their age, conformation, or condition, because commanders considered mules and horses expendable. In retrospect, after 1862 many quartermasters probably realized how desperately Confederate trains needed the animals and consciously purchased almost all available mules of any worth at all to keep traders from selling them illegally to the enemy. It could in fact have been an unofficial and unwritten but widely adhered to policy.

During the war, therefore, quartermasters, despite disclaiming such practices, relaxed standards in order to replace worn-out, disabled, and dead military animals. In connivance with mule traders, some took advantage of conditions and illegally made thousands of dollars purchasing culls for army trains, but this practice seemed not to have been widespread. Through 1863 and part of 1864, however, quartermasters did not have the luxury of checking each animal too closely, even if they had so desired. In every theater of war they were obtaining vast numbers of mules. They purchased far too many two- and three-year-old animals that became totally ineffective after a week of pulling supply wagons. New 1864 regulations for purchasing mules, however, stated that two-year-old animals could be accepted. After witnessing some of the culls and young mules being used, soldiers no doubt suspected the truth—that quartermasters purchased almost every available animal regardless of its age or condition. Far too many times they had witnessed old worn-out mules and underdeveloped, raw-boned yearlings being used ineffectively in harness. No wonder many soldiers (both

Union and Confederate) developed a bias against the animal that future army mules would never live down. Many a disgruntled officer also questioned the worth of mules in the military, yet as Meigs advised one of his quartermasters, A. R. Eddy, "a horse that will do a month's work, may in certain cases be worth his weight in silver." He could easily have said the same thing about a mule.[9]

In 1864 the charade of accepting only suitable animals reached a peak, when by statute quartermasters could be fined or imprisoned by sentence of court martial or military commission for any corruption, willful neglect, or fraud in the performance of their duties. The quartermaster's department also published new rules and regulations for the purchase of military animals. But standards for purchasing animals only two or three years old were so inconsistent with pre-war practice that one must assume that the statutes and regulations were smoke screens. For quartermasters in the field it was business as usual.

Soldiers sacrificed thousands of cavalry mounts, artillery horses, and mules. Some carnage, of course, was expected for artillery horses and cavalry mounts, but many times whole wagon trains were placed too near the fighting, and many mules were disabled or killed by enemy artillery and even rifle fire. Knowing replacements were available, teamsters did not protect or take care of their animals, unnecessarily pushing them until they dropped. Descending long hills, they rarely locked their rear wagon wheels since it would take too much time. And because most heavily loaded government wagons had no effective brakes, mules were unnecessarily injured and disabled by the thousands. Even in camp, lazy mule drivers mistreated their mules, sometimes leaving them harnessed and not allowing them to roll at the end of the day, watering them at a polluted river or stream below the camp, and neglecting their hooves by not cleaning out the mud and rocks at the end of each day. Col. Daniel H. Rucker, the commanding officer of the Washington depot, acknowledged that thousands of horses and mules had been rendered unfit by "harsh and injudicious treatment and by failure of the troops to give them ordinary care."[10]

Despite the purchase of many immature and unsuitable mules, quartermasters still knew full well the worth of the hybrid animals. So too did general officers and government officials. Meigs stated in his reports that the quartermaster corps was replacing horses with mules as quickly as possible since mules were stronger and more sure-footed. "Mules," Meigs wrote, "bear the exposure and hardships of the campaign much better than horses." So enthusiastic was the quartermaster general that at the conclusion of the war he bragged that during the entire war no enterprise had failed, "for want of means of transportation or the supplies required from the Quartermaster's Department."[11]

Mules became indispensable as the war progressed, in part because of the scarcity of horses. Cavalry regiments required 1,200 horses and artillery batteries each needed 110 animals. Disease, exposure, and hard usage consumed a great many horses, so great a number, in fact, that many wagon horses assumed new roles as cavalry mounts or artillery animals. Mules, much less susceptible to disease and abuse, replaced the horses in harness. Horses and mules had become so important to the war that they were noticed by the president. Abraham Lincoln signed General Orders No. 300, which in part stated that as of 13 May 1862, no horses or mules could be purchased for exportation from the United States and that army officers were to "appropriate any horses, mules, and live-stock designated for exportation." Secretary of War Edwin M. Stanton reiterated this general order to all commanding officers the day it was issued. The order gave quartermasters a decisive advantage over reluctant traders. It also served to restrict lucrative but illegal trade by the mule men in Missouri, Kentucky, and Tennessee.[12]

Confederate quartermasters by the summer of 1863 would have welcomed almost all suitable as well as unsuitable mules as their sources of supply continued to shrink. By then horses pulled most of their supply wagons, and even horses were becoming a premium item. During the first year of the war, Confederate buyers had experienced difficulty purchasing mules from the leading mule-producing states, Kentucky and Missouri. Both states had remained loyal to the Union, and many mule traders would accept only U.S. currency or gold. Lincoln's prohibition in General Orders No. 300 and the purchasing activities of Union quartermasters had further dried up Confederate sources. By mid-July 1863 Union troops controlled another mule-producing state, Tennessee, and also the trans-Allegheny region of Virginia. With the fall of Vicksburg early that same month, suppliers had a more difficult time importing mules from Texas. The forage shortage as well as the transportation of forage complicated the problem. Unable to depend on a steady reserve of mules, Confederates relied mainly on horses to pull supply wagons, but "seventy-five percent of Confederate horse losses came from starvation, disease, and abandonment when the animals were too weak to be of service."[13]

Even before the summer of 1863, Confederates were desperately considering alternative ways to obtain animals for the transportation service. On 4 March the quartermaster general of the Confederacy, Abraham C. Meyers, wrote President Davis in response to correspondence Davis had earlier received from A. G. Haley. Haley had offered to obtain horses and mules from Mexico, California, and Europe. Meyers informed Davis that agents had already purchased between six hundred and seven hundred mules in Texas that were being wintered in Alexandria, Louisiana, "for the convenience and cheapness of the forage, while awaiting a safe opportunity to cross the river." As soon as the animals arrived they would be put in harness to see if they were suitable. Meyers had reservations, however, "as they are generally small." But if they were suitable, Meyers said it would be advisable to increase the numbers brought in from Mexico and possibly California. Meyers was even less enthusiastic about Mexican horses and stated the obvious, that obtaining animals from Europe was "certainly impracticable.[14]

The inspector general, Maj. A. H. Cole, suggested another way to obtain horses and mules. On 2 July he wrote Meyers that already "by purchase, by impressments, and by a system of infirmaries" large numbers of animals had been returned to the transportation service and the artillery batteries. For the future, however, Cole saw that nothing was left "but to procure animals from the enemy's country." The present situation was the only "favorable opportunity" that the Confederacy had left, and if it did not avail itself of the chance while Gen. Robert E. Lee was in Pennsylvania, Cole saw little hope for victory. He suggested that a thousand convalescent troops from hospitals be sent to the areas in the rear of Lee's army "for the collection of this property." Meyers was enthusiastic about Cole's suggestion and wrote that some two thousand mules might be procured in Maryland by purchase. "Ten companies of convalescents organized as a regiment and sent on this duty might succeed admirably. About 300 can be mounted at once at Staunton." Of course the suggestion came too late. On 5 July Lee's army retreated across the Rappahannock after the defeat at Gettysburg.[15]

In contrast, by 1863 Union quartermasters and their suppliers were competently procuring mules and quickly supplying units in the field by using commercial railroads; in the conquered areas of the South they exploited rebuilt military railroads. The transfer over rebuilt lines of almost twenty-five thousand men of the Eleventh and Twelfth Corps together with ten batteries and their horses and one hundred railroad cars of baggage from the Army of the Potomac to Chattanooga in eleven days dramatically illustrated this new mobility that the railroads gave the Union armies. Following the troops and their baggage came other trains bringing more than a thousand horses and mules, spare artillery, field transport, "and all the impedimenta of a field army." Railroads and wagon mules hauled the baggage of the army and gave it a new mobility.[16]

The Peninsula Campaign in 1862 serves as an early example of the use of mule power and army logistics during the war. The shipping of thousands of horses, mules, and wagons from the coast to the James-York Peninsula made the amphibious operation near Vera Cruz during the Mexican War seem almost insignificant. "The magnitude of the movement can scarcely be understood," wrote the quartermaster and now colonel, Steward Van Vliet, "except by those who participated in it. Each division took with it its own transportation as far as it was practicable, and the remainder, together with the supply trains, were pushed forward as rapidly as possible."[17]

Despite the quartermasters' paying too much for both shipping and animals, the initial operation ran smoothly. Embarkation at Alexandria began on 17 March, and the last troops landed on the peninsula on 6 April. Four hundred steamers and sailing vessels transported approximately 110,000 soldiers, more than 14,500 horses and mules, 44 batteries of artillery, and all the equipment and supplies needed for such an army, including supply wagons, ambulances, and pontoon trains. During landings the army lost only nine stranded lighters and eight drowned mules.

McClellan planned to move up the peninsula, attack Richmond

from the southeast, and use the river system partially to ease transportation problems of supplying such a large army. Except for supplying bases in Maryland, railroads did not play a major role in the
campaign. The advance initially was by brigade, with each brigade
train following its unit. Often the scarcity of roads and the difficulty
of moving supplies to or from base camps made the initial plan im-
practical. Quartermasters soon merged the brigade trains and when
possible operated them as a single large unit. Most of the roads were
corduroyed with logs and became even rougher after constant use.
The wear and tear on the wagons and animals became a major problem in supplying the army. Almost continuous rain for days during
May made the roads practically impassable, and quartermasters
and teamsters lightened wagonloads as horses and mules were unable to handle the increased strain. McClellan's Army of the Potomac still received adequate supplies when it drove back the Confederate counterthrust fewer than ten miles from Richmond at the
Battle of Seven Pines or Fair Oaks.

After the battle McClellan waited for better weather to move the
army closer to Richmond; meanwhile, he placed his forces in a
stronger position. Lee, now in command of the Army of Northern
Virginia, acted with daring and took the initiative lest McClellan
succeed. He ordered Gen. Thomas J. Jackson's force to sweep down
from the Shenandoah Valley and attack McClellan's right flank. On
26 June the Army of Northern Virginia took the offensive and the
great Seven Days' battles began. Toward midnight on 27 June,
McClellan ordered his army to withdraw to a newly prepared base
on the James River. To keep tons of supplies from falling into Confederate hands, quartermasters ordered entire trains of supplies
burned and tons of ammunition dumped into the rivers. In this calculated withdrawal, soldiers carried cooked rations for three days
and herded 2,500 cattle. Some 2,578 wagons and 415 ambulances
pulled by 5,899 horses and 8,708 mules carried another three days'
rations and five days' forage for almost forty thousand animals. The
Army of the Potomac had lost almost half its wagons and thousands
of horses and mules. At the end of the Seven Days' battles, the
Union army was still in a strong position. Lincoln, however, was exasperated with McClellan and called off the campaign. On 3 August, Gen. Henry W. Halleck, who now controlled operations, or-

dered the Army of the Potomac back to the river that gave it birth. Not for another two years was a Union army to get as near Richmond as McClellan's had, and the Confederates had captured hundreds of good U.S. Army–branded horses and mules.[18]

The failure of the Peninsula Campaign was not attributable of the lack of quartermaster support. McClellan believed that every enemy commander was an Alexander the Great capable of countering decisively his every move. Only leisurely conducting a campaign for limited stakes, McClellan could be totally unpredictable. He gave orders for difficult logistical assignments without warning or consulting his chief quartermaster. Confusion often resulted; even so, the trains performed better than could be expected. Mule transportation had adequately supplied McClellan's men. Col. Rufus Ingalls, the chief quartermaster of the Army of the Potomac, under the circumstances in which he had to operate, did a creditable job of holding together the provisional supply system and operating it in a unified manner.[19]

Throughout the remainder of 1862 and the winter months of 1863 troops both east and west of the Appalachian Mountains received an overabundance of needed and superfluous supplies. Quartermasters combined railroad, river, and coastal transportation with well-stocked, mainly mule-drawn wagon trains to accomplish this amazing feat. Never before had army mules supplied so many American soldiers. Yet significant victories were few and far between for the Union armies, especially those in the East. Many times Confederates captured much-needed supplies and thousands of horses and mules. During the Maryland campaign, Confederate cavalry troopers captured large unescorted trains and some even that were guarded by companies of Union cavalry. Mules clearly branded "us" thereafter pulled Confederate wagons. At one time most of those wagons had also served Union troops. Throughout the war Union quartermasters unintentionally furnished large numbers of horses and mules and significantly large amounts of forage, food, and ammunition to Confederate troops.[20]

In the spring of 1863 Army of the Potomac quartermasters changed the method of supplying their army in the field, and soon quartermasters in other commands experimented with the method.

The army began using a variation of the French army's flying column, which increased enormously the soldiers' logistical capacity away from bases of supply. Soldiers in the flying column carried their own rations for as many as eight days and shared tent halves with a partner. Squads of eight divided commonly needed equipment and utensils such as a cooking kettle, mess tins, axe, pick, shovel, and hospital knapsack. To decrease weight each man carried a blanket but no overcoat, and quartermasters provided beef cattle to be slaughtered whenever needed. No soldier was to carry more than forty-five pounds at the beginning of the eight-day period. In addition to men carrying extras, two pack mules, which had been taken from the teams of ammunition and supply trains, and one wagon accompanied each company. The large wagon trains followed in the rear of the marching columns with each wagon carrying subsistence for the teamsters and forage for its team.[21]

Cavalrymen divided the load in much the same way and also carried pickets and grain for their horses. Ingalls reported that cavalry needed four six-mule wagons to each one thousand men for small-arms ammunition, one wagon per regiment for hospital supplies, one for regimental headquarters, and one wagon and two pack mules per company.[22]

Despite obvious difficulties involved in cooperation of the teams of eight and those involved with the harness mules used as pack animals, the flying column was a logistical success. Since mules were taken away from the ammunition and supply trains, certain officers and quartermasters had mixed opinions of this practice. Capt. John F. Caslow, acting chief quartermaster of the Fifth Army Corps, wrote that the "pack-mule system [was] of advantage so far as the transportation of small-stores from the trains to the commands and on short marches, but [would] not be of any great benefit, and [would] render useless many animals now doing good service." Lt. Col. William G. Le Duc, chief quartermaster of the Eleventh Corp, insisted that the system should be modified to be effective. The ammunition boxes, he wrote, galled the mules' backs and were so heavy they made it impossible for the pack mules to carry their own forage. Chief quartermaster of the First Corps, Lt. Col. J. J. Dana, reported that mules used for packing ammunition had "suffered very much" because the men used as packers were inexperienced and the mules remained saddled and packed for a long time "in momentary expectation of moving."[23]

Ingalls concluded that the pack-mule system could not be relied on for "long marches with heavy columns." He also reported that during such marches the packsaddles galled the mules badly. Ingalls intended thereafter to have a few pack mules as an "auxiliary simply to wagons, for short distances over rough country, where there are few and bad roads." He later attempted to force his plan on the Armies of the Potomac and the Cumberland, but Halleck overruled him.[24]

After its defeat at Chancellorsville, the Union army began using a modified flying column. And the army, now commanded by George G. Meade, began to move toward Gettysburg, Pennsylvania, where it was rumored that Lee was concentrating the Army of Northern Virginia. The Army of the Potomac numbered approximately 142,000 men. Ingalls calculated that with the new formation one wagon would support 50 men for seven days. This ratio, the standard 20 wagons per 1,000 men, meant that the Army of the Potomac required roughly 2,800 six-mule wagons and 16,800 mules. The army marched, however, with 4,300 wagons, "a standard of 30 wagons per 1,000 men, and with 21,628 mules, 8,889 [draft] horses, 216 pack mules, a ratio of one animal to four men." The greatly increased ratio of mules to horses showed how quickly quartermasters were replacing horses with the much more durable mules.[25]

The flying column worked superbly for the Battle of Gettysburg. The wagon trains and all possible impediments to the army remained twenty-five miles to the rear. No baggage was allowed at the front, and officers and men went forward with no tents and only a short supply of food. Only some of the ammunition wagons and ambulances were allowed in the immediate rear of the lines. These arrangements made it possible for "experienced and active officers to supply their commands without risking the loss of trains or obstructing roads over which the columns march. Empty wagons [could] be sent to the rear, and loaded ones, or pack trains, brought up during the night, or at such times and places as [would] not interfere with the movement of troops." The system also had the great advantage of keeping mules from being placed in positions where many might be captured, wounded, or killed during battle. Even so, the soldiers usually received needed supplies in a timely manner.[26]

Mules were not, as we have already learned, always treated with as much regard for their welfare in all theaters. During the campaigns for East Tennessee, large numbers of U.S. Army horses and mules died, and Confederates captured thousands of others because of totally inadequate efforts to guard them.

After the battle of Stone River in Murfreesboro, Tennessee, in January 1863, Braxton Bragg withdrew his Confederate Army of the Tennessee northwest of Tullahoma. There he established a defensive line and prepared to meet Rosecrans and his Army of the Cumberland. Rosecrans knew that his army was in no condition to pursue Confederates until provisioned and supplied with adequate forage for the horses and mules. His quartermaster, Col. J. W. Taylor, revealed on 31 March 1863 that the Army of the Cumberland of approximately sixty thousand men could rely on only 3,747 draft horses and 23,859 mules to pull wagons. Yet a week earlier the army had had 19,164 draft horses and the same 23,859 mules. The attrition of horses, Rosecrans observed, was because of a lack of "long forage." Until he could be assured of adequate forage for his animals, Rosecrans refused to move. He waited for the spring crops, especially corn, to ripen and to supplement his forage before advancing. Not until 23 June, after a delay of six months, did the wagons and pack mules of the Army of the Cumberland advance toward East Tennessee.[27]

The Army of the Cumberland relied heavily on mules. For transportation it depended on approximately three thousand six-animal wagons and some fourteen thousand pack mules. Using the conversion of 250 pounds per pack mule and assuming that approximately 2,500 pounds of supplies were hauled in each wagon, the fourteen thousand pack mules carried the equivalent of 1,150 wagonloads of supplies. Although about a third of the wagons were used to carry forage for teams and pack animals, the army was still well supplied. Assuming that at least half the wagons were pulled by mule teams, there was one mule for roughly every three soldiers.[28]

The less than popular packtrains were well suited for the hills and early summer rains of East Tennessee. The Army of the Cumberland's quartermasters, having an excess of available mules, organized the packtrains. The reasons that more quartermasters did not employ packtrains were numerous. In addition to the reasons already given by Ingalls and some of the quartermasters of Army of the Potomac, keeping up regular packtrains was an expensive proposition. Neither were the packtrains especially successful since quartermasters usually commandeered lead mules from the supply wagons. Wagon mules were not accustomed to carrying 250 pounds of supplies; they balked at the new task or quickly developed back sores. Seasoned campaigners knew the fallacy in using wagon mules for packing but had been unable to prevent the general orders in 1861 that each corps was to carry two hundred packsaddles in its wagon train to be used whenever conditions warranted. After the war, those who had used pack mules insisted that harness mules seldom made good packers and refused to use them. When quartermasters spared lead mules for packing duties, they replaced them with immature two-year-old mules. Unable to pull their share of the load in a team, the young mules were used as packers, usually ineffective ones.

Further complicating the use of pack transportation was the very lack of qualified packers and mule men who understood the nature of the hybrid animals. Teamsters and wagoners were not necessarily good mule men and had no notion of how to load mules and distribute packs evenly. A lieutenant colonel with the Army of the Cumberland later complained that using pack mules in the Tennessee campaign had been a waste of time and money because of the lack of experienced packers.

Another major reason for the failure of pack transportation was the quality of the equipment. According to one quartermaster, the packsaddles' cross trees were made of "bass wood, covered with sheepskin instead of rawhide, and were fastened together with four penny nails." When the saddles were "exposed to damp weather, they almost fell apart." Although all requisitioned saddles were not as bad as the ones described, few were built to accommodate the mules or constructed to last. Until the army switched to the Mexican-style *aparejos*, it would contend with saddles that actually harmed pack mules' backs and loins.[29]

Rosecrans knew the drawbacks as well as the advantages of using pack mules. During the early days of the war he had been with

McClellan in western Virginia and had turned to pack mules in an attempt to resolve transportation difficulties. The wagons being used by quartermasters at the time each weighed in excess of a ton when loaded and could not be pulled over rough "cut up" roads. Rosecrans requisitioned a large number of mules for packing. An assistant quartermaster in Marietta, Ohio, wrote Rosecrans's quartermaster, Capt. Charles Leib: "These are the most devilish mules I ever saw. They destroy everything, eat up trees and fences, and have nearly killed half my men. Do you think of taking them away soon? If you love me, do so."[30]

Leib soon discovered that the mules were hard to catch and even harder to pack. He protested that "it seemed as though the evil one had taken possession of them" as he and his men tried to trap them. Saddling the animals was a painful experience. "The saddles," he complained "were not rightly adjusted, the packs not properly slung, and for miles the road was scattered with bad bread, flour, beans, coffee, rice, and sugar." Finally, the quartermaster found "French Creoles and Mexican Greasers" from the "far west" who were so familiar with the animals "that as if by magic, the mules became gentle and tractable." In less than two weeks the experienced packers had two hundred mules ready for packing. Leib claimed it was a sight to see "200 wild mules running loose in the streets, following, like so many sheep, an old gray horse, from whose neck was suspended a cow bell."[31]

According to Leib, Rosecrans sent the most experienced of his packers to other commands to teach teamsters and wagoners the art of packing. Wagoners and teamsters were unwilling to accept additional duties and responsibilities, however, and as Leib correctly pointed out, little benefit was derived since the packers had "no opportunity of applying their knowledge to practice."[32]

The initial phase of Rosecrans's campaign to capture East Tennessee went smoothly. Undeterred by torrential rains, the Army of the Cumberland broke Confederate defenses and forced Bragg's army to fall back to Tullahoma and eventually to Chattanooga. Rosecrans's supply and packtrains had kept the army well supplied. On 9 September Union forces entered Chattanooga after Rosecrans had maneuvered Bragg out of the city without a battle.

Humorous sketch by Frederic Remington of civilian packers tying a double diamond hitch on a "bell sharp" pack mule. (*Century Magazine*)

General Crook riding his saddle mule, Apache, and scouts Dutchy and Alchesay. (Arizona Historical Society/Tucson)

Above: Civilian packer and pack mules wearing *aparejos.* The mules here are lightly packed and the packers have used a diamond hitch. (Arizona Historical Society/Tucson)

Opposite: Diagram for tying the diamond hitch found in Captain H. W. Lawton's *Intructions for Using Moore's Improved Pack Saddle.* (National Archives)

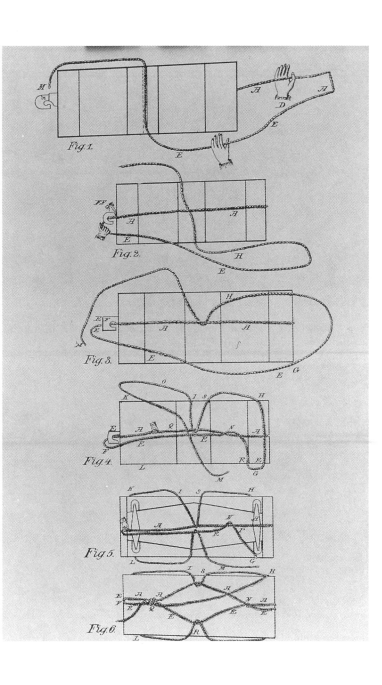

Fig. 1.

Fig. 2.

Fig. 3.

Fig. 4.

Fig. 5.

Fig. 6.

Pack company lightly loaded heading to the front in Cuba during the Spanish-American War. (National Archives)

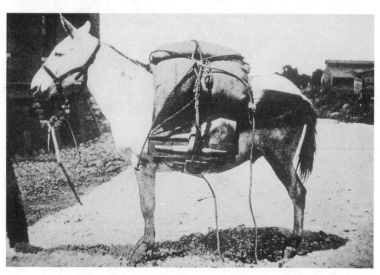

She wore a double diamond! The hitch has yet to be tightened. (Daly, *Manual of Pack Transportation*)

Packing wounded on mules using an *aparejo* during the insurrection in the Philippine Islands. (Daly, *Manual of Pack Transportation*)

Bell sharp mules of Packtrain No. 6 behind their aparejos in Candelaria, Texas, in 1917 or 1918. (W.D. Smithers Collection, Harry Ransom Humanities Research Center, The University of Texas at Austin)

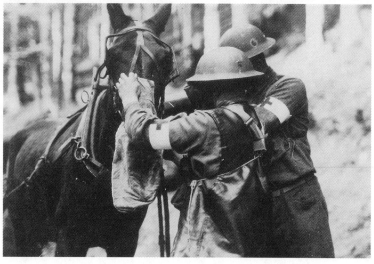

Opposite, above: Doughboys and pack mules in France. (National Archives)

Opposite, below: World War I Red Cross volunteers putting a gas mask on a mule. (National Archives)

Above: Platoon of machine gunners with their pack mules in training, Beaucourt Somme, France, 1918. (National Archives)

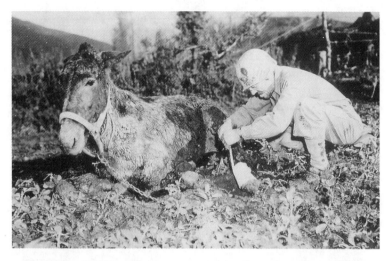

This photograph appeared in *Yank* on 18 February 1944 with the caption: "First Aid. In Italy the mule Purple Heart Mary cracked her hoof. Here she is being taken care of by veteran mule skinner Pvt. Clarence Hutchinson of Ava, Missouri." (National Archives)

Staff Sgt. Stanley P. Morrison, Hollywood, California, and Tec 5 Francis R. Smith, Fairfield, Connecticut, watering a mule near Myitkyina, Burma, on 16 November 1944. (National Archives)

Tec 4 John P. Holler of Uniongrove, North Carolina, a mule skinner with 25 years of experience, looking into the mouth of "Shrapnel," one of the mules marched from Burma to Kunming, China, supposedly to be turned over to the Chinese army. According to the Signal Corps credit, Shrapnel had been wounded 8 times while serving in Burma. Photograph date: 16 July 1945. (National Archives)

Pack mules were indispensable to soldiers fighting in Burma. A packtrain is leaving the Myitkyina airstrip carrying food, ammunition, weapons, and other essentials. Most of these mules have been well trained to follow the leader. Soldiers only lead the inexperienced ones. Photograph date: 10 June 1944. (National Archives)

Brig. Gen. Frank D. Merrill and Col. Charles Hunter watch the Marauders cross Pangsau Pass, the border line to Burma, as they march up the Ledo Road. The mule loaded with ammunition is all skin and bones. The men of Galahad had no idea how to take care of their pack mules. Photograph date: 12 February 1944. (National Achives)

Pvt. Russell Creasy of Kingsport, Tennessee, and Tec 5 Arthur Poton of Augusta, Georgia, saddle a mule with a bastro, an Italian packsaddle in the Galla Sector, Italy. Photograph date: 14 November 1943. (National Achives)

Fifth Army, Cafaggiolo Area, Italy. White mules, which make an excellent target for German gunners, are brought into the 130 Veterinarian (Italian) hospital once every two months, and are sprayed with a potassium permanganate solution. Photograph date: 11 October 1944. (National Archives)

A mule skinner of the Mars Task Force leads mules through a river on the way to Bhamo, Burma. Photograph date: 17 November 1944. (National Archives)

American mule captured from the Chinese in Korea. (National Archives)

An excellent example of a pack or artillery mule. (National Archives)

Believing Bragg's Army of the Tennessee was in full retreat, Rosecrans made a costly mistake. Instead of consolidating his widely separated forces, he ordered a general pursuit of the Confederate army into the mountains of northern Georgia. The Army of Tennessee was not demoralized or retreating and was being reinforced by troops from upper East Tennessee and by eleven thousand more under Gen. James Longstreet that had arrived from the east by rail. On 19 and 20 September the armies met on the field of Chickamauga. Bragg's army checked the Union forces and sent most of them retreating to Chattanooga the next day. Gen. George Thomas's Fourteenth Corps, unaware of the general Union reverse, held the field until nightfall on 20 September and saved Rosecrans's army from total defeat. The Confederates followed Rosecrans to Chattanooga and held the mountain ridges, forcing the Union to concentrate its defenses on the valley floor.[33]

The Army of the Cumberland seemed paralyzed from the effects of Chickamauga. Rosecrans himself acted as if he were "insensible to the impending danger." The Confederates held the high ground and passes, and it became difficult to obtain supplies. A nearly impassable mountain road from Stevenson, Alabama, to Chattanooga was the only avenue open for retreating or obtaining supplies. Early October rains virtually closed all the roads. Soldiers were reduced to three-fourths rations and then half-rations. Without adequate forage, weakened mules were unable to move supplies "with any promptness and efficacy." Teamsters doubled up teams to haul small loads. Animals began to die. The quartermaster, Capt. C. A. Dana, predicted that even if the army gained control of the Tennessee River to furnish the horses and mules with forage, it might "escape with no worse misfortune than the loss of 12,000 animals."[34]

Worse was yet to come. Above Chattanooga, Confederate cavalry fell on trains mired in the mud, and it destroyed in one day three hundred wagons and captured some eighteen hundred badly needed mules. By the middle of the month conditions had deteriorated further. Mules died in their harnesses and were left by the sides of the roads. Artillery horses died at the picket ropes. By the end of the month more than ten thousand mules had perished in transporting half-rations to hungry troops over the only open road.[35]

Toward the end of October, the Army of the Cumberland changed leadership and began a campaign to break the Confederates's virtual investment of Chattanooga. Grant had assumed command of all the forces in the West and appointed the "Rock of Chickamauga," Gen. George H. Thomas, to replace Rosecrans. By then the Lincoln administration, worried that the army would actually starve, transferred troops, mules, and supplies from Mississippi and Virginia to reinforce it. Unintentionally, the ranking Confederate commanders further aided federal efforts through their factional squabbling over Bragg's ineffective leadership.

On 27 October Union troops executed a daring move to establish another river supply line from Bridgeport. The next evening Confederate forces led by Gen. Wade Hampton tried to dislodge Gen. John Geary's division of the Twelfth Corps that was protecting the newly opened supply route, nicknamed the "cracker-line," at Wauhatchie. Frightened by the attack, some two hundred mules broke out of their corral and dashed into Hampton's troops, causing them to fall back. Perhaps the Confederate soldiers thought they were being attacked by cavalry. To commemorate the action, one Union soldier wrote a parody of Tennyson's "Charge of the Light Brigade."

> Half a mile, Half a mile onward,
> Right through the Georgia troops
> Broke the two hundred.
> "Forward the Mule Brigade!
> Charge for the Rebs!" they neighed.
> Straight for the Georgia troops
> Broke the two hundred.
>
> "Forward the Mule Brigade!"
> Was there a mule dismayed?
> Not when the long ears felt
> All their ropes sundered.
> Theirs not to make reply,
> Theirs not to reason why,
> Theirs but to make Rebs fly.
> On! to the Georgia troops
> Broke the two hundred.

Mules to the right of them,
Mules to the left of them,
Mules behind them Pawed, neighed and thundered.
Breaking their own confines,
Breaking through Longstreet's lines
Into the Georgia troops
Stormed the two hundred.

Wild all their eyes did glare,
Whiskered all their tails in air
Scattering the chivalry there,
While all the world wondered.
Not a mule back bestraddled,
Yet how they skedaddled—Fled every Georgian,
Unsabred, unsaddled, Scattered and sundered!
How they were routed there
By the two hundred.

Mules to the right of them,
Mules to the left of them,
Mules behind them Pawed, neighed, and thundered;
Followed by hoof and head,
Full many a hero fled,
Fain in the last ditch dead,
Back from an ass's jaw,
All that was left of them—
Left by the two hundred.

When can their glory fade?
Oh, the wild charge they made!
All the world wondered.
Honor the charge they made!
Honor the Mule Brigade,
Long-eared two hundred.[36]

Although failing to disrupt the new source of supplies, the Confederates did capture two hundred half-starved mules.

By the end of the first week in December, federal troops controlled East Tennessee and drove Bragg's army from Chattanooga into the mountains of northern Georgia. Gen. Ambrose E. Burnside's command captured and held Knoxville against opposition from Longstreet's Rebel forces. Union troops heavily garrisoned East Tennessee until the following spring.

Mules continued to prove their worth through the end of the war, and they also continued to receive less than good and sometimes very bad treatment from the very soldiers who depended so heavily on them. Yet in most cases the soldiers mistreated them without malice. John D. Billings in his famous account of army life during the Civil War, *Hard Tack and Coffee,* claimed that when asked the question "What became of the army mule?" thousands of old veterans "will take a solemn oath that they never saw a dead mule during the war." These men, wrote Billings, could "tell you of the carcasses of horses which dotted the line of march, animals which had fallen out from exhaustion or disease, and left by the roadside for the buzzards and crows." But they did not have the "dimmest picture of a single dead mule." Billings related that he knew better, but he was, of course, attempting to show the mule as the superior animal of the war—which of course it was.[37]

Mules were important but expendable ingredients to each side but especially to the Union, which had relied on them so heavily. Neither side made serious efforts to rehabilitate wounded mules, and in most cases Union officers refused to abandon them to force them to forage for themselves when they were starving. Throughout the conflict, Meigs insisted that quartermasters leave no animal—horse or mule—behind to be used by the enemy. Although never telling quartermasters to kill wounded or ineffective animals, one could easily read between the lines. Some of the mules' treatment could no doubt be justified in the name of war. In many cases, however, men both North and South treated the animals with callous disregard for their welfare.

CHAPTER 5

Mules in the West and Efficient Pack Mules for the Army

For the first two years after the Civil War, quartermasters in the western departments experienced difficulty obtaining serviceable mules. Before being mustered out of the service, mule drivers had swapped with civilians good mules for old and broken-down animals for a little money under the table. Since during the war many of the mules had been rushed to units needing them without being branded, the teamsters' illegal trade was difficult to prevent. Neither were officers worried about the practice; most wanted to return at once to civilian life and were not interested in pressing charges that would delay their departures. Those who were to remain in the army were more interested in retaining as high a rank as possible in the reductions-in-rank they all expected. So men in charge of mules, in effect, had an open license.

This practice of trading for a consideration was so widespread that the army lost many of its serviceable mules. To make matters worse, quartermasters could not purchase, or in many cases repurchase, replacements. QMG Montgomery C. Meigs not only issued orders halting all procurement of animals, he allowed the chief quartermasters of the military departments to auction off surplus animals. Between May 1865 and August 1866 auctioneers sold 102,954 mules for $7,685,225.96, an average of $74.65 an animal. This average was almost a third of the cost of a mule during the last

three years of the war, when quartermasters were purchasing mules
for between $170 and $180. While officers in the West were begging
for serviceable mules but could purchase none, eastern quartermasters were selling off surplus animals.[1]

The prices paid for mules during the two years following the war
varied widely as local conditions, potential purchasers, and the condition of the animals determined what surplus mules brought. In
the South, mules usually brought low prices. In Augusta, Georgia,
for example, 960 mules brought $40,615.50 or $42.31 per animal; in
Athens, Tennessee, 149 mules sold for $4,272 or an average of
$28.40; in Camden, Arkansas, 267 mules brought $10,351.50 or an
average of $38.77; and in Austin, Texas, 433 mules brought $28,907,
an average of $66.75. Yet mules brought higher prices in other parts
of the old Confederacy. In Baton Rouge, Louisiana, 195 mules were
purchased for a total of $26,829 or $137.58 an animal, and in Charle-
ston, South Carolina, successful bidders purchased 77 mules for
$9,302.89 or $120.82 average per mule. Prices in other parts of the
country reflected those in the South, but in Evansville, Indiana, two
mules brought $525 for a healthy average of $262.50, which was
exceptional. In Fort Leavenworth, Kansas, 6,574 mules sold for
$374,469.51 or an average of $56.56 per animal, and in Elmira, New
York, 482 mules were purchased for $42,191.00, or an average of
$87.53 a mule. Purchasers in Rogersville, Tennessee, had the dis-
tinction of paying less for mules than anywhere in the country.
Someone there purchased a single mule for $2.50, and two others
were sold at auction for only $30.00.[2]

The moratorium on army mule purchases lasted three years. By
1869–70 quartermasters were purchasing suitable wagon mules for
an average of $136.06 per animal. For the quartermasters to pur-
chase good animals was one thing; for the army to use them efficiently was another. By now the army needed a more rapid transportation system than it had employed from the 1850s through the
Civil War with its large trains, two or three six-mule wagons accompanying each troop, and even the use of lead mules for limited
packing. The principal duties of the army had changed significantly.
The Army Act of 1866 enlarged the cavalry from six ten-troop regiments to ten twelve-troop regiments with one hundred privates authorized for each troop; it also provided for as many as three hun-

dred Indian scouts per regiment. These scouts served under regular army officers and functioned as semiregular soldiers except in combat, when they threw away their white man's garments and fought as Indians. The bill clearly demonstrated that mobile troops, Indian and white, had primary responsibility in subduing Indians in the West. In theory these troops had to react quickly to different situations. Dependence on wagon transportation clearly limited their effectiveness. To accomplish the objective of rapid mobility, the cavalry gradually turned to troop pack-mule trains.[3]

The army's experiment with pack transportation produced indifferent results. Quartermasters had contracted for Mexican packers during the Mexican War. Trains with experienced personnel that used the Spanish-style packsaddle, the *aparejo*, had performed with amazing efficiency. Santa Anna's army also had successfully used a number of packtrains in its march to Monterrey. Other packtrains used during the war, however, had failed miserably to live up to the seemingly low standards of the day. Army pack mules were used regularly in the swamps and the back country of Florida during the 1840s and 1850s with mediocre results, because when loaded the saddles tended to gouge into the mules' backs.

In the 1850s pack transportation was successful only in Oregon and California, where the army hired civilian packers on a contract basis. These packers used aparejos and smaller than average mules. In the summer of 1864, a retired colonel and assistant quartermaster, George Ihrie, bombarded Meigs with letters proclaiming the superiority of packtrains using aparejos. In 1853 in California, he had superintended and assisted in packing about forty mules each day for about six weeks. He had letters, he also maintained, from Col. R. C. Buchanan and Gen. Edward O. C. Ord, complimenting him on his management of a packtrain of nearly three hundred mules that supplied and moved Buchanan's command during the Rouge River, Oregon, campaign against hostile tribes. His train was Buchanan's only source of supply. Ihrie insisted he could pack 250 pounds to the mule and take them "across ravines, gulches, and streams and up mountains and through chaparral where wagons couldn't go and would be useless." He bragged that he could "move any number of mules with their packs, with two packers to six mules," within thirty minutes.[4]

Ihrie's efforts were wasted, for Buchanan's command accomplished little or nothing for months except to keep itself supplied while many of the "hostiles" were already returning to the reservations. Ihrie's letters, however, pointed out a number of stark realities concerning packing. The Mexican method of packing was much superior to army packing. Aparejos were superior to crosstree saddles and together with lash ropes and blankets did not cost as much as a six-mule set of harness. Packing mules required knowledgeable packers who should have no other duties. And packtrains could be used in all seasons, especially during wet weather when wagons were useless.[5]

Although it appeared that he made no impact on Meig's thinking during the war, Ihrie at least influenced younger officers, especially George Crook, who had seen the Oregon packtrains in action during the 1850s. Crook graduated from West Point in 1852 and was initially assigned to the Fourth Infantry stationed in the Oregon Country. For the next eight years he became well acquainted with the ways of the army and the Indian. In his autobiography Crook mentioned that he and his men often rode pack mules during the campaigns in the northwest. "Both companies," he wrote, "were mounted on mules with improvised rigging, some with ropes, and others with equally if not worse makeshifts to fasten the saddles on the mules. . . . It was as good as a circus to see us when we left Fort Jones." Crook recorded that many of the men, including the commander, were drunk and that "many of the mules were wild and had not been accustomed to being ridden while the soldiers generally were poor riders. The air was full of soldiers after the command was given to mount, and for the next two days stragglers were still overtaking the command." Crook related that during this expedition the captain, Henry M. Judah, whom he referred to as a fraud, from a distance had mistaken some crows for Indians among abandoned wickiups and ordered a charge. Crook observed, "I could only see what was in front of me, but that was enough" to witness men tumbling off mules "in the most ludicrous manner." He looked back across the field "to see the men hors-de-combat, riderless mules running in all directions, men coming, limping, some with their guns, but others carrying their saddles." Crook also discovered the proper use for pack mules even though he would later prefer riding mules to horses on campaigns.[6]

During the Civil War, Crook rose from colonel to major general. After the conflict he suffered reduction in rank to lieutenant colonel with a brevet of major general, and in December 1866 he joined the Fourteenth Infantry in the Pacific Northwest where he soon confronted the Paiute Indians.[7]

Arriving at Fort Boise, Crook found that the civilians in the area were not overly fond of the former commander and many of the officers of the Fourteenth. "They were accused of all manner of things. One thing was certain," Crook realized. "They had not, nor were they, making headway against the hostile Indians. There was much dissipation amongst a good many officers, and there seemed to be a general apathy amongst them, and indifference to the proper discharge of duty." One week later a war party struck civilians near the mouth of the Boise River, and Crook went with a troop of the First Cavalry to investigate matters, intending to be gone a week. "But," he recalled, "I got interested against the Indians and did not return there again for over two years."[8]

The Paiute campaign established Crook's reputation as an energetic Indian fighter and catapulted him toward the top rank of Indian-fighting generals. During the campaign Crook led soldiers aggressively in repeated attacks on the Paiutes and gave them no rest, pursuing them relentlessly during all seasons of the year. After setbacks such as in February 1868 when Indians stampeded most of the horses and mules while the command was camped at Dunder and Blixen Creek, Crook made the best of the situation. "We had to go back to Warner Lake," he related, "by using what animals we had left to pack us in. By making two loads, we got back all right." Crook also hired competent guides, encouraged subordinates to follow his lead, and enlisted Shoshoni Indians from Idaho as auxiliaries to fight the Paiutes. Most importantly, he hired three civilian pack-trains and personally supervised them, which gave his soldiers substantial freedom from their base of supply. In fourteen attacks, the Paiutes lost 329 killed, 20 wounded, and 225 captured. In four of these engagements the Shoshoni scouts alone fought under the command of Chief Guide Archie McIntosh or one of his subordinates. Crook had made sure the hostile Indians had no rest, and he had brought to an end what others had called a seemingly endless conflict.[9]

Crook's techniques of Indian warfare that became his trademark—using pack mules, employing Indian auxiliaries, and keeping the natives on the run—marked him as a comer. Gen. Henry W. Halleck, commanding the Division of the Pacific, made Crook the temporary commander of the Department of the Columbia, even though Crook was only a lieutenant colonel by actual rank. This command was only the beginning for Crook. In his assignment to Arizona as department commander in 1871, he bypassed, to their chagrin, some forty colonels of the line. In Arizona Territory Crook perfected his transportation system and created an efficient mobile train to accompany each troop. The Crook style of organization became the standard army model.[10]

Crook's company packtrain or *atajo* (short-cut) consisted of a packmaster or *patrón*, a *cargador*, or assistant packmaster who had charge of deciding which mules carried specific loads, a cook, a blacksmith, ten packers, fifty pack mules, fourteen saddle mules, and a bell mare. Crook took complete control of the trains in his command. He replaced packers who drank too much or generally caused trouble. In their places he obtained experts at their trade, well versed in the use of all the equipment needed on the trail and how to improvise packing unusual items. On a bet, an experienced packer could saddle and pack a mule blindfolded. He could size up an animal and instinctively know how much and what kind of a load the animal could carry safely and efficiently. Packing a mule improperly could result in a troop or company losing essential supplies during a campaign. The chief packmasters for Crook's trains in Arizona Territory were Thomas Moore, who would later write a manual on pack transportation and also invent an improved packsaddle, and his assistant, Dave Mears. Officers seldom interfered with good packers who were well versed in their responsibilities. Packers had few specific rules and regulations but could be fired for abusing any animal of the train, tying a riding mule or a pack mule in front of a saloon, indulging in intoxicants to the "prejudice of good order and discipline," being absent from the packtrain without permission, being insubordinate to the packmaster or neglectful of duties on the march, and using *coronas* (saddle pads) for bedding or the aparejo as a seat, or allowing anyone else to do so.[11]

Crook also personally inspected each mule. He sold off all "bony giants and undersized Sonora rats whose withers were always a mass of sores and whose hooves were always broken and out of sorts" and replaced them with well-formed, barrel-bellied Mexican mules between 13.2 and 14 hh. Most of these hybrids were crosses of small, stout Spanish asses and Arabian-blooded brood mares. Many were gray, and all tended to be surefooted and could carry heavier loads longer distances than mules bred in the United States. Crook believed these attributes made the mule a superior mount. Many times while campaigning or merely traveling from camp to camp, Crook rode a mule rather than a horse. So did John G. Bourke, who served on Crook's staff from 1870 to 1886 and published *On the Border with Crook* a year after Crook's death. Bourke maintained a love-hate relationship with his mule, Malaria. The animal, he claimed, "had been born a first-class mule, but a fairy godmother, or some other mysterious cause, had carried the good mule away, and left in its place a lop-eared, mangy specimen, which enjoyed the proud distinction of being considered, without dissent, the meanest mule in the whole Department of Arizona."[12]

To be completely effective, pack mules had to be kept in good condition. When not on campaigns Crook kept the trains constantly on the move carrying supplies from the main depots to all posts and Indian reserves. Bourke claimed that the mules "became hardened, the packers made more skillful in the use of all the 'hitches'—the 'Diamond' and others—constituting the mysteries of their calling, and the detachments sent along as escorts were constantly learning something new about the country as well as how to care for themselves and animals."[13]

Civilian packers also had devised a system that Crook's packers used to enable all concerned with an expedition to spot new, untrained mules. When the supplier or quartermaster presented a new pack mule or saddle mule (since saddle mules had the same conformation as packers) to the train, the patrón ordered an unfortunate packer to roach the mule's mane and clip its tail leaving only a tassel. A "shavetail" was easily recognized and approached with caution, never from the rear. By the time the tail feathers had grown out, it had become a "bell sharp," which meant it would take its place at the ringing of the bell. The widely used descriptive terms "shavetail" and "bell sharp" were also given to army officers. Those fresh from West Point were all referred to as "shavetail" lieutenants, while experienced officers who had served time in rank were called "bell sharps." The latter designation was a term of respect among officers.

Crook assigned a packtrain to each troop. At the front of each train was a packer leading the most important animal, the bell mare. Sometimes the cook rode the mare. The animal was usually no taller than the mules, had a short step, and was quick and agile. The mare was often white because of the superstition prevailing among Spanish packers that mules liked the color white better than any other, but also because packers were able to see white mares better at night. By nature mules tend to be herd-bound and to establish a "pecking" order, with one animal always leading the herd. Mares always dominated mules, even the geldings. The mare therefore led her followers. Even when the mules were not able to see the mare, they followed the sound of her bell. On most occasions packers needed only to ride alongside the packed mules who strode contentedly in single file. Packers all rode mules rather than horses because no packer wanted more than one leader of the train and knew that horses would tend to dominate. On those occasions when the bell mare was killed, the mules behaved like children who had lost their mother. Mules' grief, packers insisted, seemed almost human.[14]

A trooper with Troop F, Sixth Cavalry, recalled how well pack mules followed the bell. In 1881, while chasing Apaches, Troops A and F faced crossing a swift and unusually high Gila River. They first constructed a raft that could be pulled across the river and back by using ropes, then loaded supplies and packsaddles on the raft. On the first trip across they also sent the bell mare. One of the packers then rang the bell, and the mules at once plunged into the stream and swam across. The current carried them downstream for nearly a mile, but they crossed safely and ran up the bank until they reached the mare. In contrast, the process of crossing the herd-bound cavalry mounts was slow. A soldier on the raft held on to a mount's lead rope and helped the animal across. When the raft was near the shore, the handler turned loose of the rope. About three out of every five at once turned about and swam back. This caused so much delay that by noon only twenty horses had been successfully crossed.[15]

Crook also inspected all equipment, especially every Spanish packsaddle, and watched the cargador fit it to each mule's back. Packers actually did not regard the aparejo as a true saddle. It was a grass-padded, stiff blanket contrivance with small interwoven wooden bibs that could be fitted snugly on a mule's back. Unlike other packsaddles, the aparejo distributed the weight evenly and did not slip around on a mule's back. It was designed to give its wearer more freedom because it had no breast plate or rump rigging. Only a crupper kept the aparejo from slipping forward. The aparejo came in several sizes. Mules with girths of sixty to seventy-two inches would use an aparejo fifty-four inches long. Mules with larger girths required aparejos from fifty-six to sixty-two inches long.

Setting up an aparejo with bibs and grass padding required patience. Bibs needed to be tapered from front to rear with the larger ones in front. Mules with new riggings were loaded and exercised each day until their aparejos assumed the shape of their backs and withers. In this way the aparejo protected the mule's body from all manner of loading and had a proper bearing surface on each side of a mule's backbone. As chief packer Henry W. Daly emphasized, "The aparejo must be intelligently understood, and sore mules will be a thing of the past."[16]

Everything about the aparejo and its accessories, including terminology, was of Arabic or Spanish origin. "*Jalma* was the Arabic word for packsaddle; the saddle cover was called a *suvrin-hammer*, an Anglo corruption of *sobre-el-jalma*" (over the packsaddle). Other terms for parts or accessories were *grupera* or crupper, *corona* or saddle pad, *mantas* or pack covers, *cargo* or load, and *cincha*.[17]

Aparejos were plentiful in the West. Some of the old Mexican saddles of whitish tan or rawhide color could still be seen during the war with Spain. Early in the 1870s the saddle company of Main and Winchester in San Francisco made the first non-Mexican aparejos for the army. Army contracts also went to J. C. Johnson and Company of San Francisco and the Collins Saddle Company of Omaha,

Nebraska. In 1886 Moore supervised the construction of aparejos at the military prison at Fort Leavenworth, Kansas.[18]

The aparejo alone did not insure success in army packing. A hitch was needed, and packers universally used the single diamond hitch or variations of it. If tied properly it required no adjustment during a day's march, and in an emergency it could be quickly untied simply by removing the lash rope from the cincha hook. Using the hitch a single packer could load a mule if necessary. The usual procedure, however, called for a packer on each side of the animal to hold the load with one hand and manipulate the rope with the other. For heavier, bulkier loads packers used the double-diamond hitch. This variation of the single diamond became particularly useful for packing flour, water barrels, and ammunition boxes. On occasion some packers also threw the barrel hitch and the basket hitch, neither of which varied significantly from the diamonds.[19]

The combination of dependable, barrel-bellied mules, aparejos, diamond hitches, and experienced civilian packers gave the army excellent, quick, but somewhat expensive transportation. To cut costs, officers began exploring the use of means of transportation that enlisted men could manage.

In June 1878, Capt. Nathaniel A. Constable wrote Meigs, suggesting that light, two-wheeled mule-scouting carts pulled by two mules in tandem could be used to great advantage by commands in most departments. He had constructed three or four carts in 1872 and 1873 that had been used successfully by troops of the Fourth Cavalry at Fort Concho, Texas. The carts carried thirty days' supplies for one hundred men, cost less than fifty dollars to build, and could be taken "anywhere a cavalry company will have to be sent in this department 25 days out of 30 days." On occasions when a company entered rough terrain, it could use six pack mules and leave a small detachment to guard the carts while making a detour to rejoin the command.

Meigs thought that using carts for scouts was a good idea that would save money. He wrote a memorandum to department commanders asking for their ideas on the subject, and those of their officers. Overwhelmingly, the officers responded that they preferred pack mules using aparejos. Only five of forty-three officers responding preferred using carts over pack mules. The carts would be sporadically used by some commanders, but they did not replace pack mules.[20]

In 1881, Capt. Henry W. Lawton, Fourth Cavalry, published *Instructions for Using Moore's Improved Pack Saddle.* In the preface to the pamphlet Lawton explained that the packsaddle was the result of thirty years of "intelligent effort to combine all the advantages of the Mexican *aparejo* and the American packing and riding saddle," and he believed it to be the best. The saddle, Lawton declared, simply a modification of the aparejo, was to be packed in the same way and could be used by almost anyone. He also admitted that much of his pamphlet was copied from Moore's *Instructions for Using the Aparejo.*[21]

Just how much Moore had to do with the design of the saddle named after him is debatable. In 1878 he had claimed that the aparejo was the best possible saddle for packing, and that same year *Instructions for Using the Aparejo or Spanish Pack Saddle* was published with him as the author. In all probability, however, Lawton used Moore's name with his knowledge, and Moore approved of the actual design in theory only, since Lawton implied Moore's approval in the preface of the pamphlet. Five years later Moore was still chief packer and was still using aparejos. According to the packing fraternity, the Moore packsaddle was actually harmful to the mules' withers, backbones, and kidneys, but the saddle was used to some extent until after the Spanish-American War, when actual experiments found it wanting.

Packtrains using selected mules, aparejos, and experienced packers paid large dividends for George Crook. During the winter campaign of 1872–73 in the Tonto Basin region of Arizona Territory, each mule transported a net weight of 320 pounds and averaged thirty miles a day over a thirty-day period. Guided by Apache Indian scouts and accompanied by packtrains, nine troops of the First and Fifth Cavalries entered the rugged Tonto Basin from different directions in November 1872. In the past the Apaches had used this haven to elude and defy the white soldiers. Throughout the winter, soldiers combed the basin and the mountains that bordered it, attacking and killing Apache and Yavapai Indians and totally demoralizing them. Crook used the method of converging columns of troops, "each able to look out for itself, each provided with a force of

Indian scouts, each followed by a packtrain with all needful supplies, and each led by officers physically able to go almost anywhere." Bourke stated that the mules "evoked constant praise."
They "had followed us over some of the worst trails in Arizona, and
were still as fresh as when they left [Fort] Grant." Only two mules
died during the campaign. One ate a poisonous insect and another
was struck by a rattlesnake.[22]

Late in the spring of 1873, bewildered natives began surrendering
at Camp Verde, Fort Apache, Fort Bowie, and San Carlos in Arizona
Territory and at Tularosa in New Mexico Territory. Lt. Thomas
Cruse, not a part of this campaign but rather as an officer stationed
in Arizona and New Mexico for more than twenty years, asserted
that "it was the pack trains that finally defeated the Indians, this on
the admission of all the noted chiefs with whom we talked later on.
The troops were enabled to hold on to the trail as long as the Indians
left one, and as the Apache is a temperamental person in spite of his
stoicism, this persistent following got on his nerves.'" Ultimately,
Cruse wrote, the Apache "would stop and make a stand to scare his
pursuers—and that was his undoing! He shot away his limited
stock of ammunition, lost two or three men killed, both irreplace-
able, and was finally forced to flee with the Scouts in close pursuit,
while the packtrain was right there with ammunition and supplies
for the troops. The Apaches remarked that it was very discourag-
ing." In a very real sense pack mules earned George Crook his star.
In October 1873 President Grant promoted Crook from lieutenant
colonel to brigadier general.[23]

In an attempt to emulate the success of the Tonto Basin campaign—including Crook's promotion—aggressive regimental commanders formed their own packtrains. Good packers and small
pack mules became a premium. But it was legally not possible to
obtain the type of mules needed to satisfy packers and to make
these trains perform as successfully as Crook's trains had during the
Paiute disturbances and the Tonto Basin conflict. No doubt some
quartermasters who were under pressure ignored regulations and
purchased small mules for packing, but these purchases could eventually backfire on them. What they needed was a new regulation
concerning the purchase of mules that abrogated the 1867 general

orders stating that the height of a pack mule must not be less than 14.5 hh.

Finally, Col. Asher R. Eddy, in a letter to Meigs, suggested changes in the general orders because "mules 13 hands high will pack quite as much as big mules and will not be used up so soon." Eddy also referred to Inspector General Marcy's opinion that "the short-legged, barrel-bellied Mexican mule from 13 to 14 hands high is unquestionably a more hardy animal and better adapted for packing especially in mountainous regions, than large American mules." In response to the letter, and no doubt to other information he had gleaned from other sources, Meigs asked the chief quartermasters and experienced officers in all divisions to comment on the need to change "any existing regulations as to the size of mules."[24]

The chief quartermasters and experienced officers overwhelmingly favored new regulations concerning pack mules. In fact, their recommendations to Meigs were basically the same ones that civilian packers had been making for years; they already knew the kinds of mules needed for packing, riding, and hauling wagons. Col. Langdon C. Easton, who had served in the West prior to the Civil War, as chief quartermaster of the Army of the Cumberland, and with Sherman in Georgia, had dealt with mules extensively. Easton was now army depot quartermaster at Philadelphia, and he responded that there was more endurance in middle-sized mules than in "those of larger sizes for all purposes. They will live on less and stand more exposure and hardship" than larger mules. "A small, thick set mule from 13 to 14½ hands high is best suited for packing purposes." A larger mule, he observed, had a "long racking stride in his walk" that caused "his pack to rub and chafe, while the short mincing gait of the smaller" mule made his pack less likely to cause a sore back. Easton therefore recommended that the height be lowered to 13 hands and that Mexican mules should be purchased whenever possible. "Owing to the exposure and privation that the Mexican mule has to endure as he grows up," commented Easton, "he can stand more exposure, live on less, and has more endurance than our well-cared for American mules."[25]

Capt. George W. Bradley, an assistant quartermaster serving in the Department of the South, also wrote in favor of smaller mules.

While serving in New Mexico he had fitted out packtrains and was responsible for forming the packtrain in the winter of 1868 for Maj. Andrew W. Evans's Canadian River expedition. Evans's command operated as an important part of Gen. Philip H. Sheridan's army during the winter campaign of 1868–69 in the Oklahoma country. "Not having enough Mexican mules," wrote Bradley, "I broke up a train of American mules and used them for packs." When the expedition returned to base, "the Mexican mules were found to be in the best condition." Bradley believed, therefore, that "small mules will pack quite as much as the large ones and remain in better condition." During Sheridan's entire winter operations on the Southern plains, the animals of the expedition had died by the hundreds from hunger, exhaustion, and exposure. In January 1869 Evans lost sixty-four mules during a ten-day march from the Washita River to the depot. The loss of animals had drastically modified all commanders' plans. Having smaller Mexican mules that could forage for themselves even in winter conditions was an important consideration for any officer commanding troops or packtrains. In a bit of inconsistency, Bradley also admitted that "13 inch [hands] mules" were in his judgment "too low for a standard."[26]

Chief quartermaster of the Platte, Maj. Alexander J. Perry, used Meigs's request for comments on a pack mule's size simply to request good mules and packers. Perry concurred fully with Marcy's description of mules and recommended that a well-equipped packtrain of 150 pack mules along with well-trained packers be procured in New Mexico or elsewhere and sent to the department. Perry confessed that the officers and men experienced much trouble with their packtrain. "The mules are large, most of them old, stiff, clumsy for packing, and generally return from a scout in a condition that often renders them useless for months, owing to bad packing." He added that expert packers were needed, but there were few competent judges to select from all the packers offering their services.

Lt. Col. Samuel B. Holabird, Department of Texas, concurred with other chief quartermasters that short-legged and compact mules were the best and that the standard should be lowered if "one is to be fixed at all." But he also agreed that quartermasters should be practical and purchase whatever was available when needs were pressing. Finally, in May 1873 the adjutant general issued new general orders concerning pack mules. Now "the heavily-bodied, compactly-built mule, from 13½ to 14 hands high will be the general standard for pack purposes, but when suitable in all respects, the Mexican mule, from 13 to 14 hands may be accepted. All mules purchased for the Army must be not less than four nor over 10 years of age; strong, stout, compact, well-developed, in full health, and free from any blemish or defect which would unfit them for severe work."[27]

There existed a visible bond between packers and their mules. Packers claimed mules were sensitive and intelligent animals, more so than either of their parents. Mules responded to kindness and would recognize by sight and sense of smell the individual who had shown it to them. According to Crook's long-time adjutant, Captain Bourke, the care packers gave their animals equaled "almost that given to the average baby." The mule, Bourke added, responded to such attentions. James W. Steele, an infantry lieutenant serving in New Mexico and Texas between 1867 and 1870, wrote a delightful group of essays entitled *Frontier Army Sketches*. In his essay entitled "Army Mule" Steele asserted that the companionship between a packer and his mules was "a little less than touching." Mules recognized the packer "from afar," and the packer could lead one anywhere, merely placing his hand under its chin. The animals were, said Steele, "sedate, patient, tractable, handsome," and proud of their occupation. Thomas Moore, as chief packer of the Department of Missouri, observed that "the mule has never been done justice. It is fashionable to disparage him, and people do so without knowing anything about the subject." Few would have disagreed with Steele's claim that the army mule was the chief factor in all military operations. "His corral," Steele insisted, was the "most interesting and important appurtenance of a military post, and his care is a thing of solicitude on the part of all concerned with the efficiency" of the army.[28]

Routine was important for pack mules. Packers established a set pattern and the animals responded. In February 1874 William T. Corbusier, an army physician traveling from Camp Verde with Troop K, Fifth Cavalry, was amazed at the routine and performance of the packtrain of eighty mules. "It was a sight worth seeing," he explained, "when the mules lined up to have their *aparejos* removed each evening and put on again in the morning—each mule knowing his place in line." Each animal recognized its own harness and aparejo and balked if the packer placed a strange one on its back. According to Daly, each mule in a train "was a special pet with the packers, and each knew its own name when spoken to in a voice of caution or word of encouragement, as well as a human being in a similar position would understand it." While campaigning in New Mexico in 1880, Lt. Thomas Cruse noted that as soon as the command reached camp, the horses and mules were watered and turned loose on the grazing grounds, perhaps a mile from the camp. There was little danger that hostiles would capture the herd since the scouts had carefully reconnoitered the area. The animals were always loose-herded, without lariats or picket ropes. Both soldiers and scouts were detailed to watch over the animals until nightfall. Then the herd was brought in for water and grooming, then turned loose again near the camp for the night, "in a different place and different direction from where they had been during the afternoon."[29]

There was a special relationship between the packers and their mules that few officers or men could comprehend. Steele, however, had a stab at understanding whatever it was when he claimed that a mule was a faithful worker throughout life. It would not leave its packtrain though "shelterless and unfed." It stayed by its masters all day and stood by all night, "looking his hunger with all the eloquence of his doleful face, and crying his peculiar note of distress at intervals frequently enough to accomplish his object of keeping [all others] awake and sorry." Steele observed that the horse is "the special pet of man." Yet "there was never a plebeian mule," he claimed, "doomed from colthood to unremitting toil," who was not definitely the horse's "superior in that peculiar knowledge that has never been classified, that 'sense' that is neither memory nor mind, which is inadequately described by the term sagacity, which is not distinct, and which is a marked characteristic of the long-eared thistle-eating fraternity." The mule was both docile and devilish, tricky yet faithful, always in difficulty yet never injured. He was "awkward and clumsy in gait and appearance and slow of foot," yet he "comes out fresh and vigorous at the end of journeys that wear his rider to illness and lameness." It was, "taken all in all[,] a study in natural history that will never have a definite conclusion, a creature that is a sphinx, and yet a mule."[30]

Troopers and infantrymen quickly learned to appreciate packtrains even though they might not be enamored with pack mules who were sometimes known for their late-night serenades. Perhaps the mules were only attempting to accompany packs of howling coyotes, whom soldiers throughout the Southwest sometimes referred to as the Arizona Jazz Band. Anton Mazzanovich, stationed in Arizona during the 1880s as a trooper in the Sixth Cavalry, as a soldier in the Twenty-first Infantry, and then as a civilian packer, claimed that the life of a soldier was a good life with "plenty of good fresh air and good eats as long as the packtrain" accompanied the soldiers. Breakfast with the packtrain in camp, he wrote, was "such a feed [consisting of] Baked beans with bacon, black coffee and camp-baked bread. When we picked up the Indian trail and had to leave the packtrain behind, that was a different story." On one occasion when Mazzanovich's Troop had left the packtrain far behind, he complained that it meant "no grub to most of the command for the time being." Another time the trooper was more concerned with his safety than his stomach. While engaging the Apaches in a fire fight, troopers had to conserve ammunition, and horse-holders (of which Mazzanovich was one) were forced to give up thirty-two of their rounds to those on the front line. When would the packtrain arrive?[31]

Seasoned, well-stocked packtrains performed some amazing feats in the West, but it was their endurance that was most remarkable. If traveling with the cavalry, pack mules could not keep up with the mounts during the initial fifteen miles but were pushing them at thirty miles and had the horses at their mercy in a march of seventy-five miles in a twenty-four-hour period. According to a chart in Daly's *Manual of Pack Transportation* that showed loads and rates of travel considered practicable for a well-seasoned packtrain, mules loaded with two hundred pounds of supplies could travel twenty-five miles a day at a pace of eight miles per hour for seven consecutive days. At the rate of six miles per hour the same mules with the same loads could travel one hundred miles a day for three consecutive days, or at five miles per hour the mules could travel twenty-five miles a day for 365 continuous days. When traveling at a slow rate the walk was the ordinary gait of the pack mule. As the rate of travel was increased the mule did not simply walk faster but fell into an amble or fox trot. A mule could amble along at five to six miles an hour without undue fatigue. To develop this amble young pack mules were "tailed," which meant that their lead rope was tied to an experienced mule's tail. The young mules quickly developed the amble. If a mule still had a problem ambling, packers placed the aparejo cinch sufficiently forward so the mule's elbows would rub against the cinch and become sore. The mule would then take short and quick steps in order to keep his place in line, thus readily learning the ambling gait. Steele jokingly suggested that the "jog-trot" showed "irredeemable depravity."[32]

Sometimes mules ambled steadily for long distances. In 1881, for example, a troop of Indian scouts and packtrain chasing Nana, the Mimbreño Apache who succeeded Victorio, marched eighty-five miles in twelve hours across the rugged terrain of New Mexico. Each mule carried two hundred pounds of supplies. Since their aparejos weighed from fifty-five to sixty-five pounds, each mule carried roughly 20 percent of a pack mule's average weight. Later, in pursuing the same Mimbreño Apaches, a troop of Indian scouts and a packtrain loaded with 250 pounds per mule covered some sixty miles in a day from old Fort Cummings, New Mexico, to Fort Seldom on the Rio Grande. The Indian troops and Apaches were skirmishing all the way. The Indian scouts with their pack mules then boarded freight cars and traveled by train that evening to Fort Craig. After unloading early in the morning they marched thirty miles across the valley to the San Mateos, struck the trail of Nana and party, and followed the hostiles south of the Hatchet Mountains into Mexico. By hoof and rail the mules had covered more than three hundred miles in a matter of four days.

Another perhaps more spectacular example occurred the next year when a group of Apache scouts and a packtrain made a forced march of 280 miles in only three days. The scouts were attempting to corner an Apache war party that included Juh, Chato, Natchez, and Geronimo in the Chihuahua Peloncillo Mountains that hug the Arizona–New Mexico border.

During the 1901 Garza campaign along the Rio Grande, a large

group of outlaws operating on both sides of the border from Browns-
ville, Texas, to the source of the Rio Grande committed depredations, robbing and killing anyone who resisted. Led by the wily
Garza, the band spread a path of destruction wherever it went. The
Third Cavalry under Col. Anson Mills had to cover tremendous distances and be ready to engage the outlaws whenever possible. On
one occasion a troop of Third Cavalry and a packtrain carrying 250
pounds per mule was in pursuit of the bandits and made a forced
march of 108 miles in sixteen hours. The bandits escaped but the
mules performed brilliantly.[33]

By far the best performance of pack mules in a continuous campaign was during the last Geronimo campaign in 1885–86. During
eighteen months from May 1885 to September 1886, several packtrains followed the troops and Indian scouts throughout portions of
New Mexico and Arizona Territories as well as Sonora and Chihuahua. They climbed the steepest portions of the Sierra Madres
and lost only six mules. Before attempting to move through the Si-
erras, Capt. Emmett Crawford asked Daly if his mules could make
it. Daly replied that every mule in the train "was as sure-footed as a
chamois and as careful with the load on its back as a mother with
child in her arms." He further claimed that mules recognized danger quicker than men and "knew instinctively how to avoid it."
George Crook told a correspondent for the *Los Angeles Times* that
the reason some pack mules fell while climbing in the Sierra
Madres was that when a mule came to a bad place it stopped, and
those following pushed it, causing it to fall. One mule loaded with
bacon got pushed off; it rolled down and disappeared. Two packers
far below on the zigzag trail said it "bounced over them, landed on a
big rock, bounced way up, and came down in a deep pool. It swam
out and began grazing."[34]

During the final months of the chase, mules and packers, although pushed, proved their mettle. In May 1886 Capt. Henry W.
Lawton led thirty-five Fourth Cavalry troopers, twenty infantrymen from the Eighth Regiment, twenty Apache scouts, thirty
packers, and a hundred pack mules out of Fort Huachuca in another
attempt to round up Geronimo's small band of twenty-two men and
thirteen women. Lawton doggedly pursued the Indians for four
months over two thousand miles throughout the wilds of northern

Mexico and Arizona. After a week they all walked; the horses had broken down. Lawton lost forty pounds while surgeon Leonard Wood lost thirty pounds. Fewer than twenty enlisted men endured the entire four months; others replaced them. Three different sets of officers served during the chase. Surely some of the mules and packers were also replaced during the four months, but the mule was the only animal that could be depended upon to carry ammunition and rations day after day over such rough country.

Throughout the entire chase Daly enthusiastically maintained that each pack mule carried between 250 and 300 pounds and averaged thirty miles a day except when mountain climbing. Equally important, the mules had subsisted entirely on grass and returned to their posts at the end in relatively good condition. Daly, a member of the pursuit, was of course attempting to gain recognition for himself, his packers, and the pack mules, but there is no reason to doubt his words. The mules undoubtedly did subsist on grass while campaigning, but when replaced they were rehabilitated with grain and corn. Since stripped aparejos weighed in the neighborhood of 50 pounds, the mules were actually carrying 200 pounds of supplies with certain mules packing perhaps 250 pounds of ammunition.[35]

At times packtrains were sad imitations of what they were intended to be, but poor trains usually occurred when inexperienced packers attempted to pack untrained mules, when trains used shoddy equipment, or when soldiers packed wagon mules. Such was the case for most of Gen. Alfred H. Terry's packtrains during the Little Bighorn Campaign of 1876. Bourke, who observed these trains, commented that they made the "saddest burlesque" of any he had ever seen. "One could see the other packtrain, a string of mules of all sizes, each led by one soldier and beaten and driven along by another—attendants often rivaling animals in dumbness."[36]

When the major part of Terry's command left Fort Abraham Lincoln, probably no one realized that it would face extreme transportation difficulties. A wagon train of close to 150 wheeled vehicles carried thirty days' supplies and forage for the expedition. Contract-hired two-horse wagons hauled from fifteen hundred to two thousand pounds while six-mule government wagons, depending on the condition of the teams, carried from three thousand to five thousand pounds. Herders and a few civilian packers drove the beef cattle and kept the pack mules close to the wagon train. As usual for combined expeditions of infantry and cavalry, each troop or company was assigned one wagon to transport five days' rations and forage and its mess kits as well as the mess kit, tents, and baggage of the officers and ten days' supplies for the officers' mess.[37]

Difficulties occurred, however, when the Seventh abandoned its wagons. On 8 June each troop of the Seventh received a string of eleven mules that probably consisted of seven mules trained for packing and four wagon mules. The wagon mules most likely had never carried supplies on their backs, and troopers of the Seventh had never packed even trained pack animals. With only a few civilian packers available to train a sergeant and four troopers of each troop who probably did not want to be mule packers, a scene of extraordinary confusion took place. After civilian packers demonstrated how to throw a diamond hitch, the packers of Troop K attempted to pack two empty water casks, according to Lt. Edward S. Godfrey. Using a civilian packsaddle, the five men proceeded to load the mule. When the blind was lifted, declared Godfrey, and the mule "gave a startled look first at one side, then to the other" at the empty barrels "bandaged" to its sides. It "jumped to one side causing to rattle a bung-plug that had fallen inside one of the casks." This startled the mule more, and it "snorted and brayed, bucked and kicked until the casks fell off." One of the barrels was still fastened to the saddle by the sling rope, and the mule bolted through the camp causing such a furor that Godfrey feared that it would cause a general stampede. The inexperienced packers made a second attempt, this time packing two sacks of grain. Once again the mule bucked, unloaded the sacks, and regaled itself by eating from one of the split grain sacks. "As a final effort," Godfrey remembered, "we concluded to try the aparejo and pack two boxes of ammunition. This done, the mule walked off with as little concern as if he had been a pack mule all his life." No doubt that particular mule preferred the aparejo.[38]

Two days later Terry made a decision that would seriously handicap the Seventh's operations in Sioux country. On 10 June he sent Reno with six companies on an elaborate scout that would take nine days and cover more than 250 miles through the Powder River country. Each troop of the Seventh that was not taking part in the scout supplied Reno with four of its pack mules. Although there is no evidence to substantiate a claim that Reno's packtrain received only pack mules from the other troops in the regiment, the nature of the scout and the distance covered indicates that this probably was the case. Reno's packtrain—sixty-six trained pack mules and twenty-four shavetails (or worse, wagon mules)—therefore contained most of the reliable pack mules. A packtrain consisting of experienced packers and seasoned mules in that time could have covered the 250 miles over most terrains without undue difficulty. After all, the mules would average fewer than 30 miles a day. But Reno's men were not experienced packers in any sense of the word, and even the pack mules had not been trained for such a trip. As Pvt. Peter Thompson later remembered, "I do not think there were half a dozen men in the scouting party who knew how to pack a mule without having its pack work loose." Loose packs and bad packing took a toll on the mules; most developed festering sores within a few days. Others became lame. By the time Custer's and Reno's commands united, most of Reno's pack mules were in poor condition.[39]

While Reno was wearing out and ruining many of the pack mules, the rest of the Seventh remained in bivouac at the supply camp. This gave five men from each troop time to familiarize themselves with the art of packing. "Believe me," Pvt. Charles Creighton of Troop K asserted, "we had some fun. The mules had never been packed and we were as green as the mules." When Custer left the Powder River country on 15 June, his command's train consisted of ninety-seven mules of which no more than eighteen were regular pack mules. Without enough good mules to carry supplies and without enough good packers, the Seventh's transportation difficulties multiplied. Each troop managed its own pack mules, and mules were "scattered in confusion along the advancing column." The trouble, of course, was using untrained mules and untrained troopers, many of whom must have been irritated at being given extra duties in addition to caring for their own mounts.[40]

Thoroughly irritated by the mule transportation dilemma, Custer placed the strings of mules under the command of Lt. Luther R. Hare. The mules followed the rear troop of the command. At least

Custer could not see the suffering mules. The combining of the strings evidently worked for a time, for the command arrived at the Tongue River on 16 June, where it bivouacked until ordered to meet Reno's command on 20 June.[41]

Custer again became keenly aware of mule difficulties when he marched to meet Reno. The command made painfully slow progress, for some of the mules had become unusable. Custer's troop did not reach Reno's command until after 11:00 P.M.

The next day the united command began its fatal march up the Rosebud. Terry sent it off with a grand review, but it was an inauspicious beginning, for as Godfrey wrote, "Cargo began falling off before we got out of camp." The Seventh marched a painful sixteen miles with Reno's mules in worse shape than Custer's. Probably only the mules packing ammunition boxes wore aparejos. The others used sawbuck saddles, which were easier for novices to pack but caused painful back sores on the mules. The next day thirteen of Reno's mules broke down completely. Disgusted with the events and the pace of the mules, Custer replaced Hare with Lt. Edward G. Matherly, who had taken charge of his transportation during the Washita Campaign. The change might have appeased Custer, but it had no affect on weary, sore-backed, and lame mules. Matherly reported that mules in three troops had become stubborn and almost unmanageable while others had gone lame. As a consequence of Matherly's unwelcome news, Custer assigned Capt. Frederick W. Benteen to command the rear guard battalion, "an unenviable assignment that condemned him to march in the dust of the 'lowly' mules."[42]

On 23 June the pack mules could not keep up with the command. As the Seventh followed the valley of the Rosebud, it crossed the river five times in three miles. The steep banks and the mud further wearied the already weakened mules. At one crossing, Benteen complained, "it took exactly one and a half hours to get the packtrain across, so, by that time Custer's column was all of six miles ahead of my train." For some time Benteen followed Custer's orders and stayed behind the packtrain. With each mile the mules became more scattered. Finally, Benteen used his own discretion and positioned troopers along the flank of the train to ward off a possible attack. In explaining this part of the campaign later in life he observed, "I don't begin to believe that Job ever had much to do with shaved tailed pack mules." When the train finally reached the bivouac hours after the troopers, Benteen told Custer's adjutant, Lt. W. W. Cooke, what he had done and asked Cooke to "communicate the same to General Custer so that the next officer in charge should not receive such [restrictive] orders." The command that day had covered thirty-five miles, a good day's journey for mules in excellent condition but an arduous march for those of Custer's packtrain.[43]

On 24 June the mules were able to stay closer to the command than the day before. Still at 11:00 P.M., when Custer ordered a night march to follow the heavily worn Sioux trail, all the mules had not yet crossed the Rosebud and reached camp. Capt. Miles Keogh was now in charge of the rear guard and decided to cut loose any mule packs that hindered the progress of the mule train. During the ten miles covered that night and early the next morning some of the mules' cargoes came loose, and darkness impeded repacking. At one point Custer sent Lt. Charles DeRudio and Trumpeter William G. Hardy to instruct Keogh to hurry up the packtrain. The two found a cursing Keogh at the Rosebud with sixteen mules mired in the mud. Around 2:00 A.M. 25 June, the Seventh established a camp, but all of the scattered mules did not arrive for another two hours or more. Including the night march they had carried supplies more than forty miles that day; yet they were not unpacked until sometime after daylight, something that should never have happened whether or not the Seventh needed fresh mules.[44]

The next morning the mules resumed their travel and finally neared the divide between the Rosebud Valley from the Little Bighorn. The train halted around 10:00 A.M. to await further developments. By now the animals were mostly in a sorry condition despite the efforts of several civilian packers accompanying the train. Incredibly, Custer's reaction to the weary and back-sore mules' inability to keep up with the cavalry was to increase the detail of troopers assigned to the train.[45]

Custer's plan was to locate the Sioux camp on 25 June and attack it the next day when Gibbon's infantry was due to arrive at the Little Bighorn River. Even if he had thought of giving his troopers' mounts a needed rest and the pack mules a day to recuperate, a one-day rest would have not helped the mules, many of which had large festering sores that poorly fitted packs would continue to aggravate. Custer was not noted for a concern for animals on campaign.

Custer's initial plans changed after receiving a message from Lt. Charles A. Varnum, who with a small party of Crow scouts had climbed a low mountain known to the Indians as Crow's Nest. There he discovered a large Sioux camp on the lower Little Bighorn below the mouth of a small stream later known as Reno Creek. By 9:00 A.M., when Custer reached the Crow's Nest, he could not see the camp because the sun had risen and a haze had settled over the valley. But Custer had no reason to doubt his scouts and decided to attack the camp as soon as possible. His concern and that of all cavalry officers on campaigns against hostiles was that the Indians would break camp and flee in all directions before a decisive attack could be launched. Only by attacking a large concentration of Indians in camp could he achieve impressive results.

Custer reasoned incorrectly that the Indians at that time knew of the Seventh's location. The scouts had also told him that they had seen three separate parties of Sioux that morning. No doubt Custer thought that at least one of the Indian groups had seen either the scouts or troopers and had alerted the camp. Tom Custer reinforced his brother's premonitions when he told him that a sergeant that morning had led a detail to recover a box of hardtack dropped from a badly packed mule the evening before. The troopers had come across a party of Sioux munching on their find and had exchanged fire with them. Surely these Indians had informed the camp.

Custer divided his command into three forces and began moving at noon. Not knowing the exact location of the camp and not wanting the Indians to escape to the south, he sent three troops under Benteen to the left and ordered Benteen to send men to the crest of the ridge to scan the Little Bighorn valley and then rejoin the command. Custer and Reno led their separate forces down the opposite sides of Reno Creek. The packtrain and the rear guard Company B under Capt. Thomas McDougall were to follow Custer's and Reno's troops as closely as possible.[46]

The packtrain now experienced greater problems. Before following the trail into the valley, Matherly had to halt his train, repack some cargoes, and wait for stragglers. As the train descended the trail that followed the creek, Cooke brought orders from Custer to keep the mules "off the trail, as they were raising too much dust." Matherly complied, making progress even tougher for the already weakened animals. Cooke rode back a second time to the train, and Matherly asked him if it train was causing less dust. Cooke answered, "Yes." Matherly, therefore, continued to obey the order, but the mule train was now strung out over a mile and was falling farther behind Custer's and Reno's commands.[47]

In the meantime Custer discovered that the Seventh was dealing with a major concentration of Indians, and he sent for McDougall's rear guard, the packtrain, and Benteen. Sgt. Daniel A. Kanipe was ordered to find McDougall and tell him to come "with the packtrain straight across the country. . . . If any of the packs get loose cut them and let them go, do not stop to tighten them." The wording of the message clearly showed that Custer knew the functional weakness of the train. Dust was no longer the issue, but by then the already weakened mules were mostly worn out from picking their way off the trail or attempting to get out of a muddy bog near a water hole. Custer had, in effect, made sure that the mules could not respond quickly to his command.[48]

When Benteen received the summons "Benteen. Come on. Big Village. Be Quick. Bring Packs. W. W. Cooke. P. brings pacs.," he was just returning from his scout. He already knew that a battle was starting, because Kanipe had ridden past his command shouting "We got 'em, Boys!" Benteen made no attempt to take charge of the train. He later claimed that the pack mules were more than seven miles away from his column and that it would have taken an hour for them to reach his position. Instead of taking charge he ordered a trot rather than a gallop and headed down the trail, ultimately to reach Reno's hilltop defensive position.

When he first sighted Reno's defensive position, McDougall did not know if the men there were troopers or Indians. He now had one platoon ahead of the mules and one behind them. As a defensive measure he ordered the thirteen ammunition pack mules placed together in line and gave orders that if attacked the lead platoon should deploy and try to hold the Indians off. If the troopers were unsuccessful, the enlisted men with the mules carrying the ammunition should encircle them, shoot them, and use the carcasses as a shield. If necessary they could subsist on mule meat for a few days.[49]

When the strung-out rear guard and pack mules reached Reno's Hill, all was confusion. Several mules wandered off and were captured by the Indians. One of them, an ammunition mule named Old Barnum, tried to stampede down the hill. Sgt. Richard P. Hanley, who had been detailed to the ammunition mules, knew that he would be blamed if the mule escaped, so he drew his revolver and went after Old Barnum. If he couldn't catch him, he would shoot him and possibly keep the Sioux from getting the ammunition. The mule ran about half way to where the Indians were before Hanley finally turned him back into the herd. For his bravery Hanley later received the Congressional Medal of Honor.[50]

Most of the pack mules of Custer's Seventh made their last stand on Reno's Hill. Many of them were wounded. Some of them were killed by the troopers to shield the wounded who lay in a shallow place on the bluffs. Not until the evening of 26 June could the surviving animals be taken to the river to drink; they had been more than twenty-four hours without water. It is hardly surprising that only 50 of the original train of 175 mules were still fit for any service on 6 July.[51]

No doubt the lack of enough seasoned pack mules and packers had an impact on the Seventh's Little Big Horn battle. Custer should be blamed for not taking better care of the animals of the Seventh's packtrain. But even in his disregard for the mules, they should have been able to perform effectively from 15 June until the battle, despite poor packing and the animals being out of shape. The major blame for the lack of the mule train's performance during this part of the campaign should be placed on General Terry, who sent Major Reno's command on a long-range scouting expedition with all or most of the pack mules. Barely trained troopers who used mainly sawbuck saddles and threw ineffective diamond hitches had most of the best mules badly sore-backed before the critical part of the campaign began. Blame should also be shared by Reno, who wandered miles farther than ordered and who showed little concern for his packtrain.

In direct contrast to the packtrains in Terry's column were those in Crook's. On 29 May 1876, when Crook's column of more than one thousand men left Fort Fetterman for the second time and marched up the Bozeman Trail, it was accompanied by a magnificent supply train of 120 wagons pulled by 720 wagon mules and more than a thousand "Crook-approved" pack mules. Bourke praised Crook's trains, calling them a "marvel of a system" that moved "with a precision to which the worn-out comparison of 'clockwork' [was] justly adapted." The mules, Bourke noted, "had been continuously in training since the preceding January, making long marches, carrying heavy burdens in the worst sort of weather." They were, therefore, "hardened to the hardness and toughness of wrought-iron and whalebone. They followed the bell, and were as well trained as any soldiers in the command."⁵²

Chicago Times correspondent John Finerty, unable to compare other trains with those of Crook's command, was not nearly as complimentary as Bourke had been. Finerty expressed only grudging admiration for these "average mules" who were "morose in manner and filthy, not to say immodest in habit" and "were girthed so tight" that they were "almost cut in two." Before the end of the campaign, however, he spoke of the "splendid mule packtrain." He was further astonished at the packers' language, stating that "ears polite would be immeasurably shocked by the sounds and observations" that began "the starting of a packtrain from camp." The packers, wrote Finerty, "swore in a most artistic and perfectly inexhaustible fashion." Crook established his base camp on Goose Creek, where on 14 June, 224 Crow and Shoshoni Indian auxiliaries joined him.⁵³

Crook anticipated an engagement with the Sioux and Northern Cheyennes. Concerned with the mobility of his troops, he ordered Col. Alexander Chambers to recruit 175 to 200 infantrymen who were willing to become wagon mule cavalrymen. "The first hour's experience with the reluctant Rosinantes," wrote Bourke in reference to Don Quixote's steed in Cervantes' classic tale, "equalled the best exhibition ever given by Barnum." Commenting on the circus, Finerty noted that the unwilling mules had had regulation bits forced into their jaws and regulation McClellan saddles placed on their backs. "Then the fun began. A cloud of mule-heels shod in iron would rise simultaneously in the air, while the shrill neighing and squealing of the brutes displayed the great indignation that possessed them." The inexperienced infantrymen were then ordered to mount the mules. "Many of the infantry had never been in a saddle," recalled Frank Grouard, one of the scouts of the expedition, and "none of the mules had ever had a saddle on their backs. . . . The valley for a mile in every direction was filled with bucking mules, frightened infantrymen, broken saddles, and applauding spectators." Finerty claimed that some of the mules did not move but bucked where they stood, "and then a soldier might be seen shooting up in the air like a rocket, and his very 'dull thud' would soon be heard as his body struck mother earth in his fall from among the clouds." But in the end, as Maj. Andrew Burt, Ninth Infantry, noted, the objective was accomplished after a "much vexatious delay."[54]

On 16 June Crook cut loose from his wagon train and crossed from the Tongue to Rosebud Creek. The next morning the column set out early. Halting at about 8:00 A.M. for a rest near the great bend of the Rosebud, the force was unexpectedly attacked by the Sioux and Cheyennes. The Shoshonis and the Crow scouts held the field until the troops had a chance to get organized. The Battle of the Rosebud lasted all day and featured some of the hardest fighting of the Indian wars. Both sides acquitted themselves well during the engagement. The Crows more than once kept Crook's troops from being overrun and probably saved the large packtrain from capture or destruction. But the Cheyenne and Sioux warriors fought with a tenacity not normally seen during battles with the Indians. They were fighting not only their hated enemy, the Crows, but also some of the same troops that had attacked their women and children in March. Crook's men were unable to gain any advantage until a flanking movement late in the afternoon carried a squadron of the Third Cavalry behind the Indian lines. Now pressed from the rear, the Cheyenne and Sioux warriors broke off the fight and abandoned the battlefield. Having retained possession of the field, Crook claimed a victory, but in fact he had been badly beaten. The next morning he headed back to Goose Creek to resupply. His retreat to the Tongue reflected the full measure of his defeat because it neutralized him at the most critical juncture of the campaign. Custer encountered the same Indians a week later with consequences far more disastrous than Crook had suffered.[55]

The next year pack mules performed well for the highest officer in the U.S. Army. Lt. Gen. William T. Sherman took one of his famous tours of inspection and vacation to the West. This time Sherman and his entourage, which included his son Tom, went into the Big Horn Mountains of northern Wyoming and into the wilds of Montana Territory. The only feasible transportation for this tour was a packtrain, and the army provided well for the commanding general. Chief Packer Tom Moore, technically still in command of Crook's packtrains, was placed in charge of a train of the most skilled packers and best mules. "Tables, chairs, lounges, mess-chests, and an immense cooking-stove" were carried by pack mules over some of the roughest terrain in the West. Moore knew the importance of providing all that was needed and more to impress the general with the utility of his packtrain and agility of his mules. "Everything did go, and not a cup or a dish was broken on the entire trip" by a pack mule. "It must have been an amusing sight to look behind and see a powerful mule, laden with the cooking-stove, coming down a steep hill, picking [its] way as carefully and gingerly as though walking" on eggs "that must not be broken." The expertise of Moore's mules and packers was not lost on the general, who at the end of the trip praised the packer for a job well done.[56]

During the post–Civil War Indian conflicts, mules played a constant and vital role. They hauled the supply wagons as packers helped the cavalry remain mobile and in emergencies and other special circumstances turned infantrymen into instant, although not necessarily effective, cavalrymen. Mules had become important fixtures in the army, and departmental quartermasters kept accurate records of the numbers of animals purchased, sold, and on hand at the beginning of each year. The number of mules in a given department could testify to the effectiveness of the quartermasters and other officers.

In the western departments where mules were used most extensively, their numbers were impressive. Between 1876 and 1881, for example, within the Department of the Platte, the numbers of mules on hand each 1 January were 1,923 ('77), 1,666 ('78), 1,772 ('79), and 1,757 ('80). During that same period departmental quartermasters purchased 709 mules for $84,115.62, or an average of $118.64 an animal, and sold 482 worn-out and condemned mules for $17,262.26, or an average of $35.81 per mule. During the same years in the Department of Dakota the numbers of mules on 1 January were 1,659; 1,688; 1,923; and 1,991. Purchases for the department occurred only during 1876–77 when 63 mules were bought for $10,035.00, or an average price of $159.00. During those years, however, quartermasters sold a total of 333 mules for $9,825.19, an average of $29.51 an animal. In 1878–79 a quartermaster sold one mule for only $8.00.

In other departments the numbers were almost as impressive. In Texas during the four-year period the number of mules on hand averaged 1,489, and quartermasters sold 367 mules for $7,855.69, or an average of $21.41 each, and purchased 3 mules for a total of $90.00. In Arizona the army had on hand 591 and 708 mules each year, and quartermasters had purchased 61 mules for $6,670, or an average of $109.34 a mule. They had sold 232 mules for $8,268.77, an average of $35.64 a mule. In these transactions one thing was certain: the army paid a lot more for mules it received than for the animals it condemned. One certainly wonders how many of those condemned mules served farmers, ranchers, and others for years to come.[57]

The army would not maintain such large numbers of mules for many more years. During the 1880s, bureaucrats and government economizers looked for ways to rid the army of "excesses." In army appropriations for 1889, Congress limited purchases of mules to five thousand and kept the limitation during subsequent years. In 1898 army quartermasters began selling surplus army wagons and harness mules. The Indian wars were over, and they reasoned that when the army needed occasional transportation, private contractors could perform the job cheaper than the army. So in the name of economy, quartermasters auctioned off most of the four-mule escort wagons, six-mule army wagons, and hundreds of mules, including pack mules. They also sold for $2.00, harness sets that had cost $40.00. The army would no longer maintain more than five company packtrains. No longer would many troopers in the western states and territories hear the "creaking wheels of supply wagons and ambulances" or "the cracking whips and, more explosive still, the language of drivers, mule-skinners who reduced profanity to a science, if not a fine art."[58]

Still, officers, soldiers, and some civilians enjoyed anecdotes about army mules. In October 1883 one tale making the rounds concerned Mexique, an old gray animal stationed at Mount Vernon Barracks, Alabama. A veteran of the Mexican War, he had finally been condemned and declared surplus and was to be auctioned off. Officers at the post decided to purchase him and sent a letter of request through channels to get permission. The letter finally reached William T. Sherman, recently retired lieutenant general of the army. In response Sherman wrote:

> I have seen that mule, and whether true or false the soldiers believe it was left at the Big Spring, where Mount Vernon Barracks now are, at the time General Jackson's Army camped there about 1819–1820. Tradition says it was once a sorrel but now it is white from age.
>
> The Quartermaster's Department will be chargeable with ingratitude if that mule is sold, or the care and maintenance of it thrown on the charitable officers of the post. I advise that it be kept in the Department, fed and maintained till death.
>
> W. T. Sherman, General
> P.S. I think that mule was at Fort Morgan, Mobile Point, where I was then in 1842.[59]

Secretary of War Robert Todd Lincoln ordered that the old mule, at least sixty-five years of age, "be kept and well cared for as long as he lives."[60]

Another mule story concerned the mule who played dead. In Arizona during the 1870s, a pack mule lost her footing near the top of a steep hill and turned several somersaults before reaching the bottom. "Though lying as if dead when the packers reached her, she was little injured, her load of officers' bedding having saved her." But she would not move. The packtrain had already left. With some difficulty the packers unloaded and even unrigged her. Only then did she go "galloping and braying to catch up with the bell," leaving the two packers the task of packing load and rigging up the hill on their own backs. "That hill was dubbed 'Packers Delight' on the spot."[61]

By the mid-1880s most enlisted men and many officers had no experience in campaigning against Indians, making long marches, and all that living in the field involved. Ambitious officers held yearly maneuvers and simulated field combat exercises, but they paid little attention to pack mule and wagon transportation. Civilian packers and teamsters with their wagons were usually too expensive to be hired for mere exercises.

When the army employed civilian transportation, the results were not encouraging. During yearly maneuvers in August and September 1894, QM Thomas Cruse gave a contract to a large transportation company "for so many pounds, so many days, daily movement not to exceed twenty miles." The march was only from Fort Myer to the Shenandoah Valley, and the roads were in reasonable condition. "But the wagons never got in until late at night, the horses (unaccustomed to long straightaway travel) died, the soldiers suffered, and the contractor returned with his train wrecked." This was one of many incidents that made the army regret losing most of its own transportation—six-mule wagons and pack mules.[62]

CHAPTER 6

Army Mules near Home
and Abroad, 1898–1917

After the final Indian campaigns, government officials had rele-
gated the "Old Army" to routine garrison duty. More and more congressmen looked upon the army as a necessary if unofficial con-
stabulary force that provided needed government subsidies for their
districts. If it were not for that function, some congressmen would
have favored even more drastic cuts in the army's budget. On 1 April
1898 the regular army numbered only 2,143 officers and 26,040 enlisted men who were stationed at some eighty army installations
located mainly in the West. Officers faced an almost impossible
task of offering rudimentary, systematic regimental instruction to
companies and troops that were located in many, often minuscule,
stations. Never generous to the army, Congress had drastically cur-
tailed its budgets during the 1880s, further eroding army strength.
New guidelines, for example, limited quartermaster purchases of
horses as well as pack mules and harness mules, and the army had
funds to maintain only five packtrains. Quartermasters sold surplus mules, most of the service's four- and six-mule wagons, and a
large number of harness sets. Lt. Tom Cruse lamented that "half a
dozen of the finest trains the Army ever saw were dissipated by orders. Wagons that cost two hundred dollars were sold to farmers for
fifteen—and their stock were unable to pull them!"[1]

Less than three weeks before Congress declared war on Spain,
the service had only 500 four-mule escorts, 504 six-mulers, and 96

Red Cross ambulances. Only 2,021 mules were available and only 81 of these were pack mules. Yet supply officer Col. C. P. Miller, in charge of procurement of wagons and animals, estimated that if the United States went to war, the army would need about 5,000 wagons to supply troops in Cuba and Puerto Rico and 23,500 mules just to pull the wagons. Recently promoted, Captain Cruse estimated that the army would need at least 100 packtrains for operations in Cuba alone.[2]

When Secretary of War Russell A. Alger asked Clem Studebaker, president of the largest wagon and carriage company in the United States, to supply 200 six-mule supply wagons and 1,000 four-mule escort wagons within two months, Studebaker replied that the company could not turn out 200 six-mulers in a year. "When you people sold off all your big wagons some two years ago," he noted, "we used up all our stock. Now we have neither materials nor machinery to make them." The army was forced to take whatever stock manufacturers had on hand or could build from surplus materials. Furnishing parts in the field would be a nightmare for supply officers.[3]

On 3 April Alger quizzed Cruse about his previous experience with packtrains, then ordered him to proceed to St. Louis and purchase mules to form 20 packtrains of 75 packs each. As Cruse was leaving the office, Alger added that he had better buy good mules, "for you'll probably go to Cuba with them." Counting 14 riding mules for each train, Alger had given this assistant quartermaster the responsibility of purchasing initially at least 1,780 mules suitable for packing, without advertising for them in advance. This order made the assistant quartermaster a most popular man at "East St. Louis, mule mart of the world."[4]

Mules were readily available and fairly inexpensive. The panic of 1897 had a depressing effect on the mule market as did the Cuban insurrection since Cuba purchased most of the sugar mules and had bought none for three years. Also, contractors had sent thousands of sugar mules yearly to the South African nations, but very few had been sent during the last year because of the Jameson raid and subsequent troubles. Sugar mules and pack mules had the same conformations. Cruse purchased high-quality mules for $122 apiece and commented later that after two years of service, when the least desirable ones were sold as surplus, each brought $165. Of course the mule dealers also knew the worth of the animals and began edging prices upward. One day all along the line every dealer asked $142 a head. "I made no objection," stated Cruse. "I simply did not buy. They sat back waiting for us to accept the inevitable, but by the next day my outfit and I were on the road to North Texas." There Cruse purchased twelve hundred mules "as fine as I had ever seen, for $118 a head." Most of the animals he shipped to New Orleans and then to Tampa, but for "moral effect it seemed good tactics to route twelve cars via St. Louis to Chattanooga." In St. Louis the mules were unloaded, watered, and fed, "and all day the corral fence was lined with dealers. They were astonished at the quality and price" of those Texas mules. The next day Cruse "resumed business at normal prices." Cruse formed several packtrains that went to Cuba with Gen. William R. Shafter's expedition. That spring and summer Cruse purchased more than 25,000 mules for the army and earned the title of respect given him by the dealers—Mule Man of the Army. Supply officers altogether bought a total of 36,800 animals during the war—16,618 horses and 20,182 mules. Of that number quartermasters issued 36,033 animals—16,483 horses and 19,550 mules. The remaining animals—135 horses and 632 mules— were later declared surplus.[5]

Only a small fraction of the wagons and mules could be sent to the islands. The initial expeditionary force landing in Cuba had 114 six-mule wagons, 81 escort wagons, 7 ambulances, 1,336 pack mules, and 964 draft mules accompanied by 272 teamsters and packers. More mules and wagons were available but there was no shipping space for them. Supply officers would ship another 84 wagons from Mobile. Cavalry horses had to be left behind.[6]

Confusion reigned on the loading of supplies, soldiers, and animals at Tampa. Reporter Richard Harding Davis wrote that God took care of "drunken men, sailors, and the United States," and cited the expedition bound for Cuba as "a severe test of the axiom." The two railroad lines leading into Tampa could in no way handle all the boxcars that were lined up as far away as Columbia, South Carolina, waiting for twelve hired civilians using five army wagons to unload supplies in the boxcars already in Tampa. No one knew what any car contained until it was unloaded. Supply officers had not received the invoices and bills of lading, and they could not always find needed supplies. Most of the ammunition boxes, for example, were found eighteen miles from Tampa. When soldiers began loading the guns and caissons of the light artillery aboard the hired second-class ships, they had to search cars for the breech mechanisms and fuses for the projectiles.[7]

They loaded the mules on transports with little regard for enough food and water or suitable stalls. As commander of the expedition, Shafter planned to load the mules after all supplies were aboard and before embarking the troops. By 11:00 A.M. on 6 June, teamsters and packers got their mules aboard various ships without much trouble. Troops began loading that afternoon and the next day, but the ships did not leave for Cuba until 14 June. Most mules remained aboard the transports with no chance for exercise.

The army landing at Daiquiri, Cuba, commenced in heavy seas on the morning of 22 June and continued the next day until the sea became too rough. By then Shafter had shifted the landing of troops to Sibony. Merchant captains at the Daiquiri landing refused to bring their ships close to shore, which lengthened the distance the mules would have to swim. The mules, which had been inactive for twenty-two days and without adequate food or water, were pushed out of the vessels through the side hatches to force them to attempt the swim to shore. Some 50 out of 450 animals on one vessel swam out to sea and were lost. No doubt they were homesick. Others merely gave out before reaching shore, and some swam to the wrong side of the cove and were drowned under the rocks.[8]

Even if conditions had been ideal in Cuba, land transportation would have been barely sufficient. Within days, furthermore, wagons were mired up to their axles on most roads, and the pack mules experienced difficulty even though packers reduced their loads by as much as 50 percent. Maj. Gen. Adna Romanza Chaffee later lamented that at times pack mules which ordinarily carried 250 pounds of supplies could barely transport two boxes of crackers weighing 100 pounds. Packtrains operating from the supply bases were making frequent trips to the front positions but only with a day's supply of basic rations and boxes of ammunition. Packtrains from Sibony made daily trips while those from Daiquiri required two days to deliver their often reduced loads. Much of the pack mules' efficiency depended on the packers, and when some of them were disabled by fevers and measles, pack transportation suffered. Soldiers from the ranks who had prior experience with mule teams could handle wagons in an emergency, but few soldiers possessed any experience as packers.

During the initial advance toward Santiago, commanders became irritated with the slow pace of packtrains in moving the supplies for an army as big as Shafter's and convinced the general to give priority to the unloading of sixty six-mule wagons in an effort to increase efficiency. The six-mulers, however, could not compete with packtrains. Priority supplies—ammunition and rations—moved by pack mules. Wagons followed at a more leisurely pace when they could be moved through the mud, and carried less essential items such as tents and stoves. Pack transportation once again proved to be the competent way to supply troops. To operate efficiently during the summer months in Cuba, the expeditionary force needed more experienced pack mules, more civilian packers, and fewer wagons.[9]

Mules and horses were landed under more favorable circumstances at Guánica on the southeast coast of Puerto Rico. There engineers used a pontoon bridge to make a floating wharf and more than a thousand animals ambled to shore without difficulty. Occupying the port of Ponce, Gen. Nelson A. Miles's force, reinforced by additional men and mules, began a four-column advance toward San Juan. There was little bloodshed, for most Puerto Ricans welcomed the Americans. Operations halted on 13 August after Miles received word from Cuba that Spain had signed a peace protocol the day before.[10]

During the late spring and summer of 1898 the army sent two thousand regular troops and thirteen thousand volunteers to the Philippines. These troops embarked, along with supplies for six months, wagons, harness mules, and more than three hundred pack mules principally from San Francisco, with little confusion or difficulty. Quartermasters had purchased thousands of mules from the large mule markets and sent them by railroad to San Francisco and other West Coast ports. The combined animal and troop transports usually made the trip to the Philippines with a stop of a week to ten days in Hawaii so the mules would be in better condition on arrival at Manila.

As more troops arrived in the islands, however, transportation became a major problem, and the expedition quartermaster could not wait for promised mule deliveries. He began hiring or buying pony carts, bull carts drawn by *carabos* (water buffalo), and employing natives and Chinese coolies to pack in stores to the troops surrounding Manila. Pony prices soared from $15 to as much as $150 an animal. For a time quartermasters hired four Chinese coolies for each company to provide services such as bringing up ammunition and food or carrying the wounded or dead to the rear. After Manila fell, commanders "discharged these coolies lest the troops become 'spoiled' from having Chinese do all the dirty work." By then mules were arriving from the states.[11]

American military forces remained in Cuba until 1902, and the protracted occupation gave the army ample time to experiment with its proven pack transportation. For years civilian packers with the packtrains had contended with attempts to eliminate them and thereby save money by simplifying the entire system. Until the army committed a large amount of money and time to training army personnel to be packers, civilian packers were relatively safe from being dismissed. The *aparejo* was custom fitted to each mule's back, and fitting it, balancing loads, and throwing combinations of diamond hitches took knowledge, experience, and more extra duty than most soldiers were willing to master. Because of the number of civilian packers disabled during the war in Cuba, and since certain high-ranking officers seemingly did not understand such things as the differences between pack mules and wagon mules and weights and loads depending on conditions, officers of the Miles school of campaigning revived the possibility of using the 1881 Moore packsaddle. Although the packing fraternity pointed out that the Moore saddle injured the mules' backbones, withers, and kidneys, these officers insisted on comparing the two saddles in actual demonstrations in Cuba.

Packers conducted the experiment in June 1901. One packtrain used the Moore saddles and another used aparejos. The conditions of the trial required that packers and their mules march twenty-five miles per day for thirty days continuously with each mule loaded with 250 pounds of supplies. The results showed conclusively that mules using aparejos remained in much better condition, and the officers withdrew the simplified saddle from further consideration. In much the same way, packers later eliminated the Pullman packsaddles and panniers. The Pullman device was even more harmful to the mules than the Moore saddle. The only new packsaddle accepted by the army for supplies until after World War I was the Daly Aparejo Pack Saddle, which involved mainly a change of name. Henry W. Daly became chief packer in 1903, and rank had its privilege.[12]

While the army experimented with packsaddles in Cuba, it subdued rebels in the Philippines. The Philippine insurrection was the last time that mules would not have to compete with mechanized land transportation, and the mules performed amazingly well. Expert packers devised innovations that worked well, saved lives, and made conditions more bearable for soldiers in the field. Packers rigged up mule litters to transport the wounded, which worked so well the quartermaster department purchased poles and stretchers to be used with aparejos.[13]

During the initial months of the conflict, artillery units began using the newly acquired British-made weapon, the Vicker-Maxim 2.95. This mountain artillery gun soon proved to be a most effective weapon; it required thirteen pack mules for each gun. Four mules outfitted with modified pack frames for their aparejos carried the parts of the gun, with one mule carrying the wheels and accessories, one mule the cradle, one the frame, and one the gun itself. Nine mules using ammunition cinchas and aparejos carried the boxes of ammunition. The component parts of one Vicker-Maxim 2.95 were somewhat more specialized than those of company mule pack outfits, but the packing fraternity easily adapted to the new components to make the field artillery piece transported by mules a superior mountain weapon. All mules of the mountain artillery, including riding mules, eventually had to meet the conformation requirements of pack mules, since saddle mules could not be packed and pack mules could be used for either riding or packing.[14]

Pack transportation was considered so critical during the guerrilla campaigns that the military commander ordered all officers below command rank to attend special courses on mule packing. The officers were graded by civilian packers, and the results were given to the commander. Many pack mules and officers became closely acquainted.[15]

Those seventy thousand soldiers in the Philippines had ample opportunity to become quite neighborly with mules. From 1898 to 1901, the Army Transport Service shipped thousands of mules from San Francisco and other West Coast ports to Luzon. From 1 August 1898 to 1 November 1900, for example, transports from San Francisco to Manila delivered 6,275 horses and 3,259 mules. Steamers especially equipped to handle mules and horses made almost continuous trips from San Francisco to Honolulu, where the animals were unloaded to rest from seven to ten days. The mules were then reloaded and shipped to Manila. This was an effective method of transportation, and the mules arrived in reasonably good condition with few casualties. Animals lost for any reason came to only 7 percent.[16]

All was not smooth steaming in the Pacific. In July 1900 an army transport, the *Siam*, carrying four hundred mules, ran into a typhoon between Hawaii and the Philippines and lost close to three hundred mules. Members of an army board of survey blamed the loss on flimsy stalls.

Just as the news of the *Siam* disaster was heard, Tom Cruse arrived in San Francisco with orders to take charge of the army transport *Leelanaw* and a consignment of horses and mules for the Philippines. Now a major, Cruse and port quartermaster Col. Oscar Long, therefore, spent three weeks in outfitting the *Leelanaw* with special care. Each animal had a padded stall, and the system of watering and feeding was machinelike. A veterinarian and fifty teamsters accompanied the horse and mule shipment of 570 animals.

On the first leg of the journey to Honolulu only one mule died. "By judicious feeding of half rations, with frequent bran mash," noted Cruse, "the mules were put in better condition than when they were loaded after a hard rail trip from Utah and Idaho." After ten days in Honolulu the transport continued across the Pacific and was within three days of Manila when it experienced the worst typhoon of the year. "Within the first half-hour every horse and mule was dead, either drowned or smashed in its stall."[17]

The *Leelanaw* just managed to survive. The next day the dead animals began to smell, but the sea was still too rough to hoist the animals into it. When the men did hoist the dead animals from their stalls, they found horses and mules with broken necks and backs, "and otherwise mangled; some were drowned." All the fittings and stalls were still intact. As they cleared the ship of carcasses, a teamster found one mule still alive. "He was doctored and petted and watched by all hands. Five days after the typhoon he got to his feet and nibbled at hay." As the *Leelanaw* rounded Corregidor, the survivor was still standing. "But just as the anchor dropped" at Manila, "so did the mule—stone dead." The postmortem showed that the animal should not have lived a day; "his entrails were badly ruptured." A mule ship that had sailed from San Francisco three days after *Leelanaw* experienced no difficulties except losing twenty-five animals from sickness. Most mules readily adapted to ocean crossings.[18]

A board of survey later exonerated Cruse of any blame for the tragedy. The stalls he designed had been constructed to minimize the mules' space. But sometimes it is impossible to protect men and animals from injury in a severe typhoon. The board also observed that mules' stalls should not have breast plates or feed boxes. Evidently, the feed boxes had been responsible for causing some of the deaths. Although officially cleared, Cruse faced being reminded of the incident for years to come. A Manila newspaper reporter incorrectly heard that only 1 mule out of a load of 570, which had cost the U.S. government $350,000, had survived, so that a single animal supposedly had cost the government more than a third of a million dollars. This account was picked up throughout the Far East, including Peking, where officers of the international force who had marveled at American transportation twitted officers of Cruse's Sixth Cavalry with the observation, "No wonder you Americans have such magnificent transportation. Look what you pay for mules." The teasing was later passed on to Cruse.[19]

After arriving in the Philippines, some of the pack mules were used for purposes "usually reserved for horses." The platoons of Battery F, Fifth Artillery, better known as Reilly's Battery, were able to transport to the islands in 1899 only twenty-four out of a hundred artillery horses. So Capt. Henry J. Reilly "horsed" and "muled" the platoons, with two mules being leaders and two horses being wheelers. Lt. Manus McCloskey, an officer with the battery, observed that the mules "behaved nobly" and seemed "very proud of their red artillery blankets and brass-trimmed harness." The horses, however, "seemed to feel a little put down" but "gradually became accustomed to the mules being in front of them."[20]

Artillerymen, of course, were not as well informed about mules as they were about artillery horses, and they thought that the peculiarities of their mules were universal mule characteristics. "Both the horses and mules," McCloskey noted, "had a strong aversion to water in their ears." Several times the animals had to swim the Imus River, and "if a drop of water got in a mule's ear, he would roll on his side and stop swimming so that he had to be towed across." If water got in a horse's ear, "he would shake his head and swim so fast that the soldier with him could not keep up and would have to hang on to the horse's tail and be towed ashore." In either case, McCloskey observed, "the men's language was exceedingly colorful."[21]

The most amazing feat performed by a pack mule and his packer occurred during the Jolo Island invasion in 1906. Assistant Chief Packer Mora E. Smith loaded one mule with the cage mount of a naval rapid-fire gun weighing 540 pounds. The mule carried the cage mount three miles inland where the weapon was used against a Moro fort. The same mule then transported the weapon back to shore.[22]

In the summer of 1900, pack and wagon mules accompanied American troops sent to China from the Philippines, Cuba, and the United States. The great powers' exploitation of China had created an antipathy to foreigners among the Chinese people, and in June 1900 a secret organization of Chinese—called "Boxers" in the West—tried to drive the foreigners out of their country. The Boxers massacred nearly three hundred foreigners, mainly missionaries and their families, and forced two hundred members of foreign legations (including the U.S. embassy staff) to barricade themselves in the British Embassy in Peking. The U.S. Army contingent became part of an international army consisting of British, French, German, Russian, Austrian, Italian, and Japanese forces, who were rushed in to break the siege.

The American army made an excellent showing. The international force starting from Tientsin included more than twenty-five hundred American infantry and cavalry troops. After receiving orders at Luzon, the Ninth Infantry Regiment reached China in just nineteen days, and a troop of Sixth Cavalry received mounts in time to join the expedition. Before the armies left China, the United States had committed thirteen thousand soldiers to the cause and some ten thousand of them had landed in China. According to the quartermaster, Tom Cruse, American troops were landed in China with more complete equipment of every class and larger and better stores of all supplies than those of other countries. The American army, noted Cruse, had "magnificent transportation, superior to anything" in the others' armies. It had four-mule escort wagons using sleek, well-formed harness mules and packtrains of smaller barrel-bellied mules fitted with aparejos. The equipment was carefully chosen for efficiency. In battle, Cruse bragged, "the Americans moved with clock like precision, every officer and man automatically performing his allotted duty, but salting the performance with a certain swinging recklessness. Back to various war ministries . . . went revised estimates of the United States Army."[23]

McCloskey wrote that when the international force left Tientsin on 4 August, the enormous amount of transportation "beggared description." It included "pack animals of all kinds—horses, ponies, mules, donkeys, camels." It included carts of all sizes and shapes, from the small two-wheeled cart pulled by Japanese ponies to what were called "the huge American prairie wagons, each drawn by four enormous mules." In the matter of transportation, McCloskey noted, "none of the allies could touch the Americans." He claimed that when officers from the other armies were told that the escort wagons used were not the largest American supply wagons and that in the United States the army used much larger wagons hauled by six mules and driven by one man with a single line, "they listened politely but skeptically." These officers were amazed that the mule-drawn escorts carried from between 3,500 and 4,000 pounds of supplies and kept on schedule each day while other nations had to stop their supply trains because of mud. The officers also noticed the American system "where one man cared for four mules, and each mule hauled from 700 to 1,000 pounds of stores." By contrast, in the cart system of other allies, the "load never exceeded 500 pounds per animal, and each animal required one man to care for them."[24]

The American pack mules really surprised the officers and men in the other armies. They had never seen such efficiency, and they commented on loads that stayed on the mules' backs until unlashed and of packers using the diamond hitches with great precision. The concepts were totally new to them. Then too, the speed at which the animals ambled and the small number of packers required to pack and drive a packtrain were equally astounding. "But the one thing that caused the most comment was the manner in which the mules followed the bell mare. How 50 mules could be turned loose and kept under control, especially on herd, by a couple of men was remarkable, but when it came to driving them along a crowded road and through the labyrinthine streets of a Chinese city without decreasing the speed, losing a mule, or stopping to adjust loads, the others simply marveled."[25]

Other nations' forces also used pack transportation. The British used an immense number of pack mules that were, according to McCloskey, "small, active, vicious little beasts." The animals were led in tandem, "three in one team, the halter chains of the two rear ones running into a ring in the side of the saddle of the preceding one." A coolie was in charge of the three. He led the lead mule and took care of the three animals. The packsaddles constructed of iron or steel, "were very strong, light, and neat, with breast and breech straps," and had hooks on each side on which loads were hung. The supplies to be loaded were "lashed around with a close-twisted rope that was provided with small loops or ears, leather-covered to prevent chafing." The cargo for the animal was "simultaneously lifted to each side, and the loops hung over the hooks." In this way the cargo could be loaded quickly, "but the load did not stay on if the mule trotted or acted up—as was frequently the case." The major difference the American and British methods of packing was that the British "lashed their loads to the saddle whereas the Americans lashed theirs to the mule."[26]

The British took excellent care of their animals. Each evening the mules were groomed and blanketed for the night. They were then picketed "fore and aft" because of their "fighting propensities." The British pack system worked well for them, but in comparison to American packtrains it was antiquated. The British claimed that they could not drive their mules in the same manner as the American pack mules but admitted they had never tried. They also used two-mule carts, which worked only somewhat effectively. To pull the cart, each mule wore an iron packsaddle, and the cart was hooked to a ring on the saddle by a halter shank. Although lightly loaded, a cart could damage a mule's back because of too much play in the ring and halter shank, which caused sores on the back and withers.[27]

Japanese soldiers led a number of fierce little pack stallions "with shaggy manes and bulging eyes." McCloskey observed that the handlers and horses were "generally executing a sort of waltz in the dust" that did not demonstrate effectiveness.[28]

The other nations involved in the expedition used carts and wagons. All commands supplemented their transportation with Chinese carts and drivers. Near Peking the forces used a large number of Bactrian camels. Called the cheapest transporation in China, the Americans hired a number of them to haul coal. "They ate all kinds of refuse forage that a mule would not touch and thrived on it," observed McCloskey. "They had nasty tempers and were prone to kick and bite; so many of them had to be muzzled. They were not satisfactory as saddle animals, having a motion similar to a Philippine coastal steamer in a typhoon." Once again the army experimented with camels and again concluded that although the camel was an excellent work animal, it preferred to depend on mules.[29]

After successful skirmishes at Tientsin, Peitsang, Yangtsun, and Peking, the joint expedition relieved those in the British embassy. For more than a year afterward, until a peace settlement, an allied garrison held Peking. The Sixth Cavalry moved out in April 1901. Major General Chaffee and the Ninth Infantry left Peking on 23 May. Left behind was a contingent force from all the nations. The army with its mules (never fewer than seven) would be present in China until 1938.[30]

The army, of course, also kept a larger force in the Philippines after crushing the insurrection, and supply ships continued to carry limited numbers of horses and mules. The army had placed a limit on the number of animals that it could have in the islands at any one time. By 1910 that number was 7,243 animals—4,132 horses and 3,111 mules. From time to time the limit was exceeded. In August 1910 the adjutant general complained by cable to the commanding general that on 1 July there were in the Philippine Division 5,031 horses (114 were private horses) and 3,134 mules, or a total of 8,051 public animals on hand. He added that the army also had en route to the islands on the transport *Dix* 148 horses and 295 mules, which would increase the public animals to 8,494, or 1,251 over allowance. Until the "surplus" was greatly reduced, the division would receive no more animals. The adjutant general also ordered that strong serviceable animals "should be sent to the provinces for service at places where strong sound animals" were required and that "older and less vigorous animals" should be used in Manila where the work was "comparatively light." Old and truly disabled mules, he concluded, should be inspected and destroyed "when to sell them for work in the hands of irresponsible persons would be cruel and cause suffering to the animals."[31]

By the twentieth century, mules had time and time again proven themselves to be the most important four-legged animals in the U.S. Army, and supply officers readily rejected animals that did not meet standards. For years they had procured horses and mules under contract after advertising for bids. This procedure often resulted in delays and necessitated deliveries at large markets where animals could become infected with disease. Supply officers rarely had a good opportunity to judge the qualities and dispositions of the animals before sending them to the field. Beginning in 1908, the army established remount depots. The first was at Fort Reno, Oklahoma; others were established at Fort Keogh, Montana, and Fort Royal, Virginia. The depots initially proved to be more successful in obtaining draft horses and mules than cavalry mounts because breeders were able to provide more draft animals with acceptable conformations than horses. Now all mules accepted at the depots were branded "US" on the left shoulder to avoid confusion and repurchase. A small "w" or "p" was added below the brand to differentiate between wagon and pack mules. When a mule was condemned, it was branded on the neck with the letters IC (inspected and condemned).[32]

To supply the new depots, assistant quartermasters continued their search for animals that met army specifications. Contractors responded to the advertisements and circular instructions by filling out a formal proposal to the officer-in-charge, promising to furnish and deliver a certain number of horses and mules by a specified date. The contractors then signed a contractor's bond with penalty for nondelivery. On 27 June 1910, for example, having already filled out a proposal with quartermaster, Capt. Kirby Walker, to deliver the animals within one month, three of the largest mule dealers in Kansas City, Missouri—John D. Guyton, W. R. Harrington, and J. M. Grant—signed a contractor's bond with a penalty of $7,000.00 promising to deliver twelve light draft horses at $232.00 each, eighteen wheel draft mules at $289.00 each, eighteen lead draft mules at $281.00 each, and three riding mules at $279.00 each. The quartermaster would pay $13,881.00 on delivery. During the same period, Walker had a larger proposal from the National Stock Yards, Illinois, to deliver sixty-five wheel draft mules at $275.00 each, thirty-four lead draft mules at $289.50 each, twenty-four pack mules at $263.25 each, two pack mules for machine-gun platoons at $267.75 each, and five riding mules at $283.50 each. If all went well, Walker would pay $35,989.00 for 130 mules with the necessary conformation.[33]

By 1895 other nations' armies were purchasing American mules. Official foreign observers of the army as well as others had seen what the American mules were capable of doing and urged their quartermasters to purchase these superior animals. And so foreign civilian purchases followed those of the army. The American mule markets entered the international business in a substantial way. The British seemed to be the most interested in purchasing mules, but others showed a more than casual interest. The number of mules exported from 1895 to the 1920s overall shows a steady increase, with heavier purchases during the years of the Boer War and World War I. Mule prices likewise showed a steady but more erratic increase that depended on economic conditions, the number of mules available that met the required conditions. No more than five thousand mules were exported between 1870 and 1894.

During the Spanish-American War, supply officers paid between $122 and $145 per animal and even higher prices after the war, sometimes more than $385. With a jack and jennet and mare population large enough to produce a mule population in the United States more than 4,209,000 in 1910, more than 5,432,000 in 1920, and more than 5,681,000 in 1925, the mule dealers had no trouble in supplying foreign customers.[34]

Interest in purchasing American mules came from all over the globe—even from the small German colony of Kiaochow on the Shantung Peninsula of China. On 4 October 1911 American Consul J. C. McNally pompously wrote the secretary of state that he had the "honor" to inform the department that he had influenced the Kiaochow government by his "complimentary estimate of the American mules with regard to strength and endurance" to send a competent veterinarian to the United States to purchase "a first installment for local battery use." To aid the work of the German veterinarian, he asked that the War Department designate the best markets and breeds, and offer any other helpful information. QMG James B. Aleshire responded that the best mule markets were at Kansas City, Missouri, and East St. Louis, Illinois, and he listed John D. Guyton, Warren Bailey, J. T. Sparks, Guyton and Harrington, Sparks Horse and Mule Company, and Gillan Horse and Mule Company as "responsible dealers." The department, he explained, did not purchase a particular breed of mule but used selected specifications for conformation of desired animals. He enclosed a copy of the current regulations and the average prices officers paid for mules during the fiscal year 1911. Draft mules averaged $228.56, pack mules $205.69, and riding mules $226.29. In comparison to the average price of mules exported from the United States, the army paid substantially more and expected to receive superior animals. Evidently a German veterinarian did purchase mules for the Colony of Kiaochow that year.[35]

In August 1912 Congress passed legislation that significantly affected all army personnel and civilians connected with wagon or pack-mule transportation. On 24 August it enacted legislation creating the Quartermasters Corps by merging into one agency the Supply, Pay, and Quartermasters Departments. Secretary of War Elihu Root had originally advocated this legislation as part of his reforms to modernize the American army. The official name of the head of the new organization was Chief of Quartermasters Corps of the Army, but tradition was hard to break and a year later the chief was once again Quartermaster General of the Army. More significant than name changes and consolidation, the legislation established a service corps of six thousand enlisted men to perform work that was usually done by civilians or soldiers detailed on extra duty.

The army would now no longer use civilian teamsters, packers, or blacksmiths. These men's places were to be taken by army personnel. The Quartermasters Corps built up this function slowly through recruitment and a system of examinations, but by 30 June 1916 it had a total of 5,379 enlisted men. With civilian packers being rapidly phased out of the transportation service, new army packers had to be trained quickly. This was probably the primary reason why Packmaster Daly was officially encouraged to write a greatly expanded version of his 1901 seventy-nine-page *Manual of Instruction in Pack Transportation*, which had been used mainly to instruct cadets at West Point in the methods of packing. In 1916, as already detailed in an earlier chapter, he published the *Manual of Pack Transportation*. It would take time and some procedures had to be modified, but enlisted men became capable packers.[36]

Although the army had left Cuba in 1902, it was thereafter frequently involved in Cuban problems. In 1906 President Roosevelt ordered more than five thousand troops, complete with mule transportation, to save the Cuban government from a new rebellion. The American Army of Cuban Pacification, as it was called, remained in the country until 1909. In 1912 and again in 1917 the army sent troops with pack and wagon trains to Cuba to restore order and prop up the Cuban government.[37]

The army also found itself actively involved with Mexico. In 1910–11 that nation entered a period of revolutionary turmoil, and internal conflicts in the northern part of the country spilled over the border into the United States. There were enough incidents that President Taft first ordered increasing army border patrols and then in February 1911 ordered the mobilization of a maneuver division in Texas and two regiments in San Diego, California. Taft also ordered a force of provisional coast artillery corps to concentrate near Galveston, Texas. Twenty-three thousand men took part in this show of force, but it was not until the end of May that all soldiers were at their final destinations. The army had adequate supplies as well as wagon and packtrains but could not make arrangements for general mobilization and coordination fast enough. Railroad transportation proved slow. Not enough railroad cars, for example, had been reserved for wagons and animals, and the railroad companies were unwilling to interrupt normal service. In 1913, when the Second Division mobilized at Galveston and Texas City, it did so without organized mule-drawn ammunition or supply trains and the overall transportation needed to make some eleven thousand soldiers an effective fighting force.[38]

In April 1914 American troops occupied Vera Cruz, Mexico. As a show of force, and to embarrass the government of Gen. Victoriano Huerta, which the United States had not recognized, President Wilson had supported naval actions to provoke a confrontation. In effect Wilson was attempting to aid Venustiano Carranza in seizing power from Huerta who, Wilson claimed, did not meet the test of constitutional legitimacy. Late in the evening of 21 April, sailors and marines landed at Vera Cruz to prevent a German steamer from delivering a cargo of ammunition for Huerta's army.

Before the end of the month Brig. Gen. Frederick Funston had a force of several thousand men in Vera Cruz. On 24 April the Fifth Brigade, reinforced by two troops of the Sixth Cavalry, the Fourth Field Artillery, and a portion of the Third Field Artillery, Field Company D of the Signal Corps, an ambulance company and field hospital, a field bakery of the Quartermasters Corps, and an aviation detachment, left Galveston on four transports convoyed by four destroyers. All regimental packtrains were left behind with the tents at Galveston. Each regiment was authorized to have only twenty-two mules, which was far below the number needed for active campaigning. Twenty-two was only enough mules for each regiment's machine guns, three wagons, and the medical pack and ambulance. Later joined by the battleship *Louisiana,* the expedition arrived off Vera Cruz the evening of 28 April and docked the next morning. The soldiers finally disembarked early on 30 April. The force was made up of 183 officers, 3,147 soldiers, 11 civilian employees, 155 mules, 27 wagons, 4 ambulances, 3 buckboards, and 4 newspaper correspondents. Counting marines, sailors, and soldiers, the United States maintained a force of nearly eight thousand men. Transports made bimonthly voyages between Galveston and Vera Cruz.[39]

All the fighting had ceased by the time the army troops arrived, but it seemed likely that sooner or later the Mexican army would attack. Within another week a new contingent of troops along with mountain battery outfits arrived. Correspondent Jack London noted that "beneath my window, with a great clattering of hoofs, is passing a long column of mountain batteries, all carried on the backs of our big Government mules." This invasion ended on 28 November when all troops left aboard transports for Galveston. By then new President Carranza was justly claiming that the United States had infringed on Mexican sovereignty and was interfering in purely domestic affairs. Wilson's deliberate international bad manners had aided the cause of the Carranzistas by not only depriving Huerta of munitions but also by humiliating him. Huerta resigned from office only ten weeks after the American occupation of Vera Cruz. Carranza was now attempting to get the United States forces out of Mexico and to subdue his one-time ally Francisco "Pancho" Villa, who controlled much of northern Mexico.[40]

Despite Carranza's inability to silence his detractors, Wilson decided to recognize the Carranza government. Villa, of course, resented not only what he considered Wilsonian duplicity but also the United States overtly sending munitions and other supplies to the Carranzistas. Villa instigated a series of border incidents that culminated in a surprise attack by a large number of his men on Columbus, New Mexico. The next day, Wilson ordered a punitive force commanded by Brig. Gen. John J. "Black Jack" Pershing into Mexico to assist the Mexican government in capturing Villa.

On 15 March elements of the punitive expedition crossed the Rio Grande near Columbus into Mexico. Pershing's force consisted of elements of the Seventh, Tenth, Eleventh, and Thirteenth Cavalries, the Sixth Field Artillery, and various support units and packtrains. Pershing's plan was to send from Colonia Dublán three parallel, highly mobile, and fast-moving cavalry columns with pack mules in an attempt to intercept Villa's force in Sonora. There were, however, no sharp geographical lines of distinction for the columns, nor was there a delineation of time. The general search for the Villistas was loosely based on Gen. George Crook's methods of running down hostile Apaches. Small cavalry detachments, support pack transportation, and central supply depots to replenish grain for the horses and mules and field rations for the troopers were the main features of Pershing's plan of action. In something of a new element within the plan, supply officers were located at strategic bases to provide remudas of extra horses and mules to replace those that were worn out, wounded, or needed to be shod.

In March 1916 the army established auxiliary remount depots at El Paso and Fort Sam Houston, Texas, to maintain in good condition the remuda needed for operations in Mexico. The performance of the mules across the Rio Grande equaled or surpassed those of earlier campaigns. During the first month the Tenth Cavalry Regiment and its packtrains marched 225 miles from Fort Huachuca, Arizona, to Colonia Dublán in only eight days, which meant an average of just over thirty miles per day. Two cavalry detachments then went by rail to Las Vargas in an unsuccessful attempt to trap Villa. The flying columns made up of selected men and horses from all troops of the regiment depended on large packtrains with extra mules. The trains needed the extra animals because conditions and the rate of march limited cargoes to only two hundred pounds per mule. In one incident, Packtrain No. 10 borrowed mules from the Fourth Field Artillery to supply the flying column of the Eleventh Cavalry. This column had marched more than a thousand miles during the expedition and had lost one soldier killed and three wounded. Even though exchanging animals from time to time, it had lost only thirty-two horses and five mules during its time in Mexico. Throughout the campaign packtrains were relied on for the transportation of supplies and for evacuation of the wounded. When columns were in advance of supplies and were forced to live off the land, pack mules became indispensable in collecting and distributing rations to the soldiers.[41]

Wagon mules also performed well. At the end of eleven months in the field, for example, Wagon Companies Nos. 1 and 2 had traveled an aggregate distance of approximately four thousand miles over difficult terrain. During that time the companies lost only thirty-six mules or 16 percent of their animals. In 1916 a wagon company consisted of a wagon boss and 3 assistants (all sergeants), a cook, a saddler, a blacksmith, a blacksmith assistant, 28 enlisted men, 27 wagons, 112 mules, and 6 horses.[42]

During the foray into Mexico, mules competed for the first time with mechanized truck companies. According to one motor truck advocate, any lingering doubt as to the superiority of motor trucks over mule transportation was forever settled in Mexico. An officer with the Thirteenth Cavalry claimed that "if the old order were giving way to the new, in that dawn of the mechanical age in our Service, it may be truly said that our well-tried friend, the mule, was going out in a blaze of glory."[43]

No mule went out in a blaze of glory nor did motor transportation prove its superiority in Mexico. If anything, the reverse was true. Trucks in 1916 were not up to the rigors of the terrain. Many broke down with broken axles or stalled from dust and dirt in fuel lines and carburetors. Several times wagon trains or pack mules had to deliver gasoline or parts to motor transports, or reload supplies from broken-down vehicles. "While the breakdown of one truck might delay the march from fifteen to thirty minutes," explained one officer, "ordinary breakdowns to be expected daily in a column of twenty trucks would run such road delays up to a period of many hours." On one occasion a spring on a gasoline truck broke, which took a mechanic five hours to repair. He did not have a replacement spring for the truck, which was a different make than the others in the company, and had to create a new spring. The truck company could not leave the gasoline transport since it contained half the company's supply. Overall, the army used thirteen types of trucks manufactured by eight different companies during the expedition.[44]

Where trucks could not move in the mud, mules did, and even in dry weather transports had to straddle the deep wagon ruts for miles at a time and move in low gear. Several of the army driver-mechanics were not efficient operators. One old sergeant knew nothing about driving a truck. "When asked how he got to be a sergeant chauffeur, he stated that he had taken a correspondence course in automobile mechanics, though he had never driven a motor vehicle"; he passed the final examination.[45]

During the expedition the role of the army mule subtly changed. From the beginning of the chase the army maintained more than usual coordination between cavalry troops, the wagon companies, motor truck companies, packtrains, and even scouting squadrons of army biplanes. More and more wagon companies gave way to the motor companies, especially when weather conditions were favorable. More frequently, troops were taking only small numbers of pack mules on scouting parties and even longer marches, knowing that they would be able to rendezvous with pack, wagon, or motor companies to obtain needed grain for their horses.

Coordination was evident from the very beginning of the campaign. A provisional squadron of sixty troops of the Eleventh Cavalry, for example, pursued a group of Mexican soldiers thought to be led by Villa from 24 March to 2 April 1916. Commanded by Maj. Robert L. Howze, the squadron operated with only enough mules to carry grain for the mounts. During the seven days of actual march the troops covered more than two hundred miles of almost continuous mountainous terrain. On 27 March Maj. Frank Tompkins's provisional force of two troops of the Tenth Cavalry and two troops of the Thirteenth Cavalry joined the squadron. The reinforced command rested its worn-out mounts and waited for additional supplies. On 28 March trucks brought the combined command rations and grain, and the next day Packtrain No. 11 arrived to carry the supplies. On 30 March the command covered thirty-eight additional miles.[46]

Reflecting on the experiences of his squadron after the expedition, Tompkins recommended that each troop of fifty men should have a packtrain of twelve mules with packers. One mule would carry the cooking outfit for the men, a day's rations, and three days' emergency rations. Another mule would carry the horseshoer's outfit and extra shoes for cavalry mounts; still another mule would carry the picket line and extra shoes. That left nine mules to transport five days' rations for the troops and forage for the mounts and mules.[47]

Throughout the year in Mexico, packtrains accompanied cavalry squadrons, troops, and regiments. As long as the U.S. Army maintained mounted cavalry, it needed pack mules to supply rations and grain for troopers and mounts in campaigns where there were no roads. It also needed mules to carry mountain howitzers and machine guns for both cavalry and infantry. At Aguas Calientes on 1 April, Capt. Albert E. Phillips's Machine Gun Troop employed overhead machine-gun fire to advance Troops G and E of the Tenth Cavalry against the Mexican position. Earlier the machine gun troop had prevented the Tenth's position from being overrun.[48]

The U.S. Army campaign in Mexico was not a wasted effort even though Pershing's troops failed to capture Pancho Villa. Dispersal of Villa's force and clashes with Mexican government troops ended serious border incidents. The mobilization of the expedition troops and of seventy-five thousand National Guardsmen to prevent possible invasion by Mexican forces also brought attention to the need to develop a better system of coordination between the National Guard and the regular army. Although relying heavily on mule transportation, the officers became aware of workable ways to coordinate supplies for cavalry troops with wagon and motor transportation companies. More important, Pershing's expedition into Mexico helped prepare American troops for World War I. As the chief surgeon of the expedition, Lt. Col. James D. Glennan, claimed, the "punitive expedition lived nearer to the earth and learned to get along with less than any command" in army experience. "The country has never had a more thoroughly trained and fit command."[49]

CHAPTER 7

Army Mules from World War I to World War II

In 1917 young provisional lieutenant Lucian K. Truscott Jr. joined the Seventeenth Cavalry stationed at Camp Jones near Douglas, Arizona. Here Truscott learned what instructors at officer's candidate school had not taught him. One of the most interesting schools was pack transportation, in which he discovered the importance of mule packtrains. "It was," he claimed, "a lesson none of us would ever forget: the loose pack mules trailing along behind the bell mare; the packers astride their riding mules along the flanks or in the rear; the swaying loads; and the amazing distances disappearing under the rapid, swinging pace of animals in a single day." Truscott learned his lessons well. The famous Third Infantry Division, which he commanded in Sicily and Italy during World War II, would depend heavily on pack mules.[1]

Even before Truscott became a new officer by virtue of the National Defense Act of 1916, and before elements of the U.S. Army were being trained in Mexico for participation in World War I, the Lathrop, Missouri, firm of Guyton and Harrington was purchasing mules for the British army. The exclusive purchaser for the British in the United States, the firm had maintained a cordial working relationship since the Boer War when it supplied the British army with 55,061 mules. Guyton and Harrington established a large network of American dealers to export 180,000 mules to Britain during World War I. It also sold mules and horses to Canadian mule dealers who wanted a part of the firm's action in North America. The British accepted only high-quality mules. "They didn't buy any trashy stuff," stated a one-time employee of Guyton and Harrington. "For instance," the mules "didn't have to have what was stylish and something that you'd wanna set on your front porch and see 'em grazing out in the pasture, but he had to be sound and strong, you know. And [the British] were pretty keen."[2]

The firm knew quality mules could be purchased from other mule centers as well as those in Missouri and Illinois. At Columbia, Tennessee, on 12 September 1915, for example, a Guyton and Harrington buyer shipped fifteen carloads of mules (four hundred) purchased throughout Middle Tennessee to Newport News, Virginia. There they were loaded aboard transports and shipped to England for training. The carloads, worth sixty thousand dollars, were not the first mules purchased from the region. Several weeks earlier a consignment of six hundred mules worth one hundred thousand dollars was sent to the same port by a special fast freight.[3]

Laws in Canada and the United States actually worked to the advantage of dealers in the Tennessee and Kentucky mule markets. Animals could not travel more than twenty-eight hours on a train without being off-loaded to feed, water, and rest. This was a necessary provision since most animals were not able to eat or be watered in the cars. Mules and horses traveled best if they were given only hay to eat. On longer trips from Toronto and Chicago the animals needed oats occasionally. A fast freight from Nashville to Newport News would normally take less than a day and a half. Animals could therefore make this journey without being unloaded or unduly fatigued. Freights from Lexington or Louisville could also reach the same destination within the twenty-eight hours maximum time.[4]

To ensure quality purchases, the British army sent a Royal Remount Commission of officers and veterinarians to Canada and the United States to oversee all animal purchases. These commissioners quickly learned that some American horse and mule dealers were as slick and crafty as in other places where the British purchased animals. The actions of fraudulent dealers kept British and American inspectors busy. Horses and mules unbroken or only partially broken were difficult and dangerous to inspect. Sponges placed in nostrils could hide unsoundness of wind. Teeth were scientifically filed and rounded to hide an animal's true age; ice placed in the rectum would hide a high temperature; and various medications or potions could be given to stimulate sick animals to temporary activity. Animals rejected might show up again at a different location and before another team of inspectors. Mules accepted might be substituted for rejected animals unless the purchaser took extra precautions. The British and the firm of Guyton and Harrington could end up paying twice for the same animals, including those that they had rejected originally.[5]

In shipping animals by rail and by ocean transports, the British soon learned that mules were hardier than horses. By far the most important common cause of death of the animals was a type of pneumonia called "shipping fever." This catarrhal or lobular strain of pneumonia was often accompanied by pleurisy and was especially fatal to horses, whose death rate was thirty to one compared to that of mules.[6]

When asked his opinion of the American mule, a British brigadier in France replied, "A most magnificent creature, and he has a better character than is generally given to him." American mules with the British forces from time to time made back-page copy in American newspapers. One correspondent wrote that two years of war has brought the "triumph of at least one American institution—the army mule. He has been weighed anew in the scales of battle . . . and not found wanting. In warm winter coat and with long, inquisitive ears flopping back and forth in the breeze, he marches up among the roaring guns with a steady nonchalance that lends confidence and faith to the fighting men who depend so much on him." The war correspondent, seemingly surprised over the British enthusiasm for American mules and probably anticipating American participation in the war, noted that from "Missouri, Georgia, Tennessee, Mississippi, Texas, and other stock farms in the South" the mule had gone to war and had "come into his own. The much maligned, supposedly stubborn, balky and generally pestiferous mule, has won a place in the heart of the British Army from which he can never be dislodged." The correspondent also observed that when visiting a veterinary hospital he saw hundreds of horses and only one solitary mule. When asked why only one American mule was being treated, the vet replied that it was because mules were such fine animals that few ever need "repair." No doubt American mules greeted American doughboys when they arrived in France.[7]

Enough mules were left at home to supply the needs of the American Expeditionary Force (AEF) if there had been enough shipping space allotted for them. At the time of America's entry into the war, the army possessed 27,624 draft and pack mules. Within six months it had purchased and trained 7,444 more for duty in the AEF. By September 1917, 35,068 trained mules were awaiting shipment, yet a total of only 29,910 mules were shipped to France throughout the remainder of the war.[8]

Transporting mules by ship could still be a precarious proposition. Quartermasters used portable stalls designed and constructed in 1900 and earlier used to ship mules to the Philippines, China, Cuba, and Mexico. The quartermaster with responsibility for the mules on a given transport had to be constantly on the alert for anything that could spook his charges. Rough seas and strange noises kept the mules in a constant state of agitation. The presence of a bell mare, many times necessary to lure mules aboard vessels in the first place, would keep the animals from bolting. But thousands of mules were shipped without bell mares. Depending on variables such as ventilation, rolling seas, and good feed and water, mules required from one day to two weeks to recover from a crossing. Some soldiers doubted that certain mules ever fully recovered.[9]

Many have asserted that the U.S. military was totally unprepared for participation in World War I. They point out that of more than twenty-two hundred artillery pieces used by American artillerymen in France, only a hundred were manufactured in the United States; that there were no American tanks or fighter planes; and that the principal American contributions to the war weaponry were the twelve-cylinder Liberty airplane engines that had a tendency to burst into flames when hit by bullets and then by mid-1918 the excellent Browning machine guns and automatic rifles.[10]

The insufficient attention the U.S. military paid to the care of its animals sent to France showed an even greater lack of preparation and concern. The AEF arrived in Europe with no veterinary organization. The initial absence of veterinarians resulted in the deaths of an estimated twenty-three thousand horses and mules or approximately 76 percent of the mules army quartermasters were able to ship with the AEF troops to France. The Americans' inability to attend to superficial injuries and bullet wounds, the absence of hospital facilities, and the inability to deal with spreading disease alarmed the French and British commanding officers as well as their veterinary staffs. They were correctly concerned over the spreading of disease to civilian beasts as well as their own military animals, and over the ability of American units to retain their mobility. So grave was the situation that the British quartermaster general wrote Gen. John J. Pershing offering assistance, which Pershing accepted. Wounded mules and horses with American units were thereafter sent to British veterinary hospitals. Later the French also cared for wounded American animals.[11]

Throughout the war, dead American horses and mules were sold by the wagoners to Paris butchers, sometimes informally. The AEF seemed to have no policy concerning its dead animals. Horse and mule meat, considered a delicacy in Europe, became standard fare of the French. The British shipped home some of the animals that died in their veterinary hospitals. Army details skinned the animals and removed all flesh from the bones. Hides were sent to tanners on the War Office's list and the flesh sold to slaughtering firms. Horse and mule meat supplemented the British civilians' diet during the 1918 food and meat shortages in England.[12]

The first American army mules arrived in France in July 1917, in the same convoy with the troops to which they were assigned. The American practice of shipping troops with their supply animals did not last long. Shipping space was limited, and the French, desperate for American material aid, unrealistically offered to supply all draft animals for the AEF in return for more doughboys being sent to the front lines. Later, the French reneged and offered only to loan the AEF four thousand animals with the understanding that they be replaced by 1 November. In November 1917, when the French were unable to deliver to the AEF the promised seven thousand mules each month, American quartermasters resumed shipping mules and continued supplying them until April 1918. By then American quartermasters in Europe had purchased mules wherever they could obtain them. Initially they bought 9,341 mules from France,

6,777 American mules from Britain, and 12,941 from Spain. The Germans objected to Spain selling mules to Americans. The objection and the difficulty of transporting the animals to France kept purchases lower than they might have been. Throughout American participation in World War I, quartermasters purchased a total of only 18,462 horses and mules from Spain.[13]

Army quartermasters were not especially enamored with the foreign mules, but they realized that the army's animal attrition rate made the purchases necessary. QMG Henry G. Sharpe announced that "there was no comparison between the small, poorly nourished mule secured in Spain and those purchased in Southern France and the powerful upstanding, mealy-nosed product of the Middle West." Officers complained about the small size of Spanish mules but nonetheless found important work for them. These bantam mules, between 12 and 13 hh, hauled machine-gun carts thereby releasing the heavier animals for duty with the artillery and ammunition trains. Being bred from similar type asses and mares found in the American Southwest, the Spanish animals had two of the same enduring traits as Crook's Arizona pack mules. They were tough and resilient.[14]

The AEF received stout horses and mules from the French, but the farmers were most reluctant to sell their animals at any price, for they believed that if American suppliers were unsuccessful in purchasing enough animals, they would have to import American mules that could be bought at low surplus prices after the war. No doubt, having seen some of the specimens already being used by the American, British, and French armies, these farmers were anxious to acquire American mules. Time and time again French military officials had to intercede in order to obtain any horses or mules for the AEF. The French army suppliers faced a seemingly constant and awkward dilemma. They needed to supply their own armies with replacement stock, keep civilians reasonably happy by not requisitioning too many of their animals, and resupply the Americans who were becoming the dominant force in the war. The last thing the French wanted was for American officials to replace men and supplies aboard the transports headed for France with forage and mules.[15]

Although the AEF was supplied by thousands of motor vehicles of various types, these vehicles were used more as a supplement to mules and wagons for local transportation than for long hauls. Truck convoys did at times carry supplies to forward areas but only when mules were unavailable. Too many of the trucks broke down or became unreliable on muddy roads. Soldiers in the trenches still relied to a large degree on mules for their ammunition and other supplies. Mules were more dependable than trucks and were the ones that usually brought troops hot meals. Mule-drawn wagons transported rations to the kitchen areas. Many times pack mules using *aparejos* each carried two or four marmite cans of stew to soldiers who could not come to the rear area to eat. The cans of what the soldiers referred to as slim were lashed to the aparejos using barrel hitches. Gas attacks frequently came at mealtime, which made the food useless and which many times killed or injured the pack mules. Because of the chances of gas attacks and the lack of sufficient mules, two men often carried a single milk or marmite can from the kitchen area to the trenches.[16]

All of the armies of World War I depended heavily on horses and mules. Animals rather than the gasoline engines still dominated the supply lines. Tank units often depended on mules to bring their fuel, ammunition, and supplies to the front. Successful offensives depended on availability of large numbers of supply, artillery, and pack animals. By 1917, for example, the British army employed more than a million animals on all fronts. They included camels, oxen, and elephants, but the vast majority were horses and mules in nearly equal numbers. The British would have used more mules if they had been able to obtain them. The greatest single class of supplies the British shipped to France was hay and oats—5,439,000 tons as compared to 759,000 tons of gasoline and oil.[17]

During the 1918 last-ditch German offensives on the western front, the AEF experienced transportation difficulties. Pershing later asserted that "one of the biggest, if not the biggest problem" was the shortages of animals for the AEF. On 10 August, when the U.S. Army became an independent force and Marshall Ferdinand Foch gave it a separate sector of the front, the transportation problems intensified. By the end of the month only seventy-two thousand horses and mules remained with the army for all purposes. To use the animals more efficiently, someone suggested motorizing artillery brigades and reducing each combat division from a total of 6,719 animals to 3,803 horses and mules. That suggestion was not taken seriously because the infantry needed those mules and many more.[18]

Even if sufficient truck transports and mule-drawn wagon trains had been available, heavy traffic in rear areas, especially in bad weather, caused long delays as roads became impassable. A single division with its mule trains, ambulances, and truck transports occupied nineteen miles of road. Only pack mules could carry supplies across battlefields full of debris and shell holes or cross-country, and there were never enough of these mules available. To reach combat units more efficiently engineer battalions were operating stone quarries to provide crushed rock for roads, and more than thirty thousand German prisoners were repairing roads and building new ones for the motor troop transports and wagon trains. Whenever possible, supply officers used the light railroads that the Germans had used during their spring offensives, and construction battalions built extensions to these lines.[19]

The animal transportation difficulties were so serious for American coordination in battle with French and English units that the French and English turned over to American combat troops more than 67,600 horses and mules. The British equipped divisions that trained in their sector and supplied ten divisions with horses and mules. The French turned over animals to American Remount Service officers on three different occasions. The last occurred after the American success at St. Mihiel. Foch ordered thirteen thousand animals turned over to the American army to enable it to swing around and immediately begin the Meuse-Argonne offensive. The St. Mihiel offensive had taken its toll on the animals. Some ninety thousand draft animals pulled the artillery, ammunition wagons, ambulances, and caissons for the American army's most spectacular battle yet fought—the Meuse-Argonne offensive. Yet so bad were the supply problems and so disproportionate was the large number of soldiers to the transportation necessary to supply them that Pershing almost continually asked Foch for additional animals. His pleas were to no avail since the French were also short of animals.

This last great offensive on the western front needed animal transportation. The water-logged country by the Meuse and the constant rain made it nearly impossible for motorized vehicles to navigate and extremely difficult for the animals. Engineers rebuilt roads only to have them wash out again. Thousands of horses and mules collapsed or died in their traces as they tried to pull through the mire and mud. Sometimes they did double duty by going back for needed supplies packed in the trucks that were buried in mud up to their axles along the roads.[20]

On several occasions pack mules were used successfully in emergencies. At Ergemont during the second phase of the Meuse-Argonne offensive, for example, the First Division had met stubborn resistance. On 4 October 1918 all communication with artillery in the rear had broken down, and the commander sent for new telephone wire. All division trucks were bogged down in mud, and wagon horses faltered in their traces. So Sgt. Laurence M. Lumpkin loaded ten pack mules with the needed wire and headed for the forward position. German artillerymen spotted the animals and laid down a barrage that killed five of them. The remaining mules with Lumpkin did not panic, and they delivered the wire. After unloading them, Lumpkin galloped the five animals back to the point where the other mules had fallen, removed the loads from the dead mules, repacked his remaining five and brought back the rest of the wire. For this dangerous act he received the DSC, but the mules were given no official recognition. "Their behavior under fire, however, endeared them to the First Division."[21]

By the end of October 1918, the AEF had become an experienced army with a superb fighting record. Its strength in France—including combat replacement and service troops, 1,974,400 officers and men—was growing each month by 250,000 men. Close to 35,000 civilian workers also served the army in a bewildering variety of ways. Its supplies were adequate with a total of 70 million rations; and its weapons, especially the rifles, machine guns, and automatic rifles, were top quality and plentiful. There also seemed to be enough motorized transportation with nearly 30,000 trucks, 7,800 automobiles, and 13,700 motorcycles. For animal transportation it had a total of more than 163,000 animals. This number is misleading, for it included 45,000 saddle mounts, 115,000 draft horses and mules, but only 2,587 pack mules. If the war had continued many more months, it is highly unlikely that the available transportation could have continued delivering the supplies at the tremendous rates they were being consumed or that the supplies at the rear would have been adequate until the next transports arrived from the United States. If casualties had continued at the same rate as the AEF suffered at the Meuse-Argonne (the army had 120,000 killed or wounded in six weeks or one-half its battle casualties for the whole war), ambulances would have so choked the roads that it would have been nearly impossible to continue supplying soldiers at the front.[22]

At the conclusion of the war the army sold 121,465 horses and 56,207 mules in Europe. Thousands of animals were also sold in the United States during the first six months after the war, with another 50,000 to be sold before the end of May 1919. Probably the AEF had used almost 600,000 animals during the war. The average price the army paid per mule ranged between $175 and $200. The costs at both high and low prices were between $105 million and $120 million. The army had received its money's worth from its horses and mules, but it had retained only 80,000 mules at the war's conclusion.[23]

The mechanization of war seemed to sound the death knell for mules. During the post-war years many high-ranking army officers believed that motorization, mechanization, and aviation had made mules obsolete for modern warfare. They had forgotten that despite all the modern advances during the first decade of the century, the mule rather than the gasoline engine still dominated the supply lines. They did, however, have the standard quips and enjoyed saying that these hybrids spent their lives continually in revolt against the law and order of the universe and had no respect for army regulations; that they did not know the chain of command and when ordered to move, obeyed at their leisure. Only with the most diligent efforts were a small cadre of artillery and cavalry officers able to maintain any animals in the army. By 1928 there were only 2,697 mules in the army. The cadre of cavalry and artillery officers experienced difficulty preventing further losses of animals. Yet by 1938 horses and mules had been replaced by motor transportation in most military units, including infantry. By 1940 the army maintained only two horse cavalry divisions, two animal-drawn artillery regiments, and two mixed animal and motor transport regiments, with an authorized animal strength of 20,300, that is, 16,800 horses and 3,500 mules.[24]

While in the process of mechanizing the army and eliminating horses and mules, quartermasters and artillerymen also retired the aparejos. The army readily adopted the packsaddles designed by Col. Albert E. Phillips—the Phillips cavalry packsaddle and the Phillips cargo packsaddle. Phillips claimed that after a thorough testing by quartermasters in Panama, by members of the Infantry school, and by men in Field Artillery, he had developed "a saddle of scientific yet of simple design to replace the crude and cumbersome aparejo. Many tests," he noted, "have been held, not only between the Aparejo and the Phillips saddle, but also between the packsaddles of the principal military powers," and the Phillips saddle "won first place." The new saddles, their enthusiasts pointed out, were issued ready for use. They were lighter, cheaper, and would stand rougher usage without losing their shape; both cinchas could be readjusted without removing loads, and they could be packed easier by packers and soldiers. Most important, the new saddles could be easily adjusted for different horses and mules each day, if necessary, whereas aparejos were padded for only one animal, and it required knowledgeable packers to form-fit saddles to individual mules. Most mule men probably saw the evidence presented from firsthand experience and accepted the change to save mules for the army. They were not totally convinced that the Phillips saddles were beneficial to mules' health, but they still needed their mules.[25]

In 1930 the army replaced all aparejos with the new saddles despite vocal opposition from several artillery officers who were concerned over the harm the new saddles could do to their mules. Aparejos adjusted the weight carried not only on mules' backs but also down their sides, and the cinchas were placed centrally to exert equal pressure over the mules' entire barrel. Phillips packsaddles placed the weight almost entirely on the mules' backs and withers, and cinching was like that of horses. The front cinchas exerted most of the pressure while the rear ones exerted only minimal pressure. Bunching of the skin between the front cinches and the front legs caused sores that took weeks to cure. When mules developed cinch sores, they usually also got back sores as they attempted to adjust their gait to alleviate pain. The main features of the new saddles could cause the mules more back and cinch sores and sore backs than the crude and cumbersome aparejos. Practical reasons such as ease of packing and having saddles interchangeable seemed to outweigh the best interests of the mules.[26]

In the event of involvement in another war, army leaders planned to use only American equipment and large American mules to support small segments of pack-mule artillery and small groups of infantry and cavalry. They had not considered contingency plans of using smaller mules indigenous to the countries in which they were to fight. Their oversight in minimizing the use of mules would cause hardships to American soldiers in all theaters of World War II. More practical and less visionary officers would work out better ways to use both pack and artillery mules. The U.S. Army still desperately needed mules to support its ground forces, as will be seen in the next chapter.

CHAPTER 8

Mules in World War II

With the outbreak of World War II, those who advocated eliminating mules and using motorized transportation won additional support because of the ease with which the German mechanized units swept through Poland. The speed of the Panzer divisions showed the new way of modern warfare. What many failed to realize was that support for the blitzkrieg came from horse-drawn wagons supplying the mechanized tanks, trucks, and men with gasoline, rations, and ammunition. Enough high-ranking officers, however, had a more realistic picture of the German Blitzkrieg and realized that for certain operations animals were by no means obsolete. Remount officers began purchasing cavalry horses and large numbers of mules with stocky builds that were 15 hh and weighed between 950 and 1025 pounds. The purchases for the next two years were in proportion to the number of horses and mules in the army, which indicated a lack of army decisiveness.

By 1942 officers had purchased 23,546 horses and 4,279 mules. That same year they obtained an additional 2,859 horses and 1,699 mules. But 1942 was the last year that they purchased more horses than mules. In 1943 remount officers purchased 10,217 mules but only four horses; the next two years they purchased no horses and 14,328 mules.[1]

With remount officers purchasing so many horses and mules during 1941 the army could not keep pace in supplying the remount depots with enough animal-handler recruits and other personnel. Some recruits were chosen because of their experience but most were not. A man's height and build many times determined his fate. At the induction centers someone placed a bar over a door at six feet. Men having to duck to go through to the other room sometimes found themselves mule packers.[2]

Evidently induction-center personnel wanted men from the eastern states to have equal opportunities to learn about these animals, along with those from the states where mules were plentiful. Frank Graham of Missouri recalled that he went through the induction center with a New Yorker and both were given cards marked "MP." The man was excited because he thought the initials meant "military police" when they actually meant "mule pack." On reaching their destination for training, Graham noted that he had never seen so many mules in three or four corrals. His companion stated, "just as innocently as could be, 'What in the world are those things?' He went into a state of shock." Coy McNabb related that of twenty officers assigned to remount depots there were three or four lieutenants from the East Coast who had never seen mules before. One from Boston said that he didn't know why in the world he volunteered for this assignment. "This," he claimed, "is the worst thing I've ever been in. I'm just afraid I'm going to get killed." McNabb replied that training mules was a lot safer than dodging incoming artillery shells, to which the Bostonian replied, "I'll be damned if it is. . . . I'll take my chances with those 105 shells anytime before I'd work with these mules."[3]

Because of the unusually large number of animal purchases, recruits often trained animals first and then were trained for the army. Jim Sims of Centralia, Missouri, recalled that he was inducted in April 1941 and began his army enlistment at Fort Robinson, Nebraska. The company officer told Sims and the other recruits, mainly from Missouri, that they would first train more than twelve hundred cavalry mounts and that their basic training could wait until afterward. After helping to train the remounts, Sims and the others were sent to Fort Bliss, Texas, to train mules. Sims never stated where he received his army basic training.[4]

By the winter of 1942–43 it had become evident that pack and artillery mules were needed in large numbers. In Tunisia the need for mules was glaringly apparent. In capturing Bizerte, troops abandoned the heavily mined roads of the Sedjenane valley and followed narrow trails overgrown with scrub and impenetrable by enemy tanks. To continue the Bizerte campaign in such inaccessible terrain the Sixtieth Combat Team, Ninth Division, needed pack-mule artillery and pack-mule supply. The Atlas and Aures Mountains of Tunisia were ideal paratrooper, mule packer, mule artilleryman, and horse cavalryman country. Operating in this terrain, pack mule artillery using 81-mm mortars could effectively counter mechanized columns in the valleys. Mule packtrains could keep infantrymen supplied with rations, water, and ammunition until engineers prepared roads and trails suitable for quarter-ton C&R trucks to reach the areas. Even then, mules were needed when rain and mud shut down the trucks and when infantrymen made further penetrations. Mules were also used to transport the wounded to aid stations. When reaching open country, the units used their vehicles not only for reconnaissance and supply but also to move their dependable pack mules to wherever they were needed.[5]

The army had made no preparations for using mules in Tunisia. The animals could not come from the United States because of a lack of shipping. Forage and mules had to be found in the vicinity. Finding enough good mules was one problem but not the only one. Few combat troops were experienced muleteers, and the quartermasters had no inkling of how to organize a packtrain. The Second Corps finance officer allotted $150,000, and quartermaster agents purchased or rented 218 mules, 95 donkeys, and 28 horses that were available in the towns of the immediate area. Mules and horses were rented for a dollar a day, and donkeys brought prices ranging from $295 to $385. Quartermasters borrowed packsaddles, and the British furnished forage for the animals.[6]

In Tunisia, American forces were also supplied by two British pack-transport companies, the only truly organized mule packtrains in North Africa. These companies showed how well pack mules could operate in mechanized warfare. On one occasion some of the pack mules supplied tank crews with rations. In rough terrain, pack-transport mules using cacolets and litters evacuated wounded men. The British, using many of their own army mules and purchasing others from the same sources as the Americans, kept their animals in good condition, although many of the mules purchased had to be treated for severe cases of mange. "In spite of bad weather, long marches, journeys in lorries and pack loading at night, the majority of injuries were due to gunshot wounds, which is not always the case in animal units." With the collapse of Italian and German resistance, the British collected 250 German horses and mules for use in Sicily.[7]

When the fighting moved to Sicily, the American army used many more mules. Gen. George Patton's Seventh Army used mule trains extensively in the mountainous terrain west of Mount Etna. The army transported some of the mules from Tunisia, but most of the Seventh's four thousand mules had been liberated from the Italian army. Quartermasters commandeered other animals and purchased or rented them from the Sicilians. They rented mules, horses, and donkeys for a dollar a day with an agreement that owners would be adequately compensated for killed or disabled animals; average compensation was $150 per mule, $120 per horse, and $40 per donkey.[8]

In Sicily the packers experienced trouble with their "foreign" mules, but after some experimenting they learned correct ways of handling them. Part of the problem had to be a language barrier. The mules in both North Africa and Sicily had several endearing qualities. According to one man who used them, "the Sicilian and African mules paid no attention to gunfire. And I have seen times. . . . there was one particular . . . they's walking a bunch of them down the road and a mule got a little off to the shoulder, hit a land mine, and it just blew his whole quarter and everything off and I don't know whether it quite killed him but they shot him. The other mules never missed a step, just walked right on around him."[9]

More than a third of the animals that American troops used in Sicily were killed, and many others were declared "unserviceable because of bad feet, saddle sores, or general debility." Probably the major reason that many of those animals were unable to pack supplies was that they had not received even minimal care, that is, adequate feed and water. They had been worked to the point of total exhaustion. Also, neither the British nor Americans had enough farriers and veterinarians available to service mules in need of shoes or to treat wounded mules. The few veterinarians available could handle wounds only at aid stations well in the rear of where the animals were wounded. Since operations were not prolonged and enough seasoned mules were easily obtained in the mountain regions of Sicily, the American forces adopted an unwritten policy of replacement rather than going out of their way to take care of the mules they received. No one in Sicily knew what they were doing with regard to the mules. Animals in Sicily were too often sacrificed, which unfortunately is one of the more ugly traits of warfare.[10]

According to the men doing the fighting, there were never enough pack mules in Sicily. Gen. Lucien K. Truscott Jr. "was firmly convinced that if one squadron of horse cavalry and one pack troop of 200 mules had been available" to him on 1 August at Stefano, they would have enabled him "to cut off and capture the entire German force" along the north coast road and enter Messina at least forty-eight hours earlier. Truscott was referring to being unable to prevent the Germans from escaping from Messina to the Italian peninsula. Patton concurred with Truscott and wrote that had the army possessed a "cavalry division with pack artillery in Tunisia and Sicily, not a German would have escaped." In a more realistic vein, Gen. Omar N. Bradley, "the GI's general," observed that "in contemplated operations in mountain terrain, plans should include facilities for supply by pack train."[11]

During the drive on Messina, Patton gained a degree of notoriety by killing a farmer's team of wagon mules. The mules would not budge off a narrow bridge, and a huge Seventh Army column had halted along the blocked road while the farmer and sympathetic drivers tried to coax the frightened animals into moving. Patton arrived on the somewhat humorous scene, calmly pulled his pearl-handled revolver, and shot the two mules through the head. He then ordered the men to throw the dead animals off the bridge. Later Patton explained that he had not enjoyed killing the animals but preferred it to the alternative of having the Luftwaffe arrive to strafe the column and kill large numbers of men. Nevertheless, Patton critics said that it was just another indication of the general's brutal nature.[12]

Mules became especially important during the Italian campaign. "The Apennines just shout for pack artillery," exclaimed one officer, while another took one glance at a topological map of the peninsula and murmured that he would be more confident of success if all jeeploads of supplies were placed on pack mules. The Fifth Army needed artillery set up where only mules could put it. Quartermasters conservatively estimated that the need for pack animals operating in terrain unsuitable for mechanized equipment would run five hundred animals per division. At least five times that number were actually needed. In the mountainous regions of the Italian peninsula, German infantry divisions were each using four thousand horses and mules.[13]

Truscott's Third Division was better prepared for the invasion of Italy. During the Sicilian campaign, Truscott had organized a provisional packtrain and a provisional mounted troop under the command of Maj. Robert W. Crandall, a former cavalry officer who had served under Truscott before the war. The Third would use more than four hundred mules and a hundred horses before reaching Messina.[14]

Truscott greatly expanded the use of pack and artillery mules and mounted reconnaissance troops in Italy. To head these activities he transferred from Algiers Capt. Raymond F. Baker, who had some twenty years of cavalry experience. Baker and quartermasters purchased or hired animals on a catch-as-catch-can basis. Many had been a part of the provisional units in Sicily, and most of the horses had previously been in the Italian cavalry. Baker also advertised for "cavalry" troops who could serve as packers if necessary and was rewarded by having four times as many men volunteer as he needed. He later admitted that he selected men who were at least familiar with animals and could ride a horse.

The equipment used was all Italian. The saddles were actually light packsaddles that were also used for riding. Experienced horsemen complained that they sat too high in the saddle and that the girths were too much in the middle of the barrel. For packing, the saddles were suited for the Italian mules. When some packtrains using Italian mules had received Phillips saddles, they could not use them successfully because the saddles were made for the stocky-bred, larger American mules instead of the smaller, lankier, "long-barrelled [Italian] critters."[15]

Throughout the entire conquest of Italy, most pack companies preferred and used Italian packsaddles. Capt. Donald J. Willems, in charge of organizing and supplying some of the trains in Italy, explained that even when larger European mules could support Phillips cargo packsaddles, packers would not use them. "The American saddle," noted Willems, "was the best long-range saddle ever made." But in Europe trucks transported the mules to the "muleline." Mules were used for the difficult, short hauls. Phillips saddles with full-rigging could weigh as much as 120 pounds, but the Italians saddles weighed half that much. Men needed "supplies on those mountain ridges and [packers] did not want to use up perhaps half the weight a mule could carry with a heavy Cargo Pack Saddle." Furthermore, the Italian packers knew best how to pack their own equipment.[16]

Organized into reconnaissance and heavy weapons platoons, and armed with carbines, Truscott's volunteers became cavalrymen within a month. In September they loaded their stock (at the time 355 animals) aboard LSTs and unloaded the animals at Salerno. After a month on the trail, Baker and other staff officers reorganized the provisional cavalry of the Fifth Army. The unit became three distinct organizations under one squadron command. The three units now consisted of a pack howitzer unit, a mule packtrain, and the provisional reconnaissance troop that was divided into several platoons. The howitzer unit included all artillery battalions in the Third Division, including the seventy-five artillery sections and the communication section. The mule packtrains serviced all forward units. Platoons of twenty-six mules, with their drivers and packers, were assigned to units as needed. Pack mules were also attached to the reconnaissance troops for special missions. Officers observed that the mules of the Third lost more than fifty pounds each within the first month in Italy. They desperately needed shoes and adequate forage.[17]

Maj. Gen. Mark Clark also quickly realized that artillery and pack mules were a necessity for the Italian campaign. He ordered chief supply officer of the Fifth Army, Col. Ralph H. Tate, to come up with enough mules. Tate set the goal for his staff officers to acquire thirteen hundred mules. By November officers of the newly established remount station had found only 316 mules, and the

French Expeditionary Corps had arrived on the peninsula and was demanding animals. The estimate of animals needed quickly reached twenty thousand.[18]

The Remount Branch in the United States had more than enough mules to supply the needs of the American, British, and French forces in Italy if only its officers could obtain enough priority shipping space for them. Until late in the conflict that was not possible. During the entire war, not more than fourteen thousand out of thirty thousand American mules were shipped to war, and more of those went to British and American forces in the CBI (China, Burma, India) region than to other theaters of war. Nearly thirty-five hundred were specifically "lend-leased" to British forces. In Europe the Americans were forced to solve their mule supply problems in the countries where their troops were operating. For the Italian campaign the Remount Service in the United States shipped only twenty-nine hundred mules, and most of these did not arrive until the last weeks of the war.[19]

By January 1944 the newly established but unofficial remount station had recruited no new large supplies of animals. Fighting men desperately needed mules in the Apennines. All along the front division officers stated that the high ground their men had been able to obtain had cost many lives and that those men who were holding this ground had to be supplied with ammunition and rations by pack mules or be allowed to withdraw.[20]

Clark, wanting action, leaned heavily on all concerned with the project. His displeasure and the obvious vulnerability of the forward units of the Fifth Army brought results. Officers exhausted all local resources. They paid as much as three hundred dollars for a mule that "might carry only one load of ammunition and then be suited for the auction block." They purchased two Sardinian trains, each containing six hundred mules, and expedited their arrival on the peninsula; and they set up a system of cooperation with the British army Veterinary Corps through Allied headquarters in Italy to procure, examine, and if necessary treat all new arrivals. All remounts were now designated joint property of the British Eighth Army and the American Fifth Army. The most important Allied accomplishment was making use of the Italian army's mule pack-trains. Within two months British and American officers had found seven Indian, five Cypriot, six Italian, and eight French mule trains together numbering more than ten thousand mules.[21]

A remount service took shape quickly. At first loosely organized, it became operational by February 1944 when the 2610th and 6742d Remount Depots began operating stations wherever needed. By then agents were purchasing an average of two hundred mules a week. In May 1944 veterinarians arrived to treat wounded mules. Within a year the Remount Service accumulated fifteen thousand mules and had distributed eleven thousand of them. The remount depots in Italy were busy places. Veterinarians inspected and vaccinated newly purchased mules and those captured from the Germans that were still usable. Personnel trained newly acquired animals. Trucks arrived with wounded and worn-out animals and left with replacements. It was a daily, continuous operation.

Darkening mules was one of the most important functions performed at the remount depots. In Italy gray mules are more common than brown and black ones. Packtrains of light-colored animals presented conspicuous targets for German mortars and artillery units, and hundreds of mules were lost. "Those damn Germans," noted Willems, "were too accurate with their mortars for the health of the mules. In one area we lost over a hundred mules within a couple of days." Finally, an ingenious quartermaster conceived of the idea of spraying the gray mules with a 5 percent solution of potassium permanganate, which effectively darkened and perfumed them for about two months, depending on their shedding and the amount of rainfall.[22]

The Italian packtrains were especially important to the Fifth Army. Each of the six trains was composed of four sections of 60 mules and a company headquarters section of 20 mules. Divided among the sections were a total of 12 horses or riding mules, 11 officers, and 360 enlisted men. The Fifth Army supplied each packtrain with a liaison officer to advise the Italian officers and to maintain an adequate number of replacement mules at the end of the motorized supply lines. Willems was placed in charge of the overall resupplying of the Italian pack operation. In July 1944 four new Italian pack troops became operational, and in February 1945 five more were added.

The U.S. Tenth Mountain Division in Italy initially stood out from the other pack outfits. It possessed 558 American mules and used mainly U.S. Army equipment. By February 1945, however, it was employing two Italian mule pack companies to help supply its artillery and reconnaissance troop. Its mule supply by then was 5,028 including the 558 American mules.[23]

Fifth Army officers had worked out a system of supply for pack-trains. Trucks or jeeps brought up the supplies to the mule-head, which meant the end of the line where a vehicle could operate, usually one or two miles from the forward positions. Supplies were usually packed to the front lines at night, and packers could be expected to make two trips up and back each evening. One of the liaison officers with an Italian pack company, Lt. Tommy White, later explained that depending on demands, the packers would "send anywhere from 20 to 60 mules on the run," but sometimes trains of a hundred mules were used. For short hauls the Italians packed the mules with between two hundred and four hundred pounds of supplies, and heavier loads on special occasions. Most of the time the packtrains were within range of heavy artillery. White stated that on the supply trips "maybe you'd lose eight to ten [mules] and maybe you'd make a half dozen runs and never lose any. It'd depend on whether the Germans had you zeroed in." If there was accurate shell fire, "you string 'em out" and put fifty to one hundred yards between the mules. "In fact," noted White, "when the last mule left, the first one might even be coming in."[24]

Probably the most famous American war correspondent, Ernie Pyle, reported from the front lines in Italy on 5 January 1944 a classic description of supplying troops with a mule pack outfit. The packtrain he accompanied "supplied a battalion that was fighting on a bald, rocky ridge nearly four thousand feet high. It fought constantly for ten days and nights, and when it finally came down," he lamented, "less than a third of the original men were left." Everything the soldiers received "had to go up on the backs of mules and men. Mules took it the first third of the way. Men took it the last bitter two-thirds, because the trail was too steep for mules." The mule skinners were from Sardinia and "were experienced in climbing and handling mules. They were bivouacked in an olive grove alongside a highway at the foot of the mountain." Pyle noted that the packers made no trips during the day except in emergencies, because most of the trail was exposed to artillery fire. "There were one hundred fifty-five skinners in this outfit and usually about eighty mules were used each night. Every mule had a man to lead it," and others went along to help pick up fallen animals, repack, and unload at the top. American soldiers were stationed within shouting distance of one another all along the trail "to keep the Italians from getting lost in the dark." On an average night, Pyle wrote, the train brought up "something like this—eighty-five cans of water, one hundred cases of K-ration, ten cases of D-ration, ten miles of telephone wire, twenty-five cases of grenades and rifle and machine-gun ammunition, about one hundred rounds of heavy mortar shells, one radio, two telephones, and four cases of first-aid packets and sulfa drugs." The packers loaded their "pockets with cigarets for the boys on top—also cans of Sterno, so they could heat some coffee once in a while." Mail, Pyle stated, "was the most tragic cargo, because a "large portion" of it went back down because the addressees had been killed. "On the long man-killing climb above the end of the mule trail they used anywhere from twenty to three hundred men a night. They rang in cooks, truck drivers, clerks, and anybody else they could lay their hands on." The train could go up and be back within three hours. Five days later Pyle described another function of the packtrains when he submitted the somber article "The Death of Captain Waskow." Dead men, he wrote, had been coming down the mountain all evening, "lashed on the backs of mules."[25]

Pack artillery and packtrains were used extensively throughout the Italian campaign. They supplied and carried artillery to help men of the British Eighth and the American Fifth armies and French troops operating within the Fifth Army to break the winter line. In carefully synchronized attacks by American, British, and French mountain troops, on 11 May 1944 the French troops penetrated the German lines and "unhinged" the German position in the Apennines while the Sixth Corps attacked from the Anzio beachhead. Allied troops entered Rome on 4 June. Three months later the Fifth was using mules in the northern Apennines to penetrate the new German position, the Gothic Line. In the spring of 1945 as the Fifth and Eighth armies penetrated the final defenses and entered the Po Valley, the Fifth had 4,770 mules operating in various units with

3,975 replacements in depots or veterinary hospitals, and the Eighth was maintaining 8,000 mules in units with some 7,000 replacements. By the time the Germans surrendered in Italy on 2 May 1945, Allied soldiers had captured approximately twenty-eight thousand German horses and mules, a quarter of them being mules. At that time nine mule ships had been diverted from the Burma-India run to bring an additional seven thousand American mules to the mountain troops in Italy. Only the conclusion of the European war halted that effort. The campaign for Italy played a prominent role in the outcome of World War II, and the vital use of mule power had helped make the campaign ultimately successful.[26]

Mules had been hauled all over Italy in standard two-and-a-half ton, six-by-six army trucks, using only the regulation three-foot sideboards to support American units. On one occasion a Tenth Mountain Division pack troop commander questioned the use of trucks without high racks on them. "Why," he exclaimed, "I'll have dead mules hanging from trucks all the way across the Po Valley." At that point, Willems, in charge of the remount depots, ordered the troop commander to "load those damn mules up." So he did. The mules rode across the Po Valley without a single one bailing out of the truck. Willems noted that he only knew of one mule who jumped out of a moving truck. "They're just smart enough."[27]

Mules used in Italy were shipped to France. Half of the remount depot—seven hundred mules—at Persano, Italy, arrived in France in October 1944. In November the 513th Quartermaster Pack Company, a black unit, arrived from Italy and provided excellent support for the 45th and 103rd Divisions of the Seventh Army who were fighting in a locale similar to that of the Italian Apennines. The 513th consisted of 298 mules, 2 officers, and 75 enlisted men and was the only unit of its kind in France and Germany.[28]

While pack mules mainly carried supplies, packed howitzers, and transported wounded and dead soldiers in the African and European theaters of war, they also performed more mundane but necessary tasks. One specific incident showed how mules enabled an air transport command based at Oran, Algeria, to operate efficiently in foul weather. At Maison Blanche Air Field Capt. Chan E. Livingston used French army, three-mule wagons (*camions*) to transport and load supplies aboard c-47 cargo planes during the incredibly wet winter of 1944. The planes were able to land on large metal tracks that were laid down on the muddy runways, but from that point the supply lines to outgoing planes were literally bogged down. All available trucks were stuck in mud. Livingston leased from the French ten wagons and thirty mules at twenty dollars a day for each team. The French army agreed to place its Moroccan stable sergeant on leave to care for the mules, and Livingston hired him. To find suitable drivers for the teams, he posted a notice in a nearby Italian POW camp, calling for volunteers. More than half the prisoners were willing to serve, so Livingston finally found an Italian sergeant to choose and be responsible for the men selected. The supply captain could find no grain for the animals but did discover several hundred cases of slightly moldy oatmeal. The mules actually gained weight and strength on the breakfast food. Known as the "Light Brigade" by the soldiers stationed at the field, the mule-drawn French wagons met incoming planes, hauled loads to the outgoing ones, and provided most of the base transportation for two years. The cargo pilots no doubt chuckled at such efficiency.[29]

In the Pacific, American forces used mules on New Caledonia and Guadalcanal. The Ninety-seventh Mule Field Artillery Battalion arrived at New Caledonia in March 1942 without its 805 American horses and mules. Animals needed were to be purchased from natives on the island. Strategically located with a deep-water harbor, New Caledonia served as the principal staging base for later offensives against the Solomon Islands. The Ninety-seventh along with other units had arrived to increase security in case of Japanese attack.

Initial efforts to obtain the stock necessary to support pack artillery failed. The artillerymen first purchased and attempted to train native horses for pack artillery. The native, grass-fed animals were too small and lacked sufficient bone and stamina to handle artillery parts and ammunition. They could be coaxed to eat oats but did not seem to benefit from the new diet. The battalion next imported three hundred Australian horses and were able to pack and mount one firing battery and a part of a service battery. But it was unable to find enough Australian horses suitable for packing; these animals, packers claimed, were not nearly as smart nor as strong as mules. Officers of the Ninety-seventh sent requisitions for American mules.[30]

The Ninety-seventh received two shipments of mules. The requests evidently arrived before shipping priorities had been established in the Pacific. Perhaps someone familiar with pack mule artillery processed the requests. Within months the first load of three hundred mules arrived. Two hundred of them were described as seasoned packers, and the other hundred were "fine young mules—Fort Reno's ornriest." The next load, all trained mules from a remount station, arrived at about the same time the Marines landed on Guadalcanal. By August 1942 the Ninety-seventh had a full complement of mules.[31]

In January 1943 the Ninety-seventh Battalion landed on Guadalcanal with 1,000 mules (195 more than authorized) to support the last phase of the conquest of the United States' first offensive operation in the Pacific war. Pack-mule artillery supported the march up the North coast. Col. Henry Demuth, in command of the Ninety-seventh, observed that the mules in supplying the forward 75 mm pack howitzers needed to travel only short distances—from the supply dumps on the beach to the forward positions—and that the service units also supported infantry. At other times mules experienced difficulties that their handlers had not expected. In muddy, tropical conditions they could carry their loads only a mile in an hour instead of the usual four or five miles an hour. Many mules developed diseases of the hooves, thrush and quittor, various skin infections, and sunburn. At times the battalion could not easily supply itself.

Each firing battery consisted of 117 mules—just enough animals to pack four 75 mm pack howitzers and 200 rounds of ammunition allotted to each battery. Moving ammunition forward from the depot required an additional 43 pack mules and 23 riding mules, so each battery now needed 182 mules. To feed the mules required hauling daily 1,500 pounds of oats and 2,600 pounds of hay by mules not involved with the battery. Mules did operate effectively after organized resistance ended in February. Later that month packers formed all available mules into a packtrain to supply a battalion of infantry sent into the mountains to round up straggling Japanese soldiers.[32]

Mules became especially important in the CBI theater. The Royal Indian Service Corps operated several trains in Burma and over the

Ledo Road into China. In February and March 1943 Brig. Orde Wingate's British, Burmese, and Gurka Chindits (long-range penetration group) depended largely on mules in a large-scale guerrilla operation in central Burma. More than a thousand of three thousand
men failed to return to British lines, and the Chindits had been
forced to kill most of their surviving mules for food and to prevent
the animals from being captured by the Japanese as they escaped
across the Irrawaddy River. Many of the mules were the dark
brown, large, deep-chested, American-bred animals with short,
sturdy backs that had been led out of Burma the year before.[33]

According to the commander of one of the columns, Bernard Fergusson, one of the most depressing aspects of the "miserable march
was the slaughter of the mules." Wingate had ordered the men to
take the mules off the track and kill them for food "as opportunities
occurred." The Japanese, Wingate feared, were encircling the Chindits, and the mules would slow down and perhaps expose by their
braying the small units being formed to escape back to India. In any
event the men had run out of food, and a number of the mules had to
be killed anyway for food.

Until that order the column had not lost a single mule from
avoidable causes. Each time the column came to a place where the
sound of pistol shots could not be heard for too great a distance,
"half a dozen [mules] would be led away from the track we were
making, their loads and saddlery concealed in the undergrowth, and
six shots would ring out." Wingate, who could hear the reports,
then ordered the men to slaughter the animals quietly. Now the
men, Fergusson recounted, "tried the ghastly experiment of cutting
[the mules'] throats; but the first operation sickened us so much
that I said we should try it no more. We had already disposed of sixteen animals since leaving the bivouac." Later on, as they neared
the Irrawaddy, Fergusson ordered tea brewed and instructed an officer to have the men kill a mule and distribute it for meat.[34]

On 1 April the Chindits destroyed all the remaining mules. Wingate, "acting as executioner," demonstrated to his men how to kill
the mules without shooting them, "explaining each detail of the operation like a surgeon lecturing to interns." They fed a mule bamboo to keep it quiet while tying a rope to the front and rear legs.
"Four men lifted the mule and threw him heavily to the ground."

One man, "stripped completely naked, sat on the animal's head to keep him still while Wingate deftly cut the carotid artery. . . . There was an appalling surge of blood. The naked man stood up—a monstrous figure drenched in blood from head to foot. Veterans of three years of war slipped off, nauseated, into the jungle."[35]

The Chindits immediately skinned and cut up the animal and distributed pieces to each man. The mule meat, they claimed, was sweet but tough. "The heart, liver, tongue and kidneys made excellent eating, skewered on the end of a piece of bamboo and grilled over an open fire." They ate mule meat for breakfast, lunch, and dinner for six days. On the seventh they ate the horses.[36]

Wingate's report on mules and mule men during the expedition indicated that the British in the CBI theater were almost as unprepared to use pack animals as the American forces were in North Africa and Sicily. Too few men knew how to handle mules. The Chindits had received their raw, untrained, and unhardened mules in November 1942. A training team, headed by a captain in the Veterinary Corps whom Wingate "unlawfully placed in command," received and trained the animals. Otherwise, the Chindits had neither officers nor men with any knowledge of animal management. There was "no doubt," Wingate noted, that the "man leading the mule in Long Range Penetration must be as good or better a fighting man than his comrade in the infantry company. The physical effort of mule leading is such that double pay for muleteers is underpayment."[37]

The next year the British undertook a larger, more ambitious operation. Using American supplies and mules, the revitalized Chindits once again invaded Burma. A provisional U.S. Army Air Corps group, the American Commandos under Col. Phillip Cochran, ferried more than nine thousand men of the 77th and 111th British Indian Brigade into central Burma. Wingate had insisted that his soldiers be supplied with mules and that his mules and men be supplied on the ground by air drops. The Air Commandos, referred to by the British as Cochran's Glamour Girls after a London impresario whose shows specialized in "toothsome chorines," responded by transporting 1,360 mules in C-47 Dakotas and WACO gliders and keeping men and mules well supplied on the ground.[38]

Brig. Maj. John Masters accompanied a C-47 load of mules to the landing strip known as Broadway on 8 March 1944 and graphically described the trip. As he entered the door to the aircraft, he saw what he had expected, "the stern end of three large mules jammed tight across the forward half of the cabin, their noses close against the forward bulkhead and the door leading to the cockpit." Two mule leaders and the havildar "stood in the narrow space forward of the mules soothing them as they fidgeted and nervously tossed their heads." Masters counted his men and closed the door. "Now began," wrote Masters, "the unrehearsed, and the unrehearsable."

> The lights went out. The engines started. The engines changed pitch and the plane throbbed wildly. . . . The mules threw up their heads and tried to kick, long ears back and huge teeth gleaming. The pilot opened his throttles. The plane surged forward and I felt myself being pushed down and back. The mules bucked and fought and I heard one of the bamboo poles break. The *havildar* readied his carbine. Faster, faster, the tail began to rise and the floor to level off. Five of us jumped up and pushed forward against the mules' sterns. . . . Slowly the mules calmed as we steadied on course and the bellow of the engines cut back to the throb of cruising speed.[39]

Evidently mules' response to air travel was more positive than many handlers expected. Specially equipped Dakotas could carry from four to six mules, handlers, and ten infantrymen. WACO gliders could carry two mules and six troops. Mules usually behaved, but they needed to be loaded from a truck to a plane quickly, and as soon as the plane was loaded it needed to take off. Between fourteen thousand and twenty thousand feet, mules were sleepy and quiet. It was only takeoff, sudden movements, and landing that caused mules any anxiety. Mules had to be unloaded just as quickly on reaching a destination. During flight, copilots needed to know how to soothe an unruly mule and where to aim the pistol if the mule refused to listen to reason.[40]

During the initial landing into the Indaw area, some gliders overshot the path and crashed. According to Masters, a dozen men struggled through the bamboo to reach the crashed glider, which had somersaulted and landed on its back. The soldiers "hacked through the fuselage. A British private climbed out, said 'Fuck,' without emphasis, and turned to help" get the other men out. "One by one five other soldiers and an officer followed, each making the same comment. Finally we dragged out two mules. Being devocalized, they could not say anything, but one of them tried to bite me in the arm, and I don't blame him."[41]

Veterinarians perfected a technique to excise the vocal cords of all the mules for the Chindits. During the long-range penetration of 1943, Brig. W. D. A. Lentaigne noted that the neighing of ponies and braying of mules, which carried for great distances on still days or nights, advertised to the Japanese the presence of troops who might otherwise have been relatively safe from discovery in jungle country. He asked the chief veterinarian in India if an operation could be devised for devoicing mules. A number of experiments were carried out, and a procedure was found to accomplish the operation under a general anesthetic. Of a total of 5,563 Chindit and reserve (remount) animals subjected to the operation, 43 died. A small number regained some voice, but one contended that "if a mule remained mute for six weeks after the operation it was permanently incapable of making a noise." Ten days after the operation, mules could be exercised and were capable of carrying full loads as soon as their wounds healed. The primary postoperative concern was the infestation of operation wounds by maggots, but spraying the incision with antifly solution usually controlled this problem.

Even devocalized mules had a sound all their own. According to Terence O'Brien, a member of the Chindits of 1944, a ghost of a voice remained. Although no longer having vocal cords to vibrate, mules could still force air through the vocal chamber. They made a "voice like the gasping of a water starved tap going on and on with decreasing pressure until ending at last with a prolonged rasping sigh."[42]

At about the same time, the provisional air command was also transporting mules for another operation that had the code name of Galahad. The American army had organized long-range penetration groups modeled on those of the British for special missions with Wingate's force in Burma. The 5307th U.S. Provisional Regiment, better known as Merrill's Marauders after its commander, Brig. Gen. Frank Merrill, was made up of three battalions of volunteers. According to a memorandum sent from Gen. George C. Marshall, chief of staff, to Stilwell, 950 of the volunteers would be troops who had fought in the jungle in the South and Southwest Pacific. The rest would come from jungle-trained troops from the Caribbean Defense Command and the continental United States. All needed to be intensively trained for jungle warfare as well as animal transportation and air supply.[43]

The Marauders, at first organized to serve with Wingate's command, found themselves serving under the command of Gen. Joseph "Vinegar Joe" Stilwell, in charge of American forces in the CBI theater. Stilwell, not enamored with Wingate's Chindits, had exclaimed previously that President Roosevelt had been influenced too much by British Prime Minister Winston Churchill. "The Limeys," he complained, "have his head while we have the hind tit. Events are crowding us into ill-advised and ill-considered projects." This opinion concerning large-scale guerrilla battalions was shared by several high-ranking officers and would not benefit the Marauders or their animals. Stilwell's attitude, however, did not extend to the use of mules. He knew that mules receiving forage by air could play a vital role in packing supplies and ammunition in Burma's jungles and mountains. His respect for mules was expressed in one of the many colorful statements attributed to him. "Mules are dependable and steady while horses are all prance, fart, and no sense."[44]

The Marauders' mules would not be "debrayed." As second in command, Col. Charles Hunter proclaimed, "I opposed the move, for about the only joy in life [mules] have is to bray." Hunter thought this statement could also apply to many high-ranking army officers. Anyway, Hunter could not remember a Marauder mule braying during the campaign. That was an exercise, he declared, indulged in by animals having nothing else to do. "We managed to keep our [mules] to tired to bray."[45]

As part of an offensive to capture Myitkyina in the overall building of a supply bridge to China and the linking of the Ledo and Burma roads, the Marauders did not receive adequate training or enough mules. Only one in twenty of them were experienced with animals or packing, and they received only 360 of the 700 mules they had been promised. The other 340 mules had been on a ship torpedoed in the Arabian Sea, and it sank with no mule survivors.

They were replaced with Australian horses—the same animals that had been so ineffective for Colonel Demuth at New Caledonia and which had recently served the Chinese army in India at Ramgarh. Many of the men and the 360 "big, handsome, intimidating brutes from home" reached Ledo just in time for the mission and received no extra training in jungle warfare. There was no time for conditioning marches to adjust cargo saddles on the mules' backs. One of the members of the Marauders later wrote that "it [was] doubtful if more than one in twenty of us had ever touched a mule or considered that his life lacked fulfillment on that account. Nevertheless, a leader had to be provided for every animal, and the 160 men of the two pack troops assigned to us did not stretch very far. . . . Outside the warehouse tents emergency instruction in saddling and loading was being given to men who visibly did not know what had struck them." Here and there, the soldier continued, "with all the self-assurance of 14-year-olds escorting their partners for the first time across the floor of a dancing school," soldiers led mules to water or to picket lines. "Elsewhere, helpless, skill-less, exasperated infantrymen were trying to saddle or ride horses that required breaking in all over again after their retrogression at Ramgarh."[46]

On 7 February 1944 the Marauders crossed into northern Burma. Instead of transporting his men and mules by truck eighty miles down the partially completed Ledo Road, Merrill chose to march them from Ledo as an opportunity to season them. A commander who understood mules and packing would have foregone the seasoning march. Unadjusted packsaddles caused many mules to develop sores and sore backs. With few experienced muleteers to protect the animals, their condition progressed from bad to worse. Merrill learned from the initial disaster. Later he wrote that he would rather have mule packers than infantrymen, for it was easier to make packers into infantrymen than infantrymen into packers.

From February to June the Marauders and their animals experienced more than their share of hardships. Of the almost 3,000 men who entered Burma, only 1,310 remained to see the Japanese lose control of the Myitkyina airport. Yet they cut to pieces a large part of the Japanese Eighteenth Division in the Hukawng Valley. Of the 1,310 remaining, 679 had already been evacuated to hospitals to recover from their injuries. A new group of Marauders flown to Burma from Calcutta reinforced the battle-weary survivors in the final capture of the airport at Myitkyina. By that time, 3 August, only 200 of the original men remained in the area. None of the horses was alive 1 June, and of the few mules remaining, 41 were turned over to the Chinese and later retrieved for use by the Mars Task Force.[47]

In 1945 a *Yank* magazine correspondent told the following hypothetical story about a volunteer Marauder mule handler and his mule. It seems that the Marauder's mule balked at the bottom of every rugged Burma hill. The handler had to "coax, cajole, cuss, and tug at his mule constantly. Finally, on one hill the mule stopped dead and lay down. That was the last straw. 'Get up, you sonuvabitch,' cracked the driver, who had answered President Roosevelt's call to join the volunteer Marauders. 'You volunteered for this mission, too.' "[48]

The other American long-range penetration unit to serve in Burma, the 5332d Provisional Brigade, faced the same difficult conditions and even more mountainous topography in Burma than the Chindits or the Marauders. It was ordered to circle around and assault Japanese-held positions and to protect large portions of the Stilwell (Ledo-Burma) Road. The unit's campaign required constant struggles over steep Burma hills, slick and narrow mountain trails, through forced marches, and over river crossings just to get into position to attack the enemy. To complete its task, the 5332d, better known as the Mars Task Force, required a large number of mules supplied with forage and other needed materials by air drop. Six or seven mules were needed to carry each 1,300-pound 75 mm mortar with eight other mules supplying the shells needed to dislodge the Japanese from fortified positions. Troop pack companies split up to keep the soldiers furnished with rations, small arms ammunition, and medical supplies.

Luckily the men of the 124th dismounted Cavalry and of the 475th Infantry regiments, which were the two largest groups comprising the LRPU, could depend on two excellent mule field artillery battalions and six quartermaster packmule companies. The men and mules of these outfits had all received extensive state-side training. The 612th and 613th Field Artillery had been trained at Fort Gruber in Muskogee, Oklahoma, while the 31st, 33d, 35th,

37th, 252d, and 253rd Quartermaster Pack Troops had received training at Camp Carson, Colorado.

Some of the men of the artillery battalions told of their adventures training for Mars Task Force. Randy Colvin, who had survived his basic training at Fort Bragg, North Carolina, and received instruction for a motorized vehicle with a 105 mm gun, could not walk under a bar five-feet-and-ten-inches high without ducking and so was sent to Fort Gruber along with several other of his taller colleagues.

When the men from Fort Bragg arrived, they naturally asked where the vehicles were. A corporal, who no doubt had been asked the question many times, laughed and replied, "You soBs have seen your last trucks. You're in the mule pack." The men, noted Colvin, asked, "What the hell is a mule pack?" They soon discovered what their new duties entailed. A few days later they went to the railroad dock to pick up their untrained mules that had never been "led, penned, halter shank[ed], or anything." Their first experience with these beasts had mules running loose all over Fort Bragg country. Colvin remembered that four pack battalions were being trained at that time, each with 350 first-rate Missouri mules.[49]

Lt. Maurice Ryan, thinking he was "tough," attempted to sign up for an airborne division out of Officers Candidate School. An officer had told him that there were no vacancies but that he should sign up for Pack Artillery. "It's the same thing almost, and when a vacancy occurs," stated the glib-talking officer, Ryan could transfer to Airborne. "Once I got that mule on that nameplate," said Ryan, "I couldn't have got out to save my soul. And of course I was almost a natural for it. I was pretty husky at the time and pretty tough and also I was a farm boy that knew mules and I was an Animal Husbandry graduate with a degree so I was a natural for what it was." Ryan noted that when his men first attempted to lead their new mules, most lost them. "We had mules all over the Cookstone Hills," he said. "We hunted mules for a week," and still the men could not get the mules to be led around the post. In time and with patience, however, both men and mules learned to cooperate.[50]

Mules and men were transported by ship to India. Most of the mules embarked at New Orleans under the direction of a port veterinarian, Andy Crawford, while most of the men of the 612th and

613th shipped from California. Camp Placuche, near New Orleans, maintained a remount depot for the departing animals. W. B. "Woody" Woodruff Jr., who served with the 612th, remembered that mule trains kept coming in there day after day, and before the battalion's mules left for India there were about four thousand mules at the remount depot. Woodruff was one of the battalion members who accompanied the mules on the converted *Liberty* ship. "I personally stayed with 'em from there on," he noted. "There wasn't a time from there until the campaign in Burma was over that I wasn't with the mules every day."[51]

Life aboard the mule ships for men and animals followed a fairly established routine. Each ship, equipped to carry 320 to 400 mules, contained five stable areas, which were maintained by sixty men, including one or two officers, a first sergeant, and a veterinarian or two. Woodruff remembered a lot of daily ladder climbing to feed and water the mules on the lower decks and to carry up manure. They stacked the manure on the aft part of the ship and a detail shoveled it over the side after dark to avoid submarines discovering it. If the wind "was just right, most of it would blow right back in your face and a shower was mandatory immediately following that detail." When they were in rough seas for a while, Woodruff observed, "I swear those mules were seasick, just like the men were—they sure looked it. They'd spread those legs out and brace themselves against the side of the stall and hang their head down, and they sure looked miserable."[52]

Actually, ship life proved beneficial for some of the mules. When the 612th and 613th Field Artillery men met up with their mules at Fort Landis, which was near the Myitkyina airport, they discovered them in better condition than when they had left them. Mules from a remount station pasture in the United States were almost certain to have parasites. Most of them probably had strongyles (blood worms). Since the parasites needed time in the pastures to complete their life-cycles, confined mules who could not graze in the pastures began to show decreasing numbers of strongyle egg count. Having fewer parasites and some rest, the mules' health improved. Those in the Mars Task Force were in better condition for hard work than either the Chindits' or Marauders' mules.[53]

An enormous number of mules were assembled and used during the Burma campaigns. Most of the mules used by the Marsmen were sent to Ledo by train and then herded along the Ledo Road to Myitkyina. In commenting on the large number of American mules, a Marsmen claimed, "They did get over there with a lot of mules. They had a Remount station set up . . . from Calcutta quite a ways. I did have a chance to go up there and they must have had 40 acres . . . maybe it was more. And they had all these mules shipped in there, and they had them in these pens. It was like looking at a giant stockyards. Mules from the states . . . big mules . . . farm mules . . . beautiful mules. And, as you looked down at these mules . . . [it was] just like looking at a big stockyard full of cattle, and these were all mules . . . thousands of them."[54]

The Marsmen followed the same general procedures as other mule units. They led artillery mules and wherever possible herded pack mules using bell mares. Lt. Dan L. Thrapp, a quartermaster with the Marsmen, stated what other military men had observed during previous wars, how well mules performed. "There [were] tricks to leading the mules . . . and it sometimes seemed that we might have [had] better luck if the animals had led the men. The average mule," Thrapp observed, "is one of the most intelligent and surely one of the most sure-footed animals in the world." The mule, if left to his own devices, will "never stumble, rarely slip or bog himself down, and almost never hurts himself." When the mule is led by a soldier, however, he "can perhaps get into more trouble than any other creature on the face of the globe." Although the difficulty was caused by the handler, the mule was always blamed.[55]

Eventually, even the most surefooted mules could be overworked and become accident prone. The Thirty-fifth Pack Company lost seventeen mules in one day over the side of a mountain. Some were recovered but others broke their necks or could not be found. On occasion at night "one could hear an animal roll and stop and roll some more for minutes down the mountainside." Thrapp noted that "the softly muted curses of the GIs who scrambled down through the pitch darkness after lost mules were eloquent and, on a more pleasant occasion, would have been a delight to hear." If the Marsmen had been able to keep the animals properly shod and fed, they could have used them even more effectively. As it was, the

Marsmen's mules were kept in better shape than those of any other fighting group in Burma. The task force lost less than 10 percent of its mules and to some degree this showed how well the Marsmen treated their animals.[56]

With the exception of having to overload and overwork their mules on too many occasions, the Marsmen lost animals mainly through Japanese artillery and mortar bombardments. On 20 January the Japanese, relying on mortars and direct assault, tried to drive the Second Battalion of the 475th from its position. The Second suffered only light casualties, but the mules were hard hit. The Second had been forced to protect its mules by placing them in a narrow gulch too close to their perimeter, and the Japanese bombardment killed twenty-one of them. "Picket lines were snapped by mortar shells," Thrapp explained, and occasionally "we could see animals going down, or sometimes we could hear heavily wounded mules staggering and falling into abandoned foxholes." The next day someone posted a sign naming the draw "Dead Mule Gulch."[57]

The Marsmen, as Marauders and Chindits before them, tried to protect the animals whenever possible. They kept the picket lines as far away from camp as was feasible, and mules were kept out of the immediate area of the artillery they carried after it went into operation. During a fire fight or a bombardment, the men could not easily protect loaded mules. They knew that they and their mules together were a team and that they needed to protect the animals they depended on so heavily. Thrapp related that when he and his men went into their first combat after a month's march, the company had lost but two mules, one from heat exhaustion and the "other from an unknown cause. The rest of the animals were in better shape than they were the morning we left Myitkyina."[58]

Throughout the long-range penetrations, the Marsmen, Marauders, and Chindits all had common or similar experiences with their mules and talked about similar characteristics among them. The most-mentioned subject with good reason concerned mules and water. The topography of Burma meant that they had to lure their mules across rivers and streams. "They can be diabolical," one British soldier complained, "especially if asked to swim a river." Another noted that anyone who thought a mule on land was balky "should try launching one across a 100-yard-wide river." Mules, still another noted, "just don't see any sense in swimming for a bank they can't see when there is a perfectly good bank behind them." Unless specifically trained to the water, mules must be convinced that they need to swim. then, stated Lt. Maurice Ryan of the Mars Task Force, men saw that mules "were magnificent swimmers. They can just practically swim forever." During the 1944 Chindit penetration, for example, soldiers of the Fourth Prince of Wales Gurkha Rifles attempted to swim their 240 lend-leased mules across a mile-wide stretch of the Irrawaddy River while they crossed in assault boats powered by outboard motors. Only one mule from Missouri—Maggy—enjoyed swimming, and she crossed the river three times that day. The other mules mutinied. Finally the boats dragged the mules across the river. According to Masters of the British 111th Brigade, "Close astern our two mules rode high in the water, their great hoofs flailing just behind the flimsy craft, their mouths set in a wide snarl, showing their yellow teeth. If we stopped they would try to come inboard. They would trample us under and eat us. They looked like dragons, water dragons. . . . I was glad to step ashore." Brig. Bernard E. Fergusson of the Sixteenth Brigade recounted that a column's dog, Judy, trained in message carrying, took a great interest in attempts to force mules across rivers. She would ride on the boat and "whenever she saw a mule trying to turn back to the shore or seize control, she would leap into the water and swim beside [the mule's] head to turn it in the right direction." It became so difficult crossing the Irrawaddy that the Marsmen constructed a little GI ferry, tugged by six boats with outboard motors, which could transfer a dozen mules at a time. "The fleet was swept far downstream at each crossing," wrote Capt. John A. Rand, "and the mules, jammed together aboard the ferry couldn't have been comfortable, but they took the trip placidly, as mules take most things."[59]

The men who depended on mules soon learned that they were fastidious in what they drank and ate. If mules drank the stream water, the men knew it was fairly clean. They never ate or drank too much. As one muleteer stated, "Remember, you don't drink any water from any stream unless the mule drinks first." He also said that sometimes a mule "would stop, look around, smell, then take a few steps off trail and taste of a new kind of foliage. . . . One corporal in the outfit would always eat some of whatever the mule ate." The muleteer claimed he never saw the man sick and knew "that if it ever came to complete survival in the jungle with no rations, then you could make out on whatever the mule[s] chose to eat."[60]

Soldiers also spoke of mules' dislike of elephants. A mule could get used to almost anything, Thrapp humorously noted, but drew the line at an animal that hung down at both ends. "Sensible, not knowing whether an elephant [was] coming or going, the mule [was] inclined to play safe and take off, regardless of load, underbrush, leader, column, or common courtesy." Men kept a close watch on their mules when they heard trumpeting of elephants, which could mean the enemy in the area, since the Japanese used elephants for packing, or a herd of wild elephants. In either case mules were prone to stampede.[61]

Mule handlers mentioned often the respect, admiration, and even love they had for pack and artillery mules. One mule leader on the 1943 Chindit expedition that had been forced to kill its mules for food begged to have three mules spared. "He promised they would give no trouble and swore he could bring them out alive." Wingate denied the request. "With a mournful 'Very good, Sahib' the muleteer padded away to join his animals, who were to be killed the next morning. All night he talked to them, caressed their heads, and prayed in a low monotone. At dawn he vanished into the jungle until it was over. Afterwards he wept for three days." Lieutenant Ryan recalled that when the muleteers joined his "outfit, they hated [the] mules when we got them." By the time the outfit reached Burma, "the best way to get a fight started was for somebody else to hit somebody's mule." Ryan also observed how the mules responded to their handlers. There was one man in the third section, he noted, that only used a halter shank on his mule when he tied him up at the picket line in the evening. "He did so to keep the mule from going to bed with him. . . . He would just follow him wherever he went." One could not imagine what magnificent creatures they are. In the mountains "we'd go up, and they'd go up all day. Now, whether it hurt that mule as bad going down . . . I used to think, God if I ever get to the top of that mountain, going down won't be so bad. But going down is worse because your knees start hurting. Now whether a mule's knees hurt, he can't say." Another

Marsmen in Burma later wrote that the men at first cursed them, hated them, wished they had never seen them. In Burma the mules carried the artillery, ammunition, tents, food, medicine, and transported the wounded under enemy fire. "Soon [the men] were depending upon them, [and] got to love them." They would "cling to their tails up the trails and through the streams, and a few GIs are here today because one stopped a bullet or shrapnel meant for him."[62]

The men in Burma also recognized the mules' vulnerability. They often remarked on how the need for action cost mules' their lives. Sometimes men, either too tired or in too much of a hurry, ferried mules across rivers without unpacking them. And too often mules drowned when they were spooked and fell off the rafts. Mules carrying 350 pounds of supplies or a gun mount did not have much of a chance to swim to safety. During Japanese attacks and mortar and artillery barrages, mules were extremely vulnerable. On mountain slopes, overworked mules slipped off the sides. Some mules remarkably were protected by their packs but many were killed. The deaths of mules in battle or during campaigns was a hazard of war, and men placed their own lives above those of their animals. That could be justified. But what happened to some of the surviving animals after the war in China was much harder to justify.

Between 26 May and 26 July, a group of 240 men commanded by John Rand herded nine hundred mules from Myitkyina, Burma, to Kunming, China, a distance of 750 miles. Following portions of the Stilwell Road and the Cheeve's highway cutoff, Rand's detachment led three serials (groups) of mules spaced out a day apart to put less strain on grazing spots, water holes, and ferries. The trip was rather routine in that there were no Japanese left lurking in the area, and it was taken at a fairly leisurely pace, especially after some of the mules began to tire and lag behind. Five mules totally gave out and were shot. During the entire trip, the first serial lost twenty-seven mules. Rand described his herd as being "beasts of burden for a long time. . . . [T]hey accepted calmly whatever happened to them." The mules were hitched in "files of four or five on lead ropes, and if one stopped suddenly to avoid a washout or to nip at some grass, the soggy rope that linked his group might break." If that happened, Rand reported, "we let any mules who got loose run free for the rest of the day." Continuous rain for weeks during the Burma portion dampened an otherwise routine, even enjoyable trip. "During the day, the mules slid about in the mud . . . and at night they stood in the rain with their backs arched and their hindquarters to the wind."[63]

Arriving in Kunming, the herders did not turn the animals over to the Chinese army but rather to the Field Artillery Training Command center. Rand's herders became a part of the FATC and continued to take care of the mules. At the end of the war the mules still had not been turned over to the Chinese army. Mules quickly became a glut on the market. The American mule men were now interested in getting home as soon as possible yet still retained an interest in the welfare of their mules.

Even before the end of the war, they began to notice that a small percentage of the mules in all sections had begun to lose weight and were becoming listless. Army veterinarians diagnosed the mules' conditions as surra, "a vector borne protozoan disease indigenous to the CBI and other areas of heavy mosquito and horsefly populations." Also known as equine infectious anemia, or swamp fever, the disease also affected a very small percentage of horses and mules in the United States. There was no known cure for the disease or effective vaccination against it. In Burma, veterinarians' standard treatment consisted of firing a .45 automatic pistol into the infected animals' skulls. That an epidemic would break out among the nine hundred mules in China and spread to the native mules was very remote. The disease is transmitted not by the mules themselves but by biting insects. The nine hundred and the Chinese mules, in fact, had developed some immunity to surra. On 20 August 1945, nevertheless, the chief veterinarian ordered that the uninfected mules in the first serials be immediately turned over to the Chinese and that all the mules in the second and third serials, more than six hundred mules, be killed. The men of Rand's unit were ordered to do the killing, and they did so in September.[64]

These evidently were not the only mules in China disposed of in the same way. C-47s had flown more than nine thousand mules from India and Burma to China. The Chinese and Stilwell's American forces used most of these animals. What happened to them after the war is a matter of speculation. The mules herded by Rand's soldiers deserved a better fate than to be summarily killed. Evidently, some high-ranking officer without knowledge of army pack mules and artillery mules said that no mules would be sent to the coast and shipped back to the United States or anywhere else. The logistics involved would be too great. Now that the war was over the Chinese had no pressing need for the animals, and the Americans who were concerned over their mules did not want to turn them over to the Chinese, which made the officer's decision rather easy. He instructed the veterinarian to give the order. Perhaps that seemed the only humane thing to do.

Rand agreed with the veterinarian's decision to kill the uninfected as well as mules with surra. "I knew what they were thinking, though, and I concurred when they passed a death sentence. . . . I wasn't sorry, really," noted Rand, "and, as far as I could tell, neither were my colleagues, in spite of the pains we had taken to bring the mules through. Most of us were now convinced that, well or ill, our mules were not made for Chinese life. Forcing them to fit into it . . . might be worse for them than a humane death."[65]

Some of the men with Rand's detachment agreed with their captain's assessment. They stated that the Chinese would not be able feed them properly and would mistreat and overwork them. Of course during the war these mules had been overworked and underfed by some of the very men who were now ordered to kill them. The men claimed, however, that they had never intentionally mistreated them and that they were genuinely upset to see their animals killed. As Lyman Gueck, one of the men who had come from Burma to China with the first serial, exclaimed, "The mules were shot and bulldozed over. What an ending!"[66]

CHAPTER 9

Conclusion: The Unwanted Army Mules

At the conclusion of World War II, army quartermasters in Europe disposed of both American mules and mules captured from the Germans. The general order of the day seemed to emphasize that no American mules would be shipped home, for the army had plenty of them in the states. The Italian pack companies kept all their mules, and American quartermasters gave Italians some of the large American "tube" mules to carry the heaviest part of the 75 mm artillery mortar. The quartermasters saved some of the mules that were in excellent condition for possible use in the CBI theater, but no mules were ever shipped home, and instead they handed them over to the Italians as well or sent them to Greece after the war in the Pacific ended. The Italians received approximately two thousand additional American mules and mules captured from the Germans, and American quartermasters sent another twenty-five hundred of them to Greece. The British army asked for mules instead of cash to replace the mules it had supplied for American troops in North Africa, and they received twelve hundred head of a mixture of German and American mules. In addition, some of the captured animals were slaughtered to feed POWs and hungry civilians.[1]

The American officer in charge of the captured horses and mules was not impressed with the type of mule used by the German army. "Well, he was a big mule and oftentimes would be tall," noted Capt. Donald J. Willems. The remount officer never saw a captured German mule he considered good looking. The animals "were just rough and big . . . rough lookin' mules, big feet, big boned . . . something that looked like they come out of a real big, coarse cull mare."[2]

Mules had proved themselves indispensable during World War II as they had done in previous wars. In the European and Asian theaters they had been instrumental in making the GI's conditions more tolerable and in actually saving lives as they packed medical supplies, ammunition, and food to the soldiers in forward areas. Yet in 1946 the army had retained only two animal outfits, the Fourth Field Artillery Battalion and the Thirty-fifth Quartermaster Pack Company, at Fort Carson, Colorado, for training purposes and to insure a means of expansion in case of need; it had discontinued the horse cavalry. In effect, the army high command had not appreciated enough the value of mules in combat during World War II and was repeating the mistakes of the 1920s and 1930s by almost eliminating the mule outfits entirely. It took time and effort to train mule men effectively. When pack-mule artillery and pack companies were needed during the police action in Korea, only two training units were immediately available. Evidently the army planners incorrectly believed that helicopters would take over the duties of pack mules.

In one respect the army did show a sign of progressivism where mules were concerned. It continued to investigate all aspects of transporting mules by air. During the war thousands of mules had been transported by air to Burma and China. Mules had received forage in Europe and Asia by direct airplane drops, making them more effective than ever before. The combinations of mules and planes in support of ground troops had been a logical progression in the use of mules in warfare. At the conclusion of the war the army sanctioned feasibility studies and actual experiments in transporting entire pack units by air to support ground transportation. On 3 May 1947 the Army Ground Forces Board at Fort Bragg, North Carolina, issued the Report of Study of Project No. AB-3246, *Air Transport of Animals and Equipment.*[3]

During 1946 mules and horses had been loaded into aircraft and gliders, and peacetime army personnel had perfected what others had already proven possible during the war—that when time was a critical factor, when other means of transportation were limited, and when the terrain was mountainous or swampy, aircraft could effectively transport animals safely and efficiently. The study had an interesting composite description of mules and horses placed in the various aircraft. For the transportation of mules, personnel assumed that each animal would weigh approximately one thousand pounds; its height at the poll would be seventy-five inches and at the withers sixty-five inches; its width at the ribs would be twenty-six inches, and its length from nose to tail ninety-three inches. They realized that the described mule was too tall and that most mules would be at least two inches shorter. In comparison, a horse transported by air would weigh a thousand pounds; its height would be seventy-seven inches at the poll and sixty-five inches at the withers, its width at the ribs twenty-six inches, and its length from nose to tail ninety-eight inches. Most horses would not be that out of proportion and would measure no more than ninety-seven inches long. The personnel also assumed that the weights of both animals were based on their being used daily and would factor in their existence under field conditions. Animals stabled in garrisons, they realized, would weigh more.

It was also discovered that better methods were needed to protect animals from injury aboard aircraft. One recommendation that the board approved was to provide each mule with a Shetlin animal harness and to use the Carlin tie-down device to immobilize the animals in the aircraft. These improvements over jury-rigged ropes and mule halters used during the war were named for Lt. Col. Charles G. Shettle and M.Sgt. Edward L. Carlin, the men of the Airborne Service Test Section who had designed the devices.[4]

One of the most interesting portions of the Fort Bragg report was the study of the effects of high altitude on horses and mules. Certain reports from the war indicated that animals were seriously affected by altitudes from twelve thousand to eighteen thousand feet. On 15 November 1946 three healthy mules were placed aboard a C-82 and flown at high altitudes for one hour and thirty minutes. Lt. Col. W. Smit, Veterinary Corps, accompanied the animals and reported that while climbing to twelve thousand feet, two of the animals shifted about and leaned into their stabilizing harnesses. The third mule was quiet and composed, but it was the first to show effects from a lack of oxygen later on. Between altitudes of thirteen thousand and fourteen thousand feet the animals periodically shook their heads to equalize air pressure on each side of the ear drums. Between fifteen thousand and sixteen thousand feet two of the animals yawned a few times. "All of the animals were breathing at an accelerated rate at 16,000 feet of about 60 per minute. Normal rate for horses and mules at rest on the ground is 8–16 per minute." The third mule began to show symptoms of distress. "The mucous membranes of the mouth and eyes were bluish gray." The other two mules still maintained a normal coloration of the mucous membranes. Smit observed the third mule closely at seventeen thousand and eighteen thousand feet. "Its mucous membranes indicated cyanosis was progressively pronounced." The mule began to sweat profusely at the base of the ears, and it seemed to be in a slight stupor. At eighteen thousand feet the other two mules were breathing rapidly but still seemed alert. Smit concluded that the third mule had gone as high as it could be taken safely "without the effects of asphyxiation becoming pronounced." When the C-82 descended to twelve thousand feet, all three mules became "normal in all respects." The veterinarian concluded that oxygen equipment would be necessary for animals flown for long periods at high altitudes. Pilots had reached that same conclusion, however, when they flew animals over the hump during the war.[5]

The report confirmed that all three aircraft used in the study were suitable for transporting mules but that the C-47 Dakota had limitations. The Army Air Corps's "flying mule" during World War II did not have the characteristics needed for efficient loading and transportation of the large pack animals the army used. Its ramp needed heavy modification, and the steepness of the loading ramp and the plane's floor made mules reluctant to load. The C-47's main drawback, however, was its size; it could safely hold only four mules.

Although the C-46 aircraft could carry twice the number of mules as the Dakota, it too had limitations. The height of the door sill above the ground was ninety-six inches. That height made it necessary to tilt the loading ramps to incline too steeply, which made it difficult for shod mules to retain footing while entering the plane.

The largest plane used in the experiment, the C-82, was the best equipped to transport mules. A maximum of nine mules, or a combination of fewer mules and more personnel and equipment, could be loaded. Still it required thirty-five c-82s to transport a complete Quartermaster Pack Troop while the army needed only sixty-seven of the same aircraft to transport a complete field artillery battalion, 75 mm pack howitzer. The number of planes needed for mule outfits ultimately would limit availability. Mules would have to be determined high-priority to receive a fraction of the necessary planes from supply officers.

The cg-4a and cg-15a gliders did not receive favorable consideration in the report. The cargo compartment of both varies from sixty-six to sixty inches from the front to the rear door. Since the average overall height of a mule was sixty-five inches, it would be difficult to load one without the danger of damage to the glider. Personnel determined that if it became necessary under field conditions to transport mules in gliders, two methods appeared to be feasible. The first would be to use smaller mules, and the second was to drug the animal, tie him down on his side to a pallet, and then load the pallet. But this method could not be used if the animals were needed for use immediately after landing.[6]

The army also briefly considered parachuting mules to ground artillery and pack commands to replace animals injured or killed in combat. During 1942, in fact, unsuccessful experiments in parachuting mules from planes had been attempted. Six mules were dropped in slings attached to parachutes. They all died. The slings caused too much of a jerk when the chutes opened and severed the mesentery artery (large artery that comes down the backbone) that feeds blood to the intestines. According to one of the participants, Joe Sanford, another six mules survived because the men could not push them out of the plane. During 1945 the British found a cumbersome but fairly safe procedure for parachuting mules from c-47s. The nine-hundred-pound young mules were packaged in 6½-by-4-foot crates with air bags to protect them from the jerk of the chutes. The British procedure took time and effort—almost an hour—to box the animals for flight, and several minutes to unpack them on the ground. Whether or not it would have worked in combat was only speculative since the war ended before any animals were dropped into combat zones. In 1946 the U.S. Army briefly experimented with parachuting a mule. The mule was sedated, strapped to a padded pallet, and pushed out of a c-47 at twenty-five hundred feet on a standard deployment static line. The mule did fine after the effects of the drug wore off.[7]

U.S. Army advisers became well acquainted with Greek- and American-bred mules during the Greek civil war. At the conclusion of World War II, the army sent twenty-five hundred mules that had been used in Italy to Greece. At home it transferred ten thousand surplus mules at remount depots to the Department of Agriculture. And between July 1948 and December 1949, agricultural officials sent mules to Greece to accompany American military advisers. Some of these mules, however, ended up in the hands of indigenous guerrillas in Greece. The topography and the availability of large numbers of European- and American-bred animals gave mules once again another bloody stage on which to perform. The Greek government's military used pack and artillery mules to supply its forces in pursuit of guerrilla units, while the guerrillas relied heavily on them to transport weapons and ammunition from Yugoslavia and eastern European countries controlled by the Soviet Union.

The mules performed well for both sides. It amazed the Greeks and Americans how quickly the mules acclimated to the high altitudes of Greece's mountain ranges. Government forces and American advisers used mules essentially like they were used in Europe during the war. When trucks and jeeps could no longer handle the mountainous terrain, mules packed in the supplies and artillery. They were also attached to the mechanized field artillery units to insure adequate transportation at all times under all conditions. To keep their small forces fighting, the guerrillas employed between seven hundred and fourteen hundred mules daily (mainly at night) over a distance of 120 miles. Despite mule trains being regularly strafed by Greek army fighters or attacked by ground forces, the animal trains continued. Without the trains' daily operation the guerrillas would have been unable to continue the struggle as long as they did.[8]

The civil war in Greece again proved that conventional army and guerrilla forces needed mules to operate in mountainous terrain at peak efficiency. Yet the U.S. Army sent no mules to Korea. Woody Woodruff, "an ex-muleskinner," reported that he saw "splendid opportunities to use mules to carry supplies up those steep mountain trails" and thought that a "relatively few men on riding mules herding large herds" of pack mules "with the use of a bell mare" could transport an "awful lot" of supplies. "And of course if you don't have the mules," Woodruff noted, "it means that you've got to man pack all of those things."[9]

American forces, nevertheless, used mules and other pack animals during the police action whenever possible. All mules captured from the North Koreans and Chinese were prized possessions by the men who had liberated them. Soldiers refused to volunteer information as to where captured animals were located, or in what numbers, for fear that some might be taken by another outfit. In March 1951 a machine gun unit of the Wolfhound Regiment operated north of Kumyanjumg Ni using thirty-three captured mules. In the mountain sector north of Seoul and as far as the Imjin River mules packed in barbed wire, steel stakes, mines, and other equipment. On the drive north from Seoul, the Seventh Regiment, First Cavalry Division moved its valuable captured animals in QMC six-by-six trucks, no doubt with the canvas closed to conceal the valuable cargo. Not only was the regiment using mules, it was also using Mongolian ponies. One of the mules used by the First Cavalry was a U.S. Army mule with Preston Brand 08KO. It was virtually a soldier of fortune, having served in the CBI theater during World War II, and it was later transferred to the Chinese army. It could have been one of the lucky animals with Rand's first serial that reached China from Burma.[10]

Fewer than four years after United Nations' ground forces left Korea, the question of U.S. forces using American army mules was a dead issue, for the army deactivated the mule outfits and sold the animals. Yet the high command had not completely abandoned the idea of using pack animals. It recognized that in the future U.S. special or regular army troops might have to become involved in counterinsurgency and counterguerrilla operations, and perhaps even limited wars in unsophisticated regions of the world that lacked adequate modern transportation routes and were known to have difficult terrain. Historically, pack animals, especially mules, had accompanied American troops during every conflict in which they had been involved. To cover a multitude of contingencies, and with

Korea as an actual example, the high command sanctioned studies on pack transportation.

In 1959–60 Col. Richard F. Krueger, a U.S. Army military adviser in South Vietnam, was placed in charge of supplying troops in the dense jungle-covered highlands of that country, and he experimented with using pack animals. With no mules available he used small Asian horses and old French-made packsaddles. Krueger claimed that the packtrains were used only on training maneuvers, but pack transportation would have been effective "if it only had been given a chance to prove itself." Actually, special forces had used pack animals rather extensively and effectively for patrol operations in the wooded plains and highlands of Central Vietnam since 1958.[11]

The studies on using indigenous animals to pack supplies were given a high priority in 1961 when President John F. Kennedy showed a special interest in unconventional warfare; the special warfare forces expanded sharply from fifteen hundred to nine thousand men in a year and continued to grow. By 1965, position papers and manuals appeared at many army posts. *Research Notes to the Utility of Horse Cavalry and Pack Animals in Counterinsurgency Operations in the Latin American Environment* was such a manual. Written by Hartley F. Dane, Curtis Brooks, and Curtin Winsor Jr., the manual was published in May 1965 by the Counterinsurgency Information Analysis Center of the American University in Washington DC. The authors presented a twentieth-century historical survey of the use of animals in warfare, solicited professional opinions from military officers, and included all types of maps and related materials. The conclusions were obvious: forces in army units using animals for off-road mobility would necessitate similar employment for a counterinsurgent force, and animal transport was preferable when acceptable indigenous animals were available.

In June 1965 the Special Warfare Agency of the Army Combat Development Command at Fort Bragg issued the *Final Draft Study: U.S. Army Requirements for Pack Animals.* In this somewhat remarkable 131-page bound, typed document the authors evaluated army pack animals' transport doctrine and resources, not only to determine the adequacy of the doctrine but also the resources needed to support animal use in conventional and guerrilla warfare and counterinsurgency operations. They analyzed army regulations, publications, and resources to determine voids in all aspects of using pack transportation. One of the eight appendices listed forty countries that still relied to some extent on animals in their armies as of April 1962. Of those, nineteen were using mules. Other appendices included lesson plans in packing taken from the Marine Corps schools at Quantico, Virginia, that had been developed by Kennedy Center so that special warfare instructors could teach sixteen courses on animal management and packing. The course in packing required forty hours of instruction.[12]

The primary conclusions of the study were rather obvious to veteran army officers concerned with transportation. They included such considerations as terrain, weather, and availability that dictated the use of pack animals in limited and general war or in special operations; adequate regulations covering the procurement of pack animals on an "as needed where needed" basis; the need for including instructions in field manuals (FM 25-7) for packing animals in addition to horses and mules; and the need to purchase several animals, including mules, for use in training special forces and military training teams.[13]

The recommendations in the report were logical. One of them was to revamp the army field manual on animal transportation, FM 25-7. U.S. Army developments command should provide new materials for inclusion in FM 25-7 on "care, management, maintenance, equipment, loading, training, handling, methods of evacuation" of wounded soldiers by pack animals, the training and management of local civilian animal handlers, and the "capabilities and limitations" of donkeys, Asian horses, oxen, water buffalo, yaks, camels, elephants, llamas, dogs, and reindeer. Other manuals as well should contain chapters on land transport resources, including sections on "pack animal resources of the subject areas." Yet another recommendation called for the Kennedy Center for Special Warfare to offer courses on caring for and packing animals, a course that was already being planned for conventional as well as special forces, while still another requested that the Army Combat Developments Command Combat Services Support Group prepare a study on "forage, forage logistics, and resupply problems for pack animals" in several types of operations. The last recommendation asked for the Army Combat Developments Command to "assess the requirement for further study on pack animals employment for all forms and levels of warfare."[14]

Although this document was meant to analyze official doctrine and make it possible for units to use indigenous animals when needed for packing purposes, its authors readily acknowledged that the mule was the preferred pack animal. They repeated all of the mule's positive attributes and emphasized that it would "provide the best pack transport in almost every climate and type of terrain." Using such true accolades, which were copied from the 1933 British Veterinary Service manual, *Animal Management*, and being consistent with the need for pack transportation, it seemed reasonable that the army brass would admit a mistake and reinstate at least one or two mule pack troops. If not, it would be reasonable for army personnel to concentrate on learning to pack mules, donkeys, and horses, all of which are considered the prevalent pack animals throughout the world and all of which would employ similar methods of packing.[15]

How often special forces used animals for packing after 1965 or whether there were mules purchased and used by the army at various times is not known. There still existed a need, however, for expertise not only in packing but in understanding the habits of mules. The proposed (but never taught) forty-hour course in packing indigenous animals was a poor substitute for the training in mule packing that recruits had received in the past at Fort Carson, Colorado. Field manuals in pack transportation had not been revised since the 1950s and had been out of print for more than ten years.

On 4 January 1985 Secretary of the Army John O. Marsh sent a memorandum to Chief of Staff John Wickham asking for his views on the use of mules for the reinstituted Tenth Infantry Division and the Vermont National Guard. Marsh noted that mules were still considered to be a highly effective means of moving weapons and supplies in mountain terrain. "Why don't we put a small group of these animals for testing purposes in the Tenth Division?" Marsh asked. "It would be very consistent with the role and image we have in mind for this unit. Please keep a closed hold on this, and I would appreciate your views." The secretary's inquiry sparked an interest in reestablishing four-legged recruits in the army. Parties concerned from throughout the service conferred with one another.[16]

Three days later assistant deputy chief of staff, Maj. Gen. John W. Woodmansee Jr., replied to Marsh. In his memo Woodmansee mentioned several subjects under the heading of "discussion." These included the German army's thirty-day basic muleskinner school, the operational concepts of light infantry permitting but not requiring the use of mules, doctrine still existing for the employment of mules, and the helicopters and rough terrain vehicles that had to a large degree replaced mules. However, mules still had utility when mountainous terrain, bad weather, and the enemy situation precluded resupply and movement by other means. Woodmansee also mentioned that the same problems that existed in World War II "would probably exist today. While maintaining some muleskinner expertise for special terrain requirements would be advisable in our active component, it would require the diversion of resources from higher priority missions." Expertise in the use of mules, he thought, "could best be maintained by a National Guard mountain unit, provided that unit could afford to develop and maintain a full time training program." The Vermont National Guard mountain battalion, however, could not afford to create and maintain a muleskinner program, and both the National Guard Bureau and the Vermont unit concurred. Woodmansee, therefore, recommended at the end of his two-page memo that a "muleskinner unit not be developed for the active duty light infantry division" and that the "National Guard Bureau not be asked to develop, train or maintain a muleskinner unit."[17]

In March, Secretary Marsh, not pleased with the chief of staff's response, told Wickham quietly to establish a group to undertake a serious study of the subject. The month before, Maj. Gen. Johnny J. Johnston, GS and director of training, had sent a memo to Maj. Gen. John J. Yeosock, deputy chief of staff for Operations, Army Forces Command, mentioning the German army's thirty-day course and that Switzerland, Spain, and Italy had "similar mule units oriented toward the internal defense of specific mountain areas." The Austrian Infantry school, Johnston added, taught Hoflinger horse handling as a part of its mountain instruction. Johnston ended his note with the specific request that Army Forces Command "insure Tenth Mountain Division (Lt Inf) has training in mule handling; this could include work overseas with Germans, Swiss, Italians, etc. Also consider whether we should have some number of mules at Ft. Drum for training." He was no doubt ready to institute a mule unit as an indication of support for the secretary of the army. What the ramifications of that political move were are not known.[18]

By now too many players had become involved, and someone or several people had not kept a "closed hold on this"; the subject was leaked, and newspaper reporters had a field day. Tom Wicker's syndicated column, "In The Nation," was probably the most influential and most read account. Appearing in the *New York Times* of 12 April and in newspapers throughout the country on Sunday, 14 April, it was titled "Gee-Haw for the Army," which reflected the article's flippancy. "Not since the adoption of the breech-loading rifle," Wicker wrote, "has anything more sensible been proposed by the U.S. Army than the reinstatement of the mule as a pack animal for the new Light division of mountain infantry. Today's generals, entranced with electronic buzzes and whirrs, have gone head-over-heels into high-tech weaponry beyond the public's ken. But the mule is a low-tech (not to mention low-budgeted) creature; and a spokesman, Lt. Col. Craig McNab, said its proposed rehabilitation had created much good will for the Army." The colonel had said, "People can identify with mules."[19]

Wicker then discussed Mule Day for Columbia, Tennessee, the next Saturday, the possibility of Congress naming 26 October as Mule Appreciation Day, the history of George Washington and the mule, and, of course, he quoted from William Faulkner's *Satoris* about the mule named Homer and stated that the army could use recruits of Homer's caliber. The article was a typical humorous mule piece that poked fun here and there but also pointed out the good attributes of the animals. McNab said that in the absence of qualified mule skinners, the army's Mule Committee had ordered a search for old training manuals to determine "what was doctrine on mules." "How many veterinarians, for instance, might be needed for how many mules?" Wicker wrote. "That question would merely baffle an old-time one-gallus farmer or mule skinner in General Pershing's army. They never knew mules got sick."[20]

When the working group, or as Wicker had called it, the Mule Committee, met on 12 September, the officers had to determine the adequacy of the existing doctrine concerning pack mules. Also under discussion was the level at which a pack transport capability should exist in light infantry divisions and what the implications were concerning the need for veterinarians. Someone in Logistics Command had identified a mule-training capability with the National Park Service, Department of the Interior. The committee members reported that although pack animals had been used successfully in the past, "existing doctrine [had] questionable accuracy" and did not address a "need for pack animal support of light infantry." The John F. Kennedy Special Warfare Command had determined the specific requirements for using pack animals and also stated that the Army Infantry School Command had identified potential use of animals or mules under certain limited conditions forward of brigade support area. "Any use of animals would be for resupply medevac, or lightening the burden of individual soldiers." The committee members maintained that the implications on manpower and materials did not justify a large mule unit and recommended that the mission of the Tenth Mountain Division, Light Infantry not be changed. They also recommended further study to explore the concept addressing total animal requirements in "multiple scenarios" and at all levels of a conflict. For the immediate future, any training in using mules should be limited to "specific needs of individual units based on stated mission requirements and coordinated through allied forces that maintain animal training facilities." Special forces, however, should establish whatever mule units and other animal units that were determined necessary.[21]

As of 12 September, Projects officer 1st Lt. Eve Iversen was ready to conduct further research on establishing pack mules for special forces. She had already received substantial support from the American Museum of Natural History, the Bronx Zoo, the Smithsonian Institute, and the National Archives, and from other museums and government agencies. She had also coordinated with all allied liaison representatives at Training and Doctrine Command (TRADOC) and other headquarters. She had located two retired technical experts who were willing to assist in any way. Her job was now to collect all of the documents concerning pack transportation and examine them at Fort Bragg with the goal of writing a formal report that could be used by special forces. One of the problems the U.S. Army Southern Command identified was logistical in support of the contras of Nicaragua. Distribution of materials was a major problem in other places as well. The staff study of pack-animal transport had indicated that this might be a solution to some of the problems. She would also interview the retired technical experts and anyone with substantial knowledge of mule packing and of the history of American or allied military animal transportation. These tasks kept the lieutenant busy.[22]

Iversen's efforts, as well as those of other officers who knew the worth of mules in the military, came to an end months before a terse AP announcement on 28 July 1986. Mules were wonderful animals, but there were "problems in bringing them back into the Army," Maj. Phil Soucy said in explaining the decision against returning them to active duty. "It wouldn't be worth the investment for the few contingencies in which they could be used."[23]

Many people in and out of the army disagreed, of course. Money at the time was not the issue. President Reagan had told the military establishment early on that "defense is not a budget item. Spend what you need." The president had told the Congress the same thing just four months before the announcement to "stop scrutinizing every paper clip, bolt, and bullet in the military budget." The decision to recall mules into the military would have received less flap than the issues of Star Wars or strengthening the role of the chairman of the Joint Chiefs and creating a post to oversee development and production of weapons. What had been done in reestablishing small mule units in the army had simply been image. The idea of establishing a mule unit in the army during the 1980s would have caused too many to laugh at the notion, especially in an age of advancing technology. No doubt, an old mule man from World War II would question that assumption. "Image be damned," he would state. "We have yet to win a war without mules."

Appendix

Daly's Specifications for Pack and Riding Mules

The mule must be sound in body and limbs, of blocky build, of kind and gentle disposition, with free and springy action at the walk or trot, and to conform to the following description:

The Pack mule must be in fair condition, from 4 to 6 years old; weight, depending upon height to be as follows:

Pack Mules should weigh from 950 to 1,025 pounds, and be from 14.1 hands to 15 hands high.

Head of medium size, well formed, intelligent looking, broad between the eyes; eyes clear, large and full; ears long and flexible; teeth and tongue free of blemishes; muzzle well rounded and firm.

Neck, stocky, broad and full at crest, and inclined to arch.

Wither, low and broad; indicating strength in shoulders.

Chest, low and broad, with division well defined, holding the fore legs well apart, showing good lung power.

Knees, wide in front and free of blemishes.

Back, short and straight, indicating strength in back over region of the kidneys.

Barrel, deep and large, indicating a good feeder—not hard to please in either food or water—a most essential requisite in the selection of pack mules.

Hips, broad and well rounded.

Dock, low and stiff, offering resistance, showing endurance.

Hocks, standing well apart and strongly made, showing well developed buttocks.

Pasterns, muscled, short, and strongly shaped.

Hoofs, sound, broad, full, with frog well developed, elastic, and healthy.

Riding mules will conform to the above conditions, with the exception, they must be deeper from point of withers to brisket.

Notes

1. THE ARMY MULE

1. Anna M. Waller, *Horses and Mules and National Defense*, (Washington DC: Department of the Army, Office of Quartermaster General, 1958), 61–73.

2. "Army's Combat Mules Bow Out at Review," *New York Times*, 16 December 1956, 69; Waller, *Horses and Mules and National Defense*, 71–73.

3. "The Army Mule 1775–1957," *Veterinary Medicine*, 52:200–201.

4. "The Army Mule Retires," *New York Times*, sec. 1, p. 36.

5. Jack Raymond, "Army to Retire Its Combat Mules," *New York Times*, 2 December 1956, 1, 44; "The Army Mule Retires," sec. 1, p. 36.

6. James W. Steele, *Frontier Army Sketches* (1883; reprint, Albuquerque: University of New Mexico Press, 1969), 301–5; Emmett M. Essin, "Mule," in *The Reader's Encyclopedia of the American West*, ed. Howard R. Lamar (New York: Thomas Y. Crowell, 1977), 780; Emmett M. Essin, "Army Mule," *Montana: The Magazine of Western History* 44 (spring 1994): 31.

7. Essin, "Army Mule," 31–32.

8. Essin, "Army Mule," 31–32; W. B. Tegetmier and C. L. Sutherland, *Horses, Asses, Zebras, Mules, and Mule Breeding* (London: Horace Cox, 1895), 116–17.

9. U.S. Army, Office of the Quartermaster General (hereafter OQMG, "Mules," Box 705, Consolidated Correspondence File (hereafter CCF), RG 92, National Archives, Washington DC (hereafter NA).

10. U.S. Army, Office of the Quartermaster General, *Specifications for Horses and Mules* (Washington DC: Government Printing Office, 1917), 7–8.

11. OQMG, *Specifications for Horses and Mules*, 7–8; "Mules," Box 705; Essin, "Army Mule," 36.

12. Henry W. Daly, *Manual of Pack Transportation*, U.S. Army Quartermaster Corps (Washington DC: Government Printing Office, 1917), 165–66.

13. U.S. Army, Office of the Quartermaster General, *Quartermaster Corps: Classification of and Specifications for Public Animals*, "Army Regulations No. 30-440, 18 June 1942," 1–4.

14. "Army Regulations No. 30-440," 1–4; *Public Animals: Horses, Mules, and Dogs*, "Army Regulations No. 880-5," 1 September 1953, 6. These regulations superseded all previous ones such as AR 30-435, AR 30-440, AR 30-450, AR 30-455, AR 30-2290, SB 10-115.

15. Robert Bryon Lamb, *The Mule in Southern Agriculture* (Berkeley: University of California Press, 1963), 17.

16. Lamb, *The Mule in Southern Agriculture*, 17; Tegetmier and Sutherland, *Horses, Asses, Zebras, Mules*, 118–20; Harvey Wiley, *The Mule: A Treatise on the Breeding, Training, and Uses, to Which He May Be Put* (Washington DC: French & Richardson, 1867), 41–45; Lorraine Travis, *The Mule* (London: J. A. Allen, 1990), 86.

17. Erna Risch, *Quartermaster Support for the Army: A History of the Corps, 1775–1939* (Washington DC: Quartermaster Historians Office, Office of the Quartermaster General, 1962), 184–87.

18. Essin, "Army Mule," 42.

19. Essin, "Army Mule," 33.

20. Essin, "Army Mule," 44; Lamb, *The Mule in Southern Agriculture*, 17–18.

21. Essin, "Army Mule," 44–45.

2. ARMY MULE POWER IN FLORIDA AND MEXICO

1. Risch, *Quartermaster Support*, 204–9; Maurice Matloff, ed., *American Military History*, (Washington DC: Office of the Chief of Military History, 1969), 156–57. Although the army did own and operate some wagon trains during the 1820s, it used oxen and horses as draft animals.

2. Risch, *Quartermaster Support*, 232–35; John K. Mahon, *History of the Second Seminole War, 1835–1842* (Gainesville: University of Florida Press, 1967), 325; John T. Sprague, *The Origin, Progress, and Conclusion*

of the Florida War (1848; reprint, Gainesville: University of Florida Press, 1964), 269; Lamb, *The Mule in Southern Agriculture*, 18–19.

3. Risch, *Quartermaster Support*, 230.

4. Mahon, *History of the Second Seminole War*, 321–27; Risch, *Quartermaster Support*, 234–36.

5. Risch, *Quartermaster Support*, 240–42; K. Jack Bauer, *The Mexican War, 1846–1848* (New York: Macmillan, 1974), 18–19.

6. Ulysses S. Grant, *Personal Memoirs of U. S. Grant,* vol. 1 (New York: C. L. Webster, 1885), 69–70.

7. Risch, *Quartermaster Support*, 242–43.

8. Grant, *Personal Memoirs*, 1:80.

9. Grant, *Personal Memoirs*, 1:81–82.

10. Grant, *Personal Memoirs*, 1:82.

11. Col. and Asst. QM Trueman Cross to Maj. Gen. Thomas S. Jesup, 17 February 1846, "Messages from the President of the United States Transmitting the Correspondence with General Taylor Since the Commencement of Hostilities with Mexico, Not Already Published," 29th Cong., 2d sess., H. Doc. 119, p. 345.

12. Essin, "Army Mule," 32; Lloyd Lewis, *Captain Sam Grant* (Boston: Little, Brown, 1950), 132; Cross to Jesup, H. Doc. 119, pp. 346–47.

13. Lewis, *Captain Sam Grant*, 135.

14. Grant, *Personal Memoirs*, 1:88–89.

15. Lewis, *Captain Sam Grant*, 136–37.

16. Bauser, *The Mexican War*, 46–56; Matloff, *American Military History*, 163–65; Grant, *Personal Memoirs*, 1:94–97; James M. McCaffrey, *Army of Manifest Destiny: The American Soldier in the Mexican War, 1846–1848* (New York: New York University Press, 1992), 7–9, 9.

17. Bauer, *The Mexican War*, 59, 62–63; Grant, *Personal Memoirs*, 1:96; Matloff, *American Military History*, 165.

18. Bauer, *The Mexican War*, 81–83; Lewis, *Captain Sam Grant*, 149; McCaffrey, *Army of Manifest Destiny*, 11–13.

19. Bauer, *The Mexican War*, 88.

20. Col. and Asst. QM Henry Whiting to Maj. Gen. Thomas S. Jesup, "Messages of the President of the United States and the Correspondence, Therewith Committed Between the Secretary of War and Other Officers of the Government Upon the Subject of the Mexican War: Mexican War Correspondence," 30th Cong., 1st sess., H. Doc. 60, p. 560.; N. C. Brooks, *A Complete History of the Mexican War: Its Causes, Conduct, and Consequences* (Chicago: Rio Grande Press, 1965), 167–68.

21. George Winston Smith and Charles Judah, eds., *Chronicles of the Grin-*

gos: The U.S. Army in the Mexican War, 1846–1848, Accounts of Eye-witnesses and Combatants (Albuquerque: University of New Mexico Press, 1968), 373.

22. Risch, *Quartermaster Support*, 270–71; Whiting to Jesup, H. Doc. 60, p. 686.

23. Risch, *Quartermaster Support*, 272.

24. U.S. Army, OQMG, "Mule Transportation," Box 704, CCF, RG 92, NA; Whiting to Jesup, H. Doc. 60, 686–88; Bauer, *The Mexican War*, 89; Risch, *Quartermaster Support*, 271.

25. Grant, *Personal Memoirs*, 1:105–6; Lewis, *Captain Sam Grant*, 172.

26. Lewis, *Captain Sam Grant*, 172; S. H. Drum to Gen. Thomas S. Jesup, H. Doc. 60, 737.

27. McCaffrey, *Army of Manifest Destiny*, 132–34.

28. McCaffrey, *Army of Manifest Destiny*, 132–35; Bauer, *The Mexican War*, 90–100; Matloff, *American Military History*, 169–71, 202–4; Lewis, *Captain Sam Grant*, 173–80.

29. Risch, *Quartermaster Support*, 273.

30. Hudson Strobe, *Jefferson Davis: American Patriot 1808–1862* (New York: Harcourt, Brace, 1955), 177.

31. McCaffrey, *Army of Manifest Destiny*, 142.

32. McCaffrey, *Army of Manifest Destiny*, 142–45, 145. Bauer, *The Mexican War*, 204–18; Samuel E. Chamberlain, *My Confession* (New York: Harper, 1956), 114–28.

33. John T. Hughes, *Doniphan's Expedition: Containing an Account of the Conquest of New Mexico* (Cincinnati: U. P. James, 1847), 14–15; Bauer, *The Mexican War*, 130; Risch, *Quartermaster Support*, 279; Dwight L. Clarke, *Stephen Watts Kearny: Soldier of the West*, (Norman: University of Oklahoma Press, 1961), 116–45; Leo E. Oliva, *Soldiers on the Santa Fe Trail* (Norman: University of Oklahoma Press, 1967), 61.

34. William Y. Chalfant, *Dangerous Passage: The Santa Fe Trail and the Mexican War* (Norman: University of Oklahoma Press, 1994), 10–12, 16–20; Hughes, *Doniphan's Expedition*, 18–32, 27; Clarke, *Stephen Watts Kearny*, 117; Marc L. Gardner and Marc Simmons, eds., *The Mexican War Correspondence of Richard Smith Elliott* (Norman: University of Oklahoma Press, in press).

35. Clarke, *Stephen Watts Kearny*, 157–62.

36. Clarke, *Stephen Watts Kearny*, 163, 183–94; Hubert Howe Bancroft, *History of California 1846–1848*, vol. 22 (San Francisco: The History Company, 1886), 337–40.

37. Clarke, *Stephen Watts Kearny*, 202–5, 207–8, 230; Bauer, *The Mexican War*, 186–88.

38. Risch, *Quartermaster Support*, 279; Hughes, *Doniphan's Expedition*, 15–17.

39. Hughes, *Doniphan's Expedition*, 57.

40. Hughes, *Doniphan's Expedition*, 57; Ray Allen Billington, *The Far Western Frontier, 1830–1860* (New York: Harper & Row, 1956), 186; Albert Wislizenus, *Memoir of a Tour to Northern Mexico, Connected with Col. Doniphan's Expedition in 1846 and 1847*. 30th Cong., 1st sess., 1848, S. Doc. 26.

41. Hughes, *Doniphan's Expedition*, 107.

42. Hughes, *Doniphan's Expedition*, 97–134, 115; Hubert Howe Bancroft, *History of Mexico, 1824–1861*, v. 23 (San Francisco: A. L. Bancroft, 1885), 407–8; Maurice G. Fulton, ed., *Diary and Letters of Josiah Gregg*, vol. 2 (Norman: University of Oklahoma Press, 1944), 79–133.

43. Hughes, *Doniphan's Expedition*, 143–44; Oliva, *Soldiers on the Santa Fe Trail*, 79–80.

44. Oliva, *Soldiers on the Santa Fe Trail*, 79–92; Chalfant, *Dangerous Passage*, 165–72, 190–95.

45. Bauer, *The Mexican War*, 232–42; Risch, *Quartermaster Support*, 283–89.

46. Bauer, *The Mexican War*, 244; Philip Syng Physick Conner, *The Home Squadron under Commodore Conner in the War with Mexico, Being a Synopsis of Its Services (With an Addendum Containing Admiral Temple's Memoir of the Landing of Our Army at Vera Cruz in 1847)* (Philadelphia, privately printed, 1896), 63–66.

47. Conner, *The Home Squadron*, 69, 75; Risch, *Quartermaster Support*, 290–91.

48. Gen. Winfield Scott to A. R. Hetzel, captain and assistant quartermaster, H. Doc. 60, 884.

49. Risch, *Quartermaster Support*, 291; Bauer, *The Mexican War*, 259.

50. Milo Milton Quaife, ed., *The Diary of James K. Polk during His Presidency, 1845–1849*, vol. 2 (Chicago: A. C. McClurg, 1910), 430–31.

51. Smith and Judah, *Chronicles of the Gringos*, 354.

52. Russell F. Weigley, *History of the United States Army* (New York: Macmillan, 1967), 181.

53. J. K. Greer, *Colonel Jack Hays: Texas Frontier Leader and California Builder* (New York: Dutton, 1952), 176; Floyd F. Ewing Jr., "The Mule as a Factor in the Development of the Southwest," *Arizona and the West* 5 (winter 1963): 323; Matloff, *American Military History*, 174–76; McCaffrey, *Army of Manifest Destiny*, 172; William H. Goetzmann, *When the Eagle Screamed: The Romantic Horizon in American Diplomacy, 1800–1860* (New York: John Wiley, 1966), 67–68.

54. McCaffrey, *Army of Manifest Destiny,* 178.
55. McCaffrey, *Army of Manifest Destiny,* 179–85; Bauer, *The Mexican War,* 316–19, 318.
56. Chamberlain, *My Confession,* 175–77; for difficulties with Scott's force, see Risch, *Quartermaster Support,* 293–94.
57. Risch, *Quartermaster Support,* 297–98.
58. Grant, *Personal Memoirs,* 1:181–82.

3. MULE POWER IN THE ARMY, 1848–1861

1. Risch, *Quartermaster Support,* 301, 304–8; James A. Huston, *The Sinews of War: Army Logistics, 1775–1953,* Office of the Chief of Military History (Washington DC: Government Printing Office, 1966), 154–55.
2. Percival G. Lowe, *Five Years a Dragoon ('49 to '54) and Other Adventures on the Great Plains* (reprint, Norman: University of Oklahoma Press, 1965), 133.
3. U.S. Secretary of War (hereafter sw), *Annual Report,* 31st Cong., 2d sess, 1850, H. Doc. 1, pp. 114, 26–27; *U.S. Statutes at Large,* 31st Cong. 1st sess., 438–39.
4. Teresa Griffin Viele, *"Following the Drum:" A Glimpse of Frontier Life* (New York: Rudd & Carleton, 1858), 223; Robert M. Utley, *Frontiersmen in Blue: The United States Army and the Indian, 1848–1865* (New York: Macmillan, 1967), 21.
5. Utley, *Frontiersmen in Blue,* 115–18; William Y. Chalfant, *Cheyennes and Horse Soldiers: The 1857 Expedition and the Battle of Solomon's Fork* (Norman: University of Oklahoma Press, 1989), 28–33.
6. Utley, *Frontiersmen in Blue,* 120–21; Chalfant, *Cheyennes and Horse Soldiers,* 321.
7. Utley, *Frontiersmen in Blue,* 122–23; Chalfant, *Cheyennes and Horse Soldiers,* 66–68, 105; Lowe, *Five Years a Dragoon,* 185–86.
8. Lowe, *Five Years a Dragoon,* 186.
9. Lowe, *Five Years a Dragoon,* 188–89, 215.
10. Utley, *Frontiersmen in Blue,* 122; Lowe, *Five Years a Dragoon,* 201–2.
11. Utley, *Frontiersmen in Blue,* 123.
12. Utley, *Frontiersmen in Blue,* 122–25; Chalfant, *Cheyennes and Horse Soldiers,* 181–201.
13. Averam B. Bender, "Military Transportation in the Southwest, 1848–1860," *New Mexico Historical Review* 32 (April 1957): 123–27, 137; Risch, *Quartermaster Support,* 301, 317.
14. Bender, "Military Transportation," 127–29; Risch, *Quartermaster Support,* 308; Huston, *The Sinews of War,* 155.

15. Risch, *Quartermaster Support*, 308, 311, 314; Essin, "Army Mule," 33.
16. S. G. French, *Report of the Expedition to El Paso del Norte*, Samuel G. French Papers, Carlisle Barracks, Army War College, Carlisle, Pennsylvania; Bender, "Military Transportation," 133–34.
17. Risch, *Quartermaster Support*, 310–11.
18. Utley, *Frontiersmen in Blue*, 52–53; Bender, "Military Transportation," 134; Essin, "Army Mule," 33.
19. Bender, "Military Transportation," 133–34; Essin, "Army Mule," 34.
20. "Mules," Box 705.
21. French, *Report of the Expedition to El Paso del Norte*.
22. French, *Report of the Expedition to El Paso del Norte*.
23. French, *Report of the Expedition to El Paso del Norte*.
24. French, *Report of the Expedition to El Paso del Norte*.
25. Risch, *Quartermaster Support*, 315–17.
26. Odie B. Faulk, *The U.S. Camel Corps: An Army Experiment* (New York: Oxford University Press, 1976), 24–27; Risch, *Quartermaster Support*, 319–20.
27. Faulk, *The U.S. Camel Corps*, 28–29.
28. sw, *Annual Report*, 33d Cong., 1st sess., p. 25; Faulk, *The U.S. Camel Corps*, 30.
29. John Russell Bartlett, *Personal Narrative of Explorations and Incidents in Texas, New Mexico, California, Sonora, and Chihuahua Connected with the United States and Mexican Boundary Commission, during the Years 1850, '51, '52, and 1853* (1854; reprint, Chicago: Rio Grande Press, 1965), 576–83.
30. Faulk, *The U.S. Camel Corps*, 86–87, 186; Lewis Burt Lesley, ed., *Uncle Sam's Camels: The Journal of May Humphreys Stacey Supplemented by the Report of Edward Fitzgerald Beale (1857–1858)* (Cambridge: Harvard University Press, 1929); W. Eugene Hollon, *The Southwest: Old and New* (Lincoln: University of Nebraska Press, 1968), 211–17.
31. U.S. Army, oQMG, Lt. Col. George P. Ihrie to QMG M. C. Meigs, 12 June 1864, "Pack Mules," Box 776, CCF, RG 92, NA; Martin F. Schmitt, ed., *General George Crook: His Autobiography* (1946; reprint, Norman: University of Oklahoma Press, 1960), 36–37, 45–46, 60.
32. U.S. Army, oQMG, Capt. Winfield Scott Hancock to Gen. Thomas E. Jesup, 24 April 1857, "Pack Mules," Box 776.
33. Norman F. Furniss, *The Mormon Conflict: 1850–1859* (New Haven: Yale University Press, 1960), 95–100, 104–8; Howard Roberts Lamar, *The Far Southwest, 1846–1912: A Territorial History* (New Haven: Yale University Press, 1966), 340–42; Hubert Howe Bancroft, *History of*

Utah: 1540–1886, vol. 26 (San Francisco: The History Company, 1889), 493–97; Risch, *Quartermaster Support*, 322–24.

34. Furniss, *The Mormon Conflict*, 107–9; Lamar, *The Far Southwest*, 342–45.

35. John J. Dickenson to AAG. (Col. Irving McDowell), 24 November 1857. 35th Cong., 1st sess., 1857, H. Doc. 71, 93–98; Joseph E. Johnston to AAG (McDowell), H. Doc. 71, 76–77; Eugene Bandel, *Frontier Life in the Army, 1854–1861*, ed. Ralph P. Bieber (1932; reprint, Philadelphia: Porcupine Press, 1974), 220–21.

36. Dickenson to AAG (McDowell), H. Doc. 71, pp. 100–101.

37. LeRoy R. Hafen and Ann W. Hafen, eds., *The Utah Expedition, 1857–1858: A Documentary Account of the United States Military Movement under Colonel Albert Sidney Johnston, and the Resistance of Brigham Young and the Mormon Nauvoo Legion* (Glendale CA: Arthur H. Clark, 1982), 173.

38. Bancroft, *History of Utah*, 520; Johnston to AAG (McDowell), H. Doc. 71, pp. 77, 96–97.

39. Dickenson to AAG (McDowell), H. Doc. 71, pp. 100–101; Hafen and Hafen, *The Utah Expedition*, 171, 175–76.

40. Dickenson to AAG (McDowell), H. Doc. 71, 103.

41. Randolph B. Marcy to Fitz John Porter, 35th Cong., 2d sess., H. Doc. 2, part 2, 187–97; W. Eugene Hollon, *Beyond the Cross Timbers: The Travels of Randolph B. Marcy, 1812–1887* (Norman: University of Oklahoma Press, 1955), 216–32; Furniss, *The Mormon Conflict*, 155–56; Averam B. Bender, *The March of Empire: Frontier Defense in the Southwest, 1848–1860* (Lawrence: University of Kansas Press, 1952), 182–83, 270.

42. William G. Hartley, *My Best for the Kingdom: History and Autobiography of John Lowe Butler, a Mormon Frontiersman* (Salt Lake City: Aspen Books, 1993), 341; Thomas G. Alexander and Leonard J. Arrington, "Camp in the Sagebrush: Camp Floyd, Utah, 1858–1861," *Utah Historical Quarterly* 34 (1): 16–18.

43. Alexander and Arrington, "Camp in the Sagebrush," 18.

44. U.S. Army, OQMG, "Mule Transportation."

4. MULES AND THE CIVIL WAR

1. Risch, *Quartermaster Support*, 429.

2. *The War of the Rebellion: A Compilation of the Official Records of the Union and Confederate Armies*, 128 vols.(Government Printing Office,

1880–1901), ser. 3, vol. 4, 888. Hereafter referred to as OR; OR, ser. 3, vol. 2, 797.

3. OR, ser. 3, vol. 2, 798; Russell F. Weigley, *Quartermaster General of the Army: A Biography of M. C. Meigs* (New York: Columbia University Press, 1959), 269; George Thomas Stevens, *Three Years in the Sixth Corps: A Concise Narrative of Events in the Army of the Potomac* (Albany: S. R. Gray, 1866), 223.

4. Robert Ginsberg, "Taps for the Army Mule," *American Legion Magazine* 50 (February 1941): 21, 49.

5. OR, ser. 3, vol. 2, 797–98; Russell F. Weigley, *History of the United States Army* (New York: Macmillan, 1967), 220–21, 224. Weigley, *Quartermaster General of the Army*, 255–56; Edward Hagerman, *The American Civil War and the Origins of Modern Warfare: Ideas, Organization, and Field Command* (Bloomington: University of Indiana Press, 1988), 210.

6. OR, ser. 1, vol. 23, pt. 2, 281–82, 300–304, 320–21; Hagerman, *The American Civil War*, 210–12.

7. Hagerman, *The American Civil War*, 44; John B. Moore, "Mobility and Strategy in the Civil War," *Military Affairs* 24 (summer 1960): 69–77; Risch, *Quartermaster Support*, 379.

8. "Mules," Box 705; Essin, "Army Mules," 34; OR, ser. 1, vol. 23, pt. 2, 300.

9. "Mules," Box 705; U.S. Army, Office of the Quartermaster General, "Horses and Mules," Box 415, CCF, RG 92, NA; Risch, *Quartermaster Support*, 376.

10. "Horses and Mules," Box 415; Risch, *Quartermaster Support*, 378; OR, ser. 3, vol. 4, 889.

11. OR, ser. 3, vol. 2, 799.

12. OR, ser. 3, vol. 2, 799; OR, ser. 3, vol. 3, 768–69, 201; ser. 3, vol. 5, 216; John D. Billings, *Hard Tack and Coffee, or the Unwritten Story of Army Life* (Boston: G. M. Smith, 1887), 281.

13. Hagerman, *The American Civil War*, 119–20.

14. OR, ser. 4, vol. 2, 417.

15. OR, ser. 4, vol. 2, 616–17.

16. Weigley, *History of the United States Army*, 222, 224; Marvin A. Kreidberg and Merton G. Henry, *History of Military Mobilization in the United States Army, 1775–1945* (Westport CT: Greenwood Press, 1975), 126.

17. Weigley, *Quartermaster General of the Army*, 244; OR, ser. 1, vol. 9, pt. 1, 158.

18. Huston, *The Sinews of War*, 222; OR, ser. 3, vol. 2, 797–98; Hagerman,

The American Civil War, 51; Matloff, *American Military History*, 221–24.

19. Hagerman, *The American Civil War*, 51.

20. OR, ser. 1, vol. 27, pt. 3, 212–13, 230–31; OR, ser. 1, vol. 25, pt. 2, 554–55; Hagerman, *The American Civil War*, 62–69; Weigley, *Quartermaster General of the Army*, 276–77.

21. Hagerman, *The American Civil War*, 70–72.

22. OR, ser. 1, vol. 25, pt. 2, 546.

23. OR, ser. 1, vol. 25, pt. 2, 552.

24. OR, ser. 1, vol. 25, pt. 2, 552.

25. OR, ser. 1, vol. 25, 544, 547–48, 552, 554.

26. Hagerman, *The American Civil War*, 73–74.

27. Hagerman, *The American Civil War*, 74; OR, ser. 1, vol. 27, pt. 1, 221–22.

28. OR, ser. 1, vol. 23, pt. 2, 281–82, 300–304; Hagerman, *The American Civil War*, 210–11.

29. Hagerman, *The American Civil War*, 331–32.

30. OR, ser. 1, vol. 25, pt. 2, 547–57; Risch, *Quartermaster Support*, 374; Charles Leib, *Nine Months in the Quartermaster's Department or the Chances of Making a Million* (Cincinnati: Moore, Wilson, Keys, 1862), 119; Ihrie to Meigs, 4 July 1864, "Pack Mules," Box 776.

31. Leib, *Nine Months*, 85, 109.

32. Leib, *Nine Months*, 109–11.

33. Leib, *Nine Months*, 119.

34. James M. McPherson, ed., *The Atlas of the Civil War* (New York: Macmillan, 1994), 128–34; J. G. Randall and David Donald, *The Civil War and Reconstruction* (Boston: D. C. Heath, 1961), 412–15; Hagerman, *The American Civil War*, 209–18.

35. OR, ser. 1, vol. 30, pt. 1, 218–19, 221.

36. OR, ser. 3, vol. 4, 879; OR, ser. 1, vol. 31, pt. 2, 29; Hagerman, *The American Civil War*, 220.

37. McPherson, *Atlas of the Civil War*, 134; Randall, *The Civil War*, 414–15; John D. Billings, *Hard Tack and Coffee*, 295–97.

5. MULES IN THE WEST AND EFFICIENT PACK MULES FOR THE ARMY

1. Risch, *Quartermaster Support*, 469–70; sw, *Annual Report*, 39th Cong., 2d sess., H. Doc. 1, appendix, ser. 1285, p. 50.

2. U.S. Army, OQMG, "Register of Mules, Artillery Horses, and Cavalry Horses Sold at Various Stations," Entry 1286, Box 1, CCF, RG 92, NA.

3. Robert M. Utley, *Frontier Regulars: The United States Army and the Indian, 1866–1891* (New York: Macmillan, 1973), 52–53.

4. Ihrie to Meigs, 12 June 1864, "Pack Mules," Box 776, RG 92, CCF, NA.

5. Ihrie to Meigs, 12 June, 18 June, 4 July 1864, "Pack Mules," Box 776; Utley, *Frontiersmen in Blue*, 184–85.

6. Schmitt, *General George Crook*, 36–37.

7. Schmitt, *General George Crook*, 31–113; Essin, "Army Mule," 36.

8. Schmitt, *General George Crook*, 143–44.

9. Utley, *Frontier Regulars*, 179–80; Schmitt, "George Crook," *Reader's Encyclopedia*, 276–77.

10. Utley, *Frontier Regulars*, 178–81; Essin, "Army Mule," 36.

11. Essin, "Army Mule," 36; Daly, *Manual of Pack Transportation*, 160; Dan L. Thrapp, *The Conquest of Apacheria* (Norman: University of Oklahoma Press, 1967), 105–7.

12. John G. Bourke, *On the Border with Crook* (1891; reprint, Lincoln: University of Nebraska Press, 1971), 150–51, 201; Essin, "Army Mule," 36; Emmett M. Essin, "Mules, Packs, and Pack Trains," *Southwestern Historical Quarterly* 74 (July 1970): 61.

13. Bourke, *On the Border with Crook*, 166.

14. Bourke, *On the Border with Crook*, 150–54; Daly, *Manual of Pack Transportation*, 164; Essin, "Mules, Packs, and Pack Trains," 53–55; Donald E. Worcester, *The Apaches: Eagles of the Southwest* (Norman: University of Oklahoma Press, 1979), 150–51.

15. Anton Mazzanovich, *Trailing Geronimo* (Hollywood: A. Mazzanovich, 1931), 126–27.

16. Thomas Moore, *Instructions for Using the Aparejo or Spanish Pack Saddle* (Chicago: Jameson & Morse, 1878), 3–4, found in "Pack Mule," Box 776; U.S. Army, OQMG, *Report from Thomas Moore, March 16, 1878*, Quartermasters Confidential Correspondence (hereafter QMCC), Special Subjects File, Correspondence 1871–90, Entry 1323, Box 1, CCF, RG 92, NA; Daly, *Manual of Pack Transportation*, 24, 42–43, 146.

17. Worcester, *The Apaches*, 151; Bourke, *On the Border with Crook*, 151; Daly, *Manual of Pack Transportation*, 26.

18. Daly, *Manual of Pack Transportation*, 21; "The Pack-Train in the Army," *Frank Leslie's Popular Monthly* 15, 4 (April 1983): 186.

19. "The Pack-Train in the Army," 21–23; Essin, "Mules, Packs, and Pack Trains," 62.

20. U.S. Army, OQMG, "Extract from Annual Report of Captain N. A. Constable, Assistant Quartermaster, Fort Concho, Texas for the fiscal year ending June 30, 1878," QMCCF, Entry 1323, Box 1, CCF, RG 92, NA; U.S. Army, OQMG, "Meigs Memorandum, December 1, 1877," QMCCF, Entry 1323, Box 1, CCF, RG 92, NA; U.S. Army, OQMG, "Abstracts of answers received from officers of the line and staff on relative merits of Cart,

Travois, and Pack Mules," QMCCF, Entry 1323, Box 1, CCF, RG 92, NA; U.S. Army, OQMG, "Horses and Mules," Box 705, CCF, RG 92, NA.

21. Henry W. Lawton, *Instructions for Using Moore's Improved Pack Saddle* (Washington DC: Government Printing Office, 1881), 6.

22. Bourke, *On the Border with Crook*, 181, 187.

23. Utley, *Frontier Regulars*, 196–98; Bourke, *On the Border with Crook*, 151, 154, 181, 186, 188–202; Worcester, *The Apaches*, 220; Thomas Cruse, *Apache Days and After* (1941; reprint, Lincoln: University of Nebraska Press, 1987), 54–55; Donald E. Worcester, "Apache Scouts and Pack Trains," *True West* 43, 2 (February 1996): 16–21.

24. "Mules," Box 705.

25. "Mules," Box 705.

26. "Mules," Box 705; Utley, *Frontier Regulars*, 153–59.

27. "Mules," Box 705.

28. James W. Steele, *Frontier Army Sketches* (1874; reprint, Albuquerque: University of New Mexico Press, 1969), 306, 313; Henry W. Daly, *Manual of Instruction in Pack Transportation* (West Point: Press of the U.S. Military Academy, 1901), 74–75; Agnes Wright Spring, "Prince of Packers," *True West* 38 (October 1970): 24–25.

29. William T. Corbusier, *Verde to San Carlos: Recollections of a Famous Army Surgeon and His Observant Family on the Western Frontier, 1869–1886* (Tucson: D. S. King, 1968), 18–19; Henry W. Daly, "The Geronimo Campaign," *Arizona Historical Review* 31 (July 1930): 31–32; Worcester, *The Apaches*, 151; Cruse, *Apache Days*, 55.

30. Steele, *Frontier Army Sketches*, 313.

31. Mazzanovich, *Trailing Geronimo*, 146–47, 164.

32. Daly, *Manual of Pack Transportation*, 145; Steele, *Frontier Army Sketches*, 303.

33. Daly, *Manual of Pack Transportation*, 144; Utley, *Frontier Regulars*, 375; Worcester, *The Apaches*, 220–25; William A. Ganoe, *The History of the United States Army*, (Ashton MD: Eric Lund, 1954), 367.

34. Daly, "The Geronimo Campaign," 31; Spring, "Prince of Packers," 42–46.

35. Utley, *Frontier Regulars*, 386–88; Daly, "The Geronimo Campaign," 31–32.

36. Bourke, *On the Border with Crook*, 353.

37. Edward S. Godfrey, "Custer's Last Battle." In Paul F. Hutton, editor, *The Custer Reader* (Lincoln: University of Nebraska Press, 1992), 259–60.

38. Richard G. Hardorff, "Packs, Packers, and Pack Details: Logistics and Custer's Pack Train," in Gregory J. W. Urwin, editor, *Custer and His*

Times: Book Three (Conway: University of Central Arkansas Press, 1987), 226–27; Godfrey, "Custer's Last Battle," 264–65.

39. Hardorff, "Packs, Packers, and Pack Details," 227–28, 240.
40. Hardorff, "Packs, Packers, and Pack Details," 227, 228.
41. Hardorff, "Packs, Packers, and Pack Details," 228.
42. Hardorff, "Packs, Packers, and Pack Details," 229; John S. Gray, "The Pack Train on George Custer's Last Campaign," *Nebraska History* 57 (spring 1976): 62–63; W. A. Graham, *The Custer Myth: A Source Book of Custeriana* (New York: Bonanza Books, 1953), 134, 177–78; Kenneth Hammer, *Custer in '76: Walter Camp's Notes on the Custer Fight* (Provo: Brigham Young University Press, 1976), 127.
43. John M. Carroll, ed., *The Benteen-Golden Letters on Custer and His Last Battle* (New York: Liverwright, 1974), 166, 177–78; Robert M. Utley, *Cavalier in Buckskin: George Armstrong Custer and the Western Military Frontier* (Norman: University of Oklahoma Press, 1988), 177; Hardorff, "Packs, Packers, and Pack Details," 229–31.
44. Hammer, *Custer in '76*, 83; Hardorff, "Packs, Packers, and Pack Details," 231, 242–43; Graham, *The Custer Myth*, 241.
45. Hardorff, "Packs, Packers, and Pack Details," 232.
46. Utley, *Cavalier in Buckskin*, 181–83.
47. Hammer, *Custer in '76*, 78; Hardorff, "Packs, Packers, and Pack Details," 232.
48. Hammer, *Custer in '76*, 93–94; Hardorff, "Packs, Packers, and Pack Details," 233.
49. Hardorff, "Packs, Packers, and Pack Details," 234; Hammer, *Custer in '76*, 70.
50. Hammer, *Custer in '76*, 125, 127–28; Hardorff, "Packers, Packs, and Pack Details," 234.
51. Hardorff, "Packers, Packs, and Pack Details," 234.
52. Bourke, *On the Border with Crook*, 353.
53. John F. Finerty, *War-Path and Bivouac: The Big Horn and Yellowstone Expedition, or The Conquest of the Sioux* (1890; reprint, Lincoln: University of Nebraska Press, 1966), 53, 116; Utley, *Frontier Regulars*, 253.
54. Bourke, *On the Border with Crook*, 305; Joe De Barth, *Life and Adventures of Frank Grouard* (1894; reprint, Norman: University of Oklahoma Press, 1958), 115; Finerty, *War-Path and Bivouac*, 112–14; Merrill J. Mattes, *Indians, Infants, and Infantry: Andrew and Elizabeth Burt on the Frontier* (Denver: Old West, 1960), 217.
55. Utley, *Frontier Regulars*, 255–56; Robert M. Utley, *The Lance and the Shield: The Life and Times of Sitting Bull* (New York: Henry Holt, 1993), 140–42.

56. "The Pack-Train in the Army," 490; Robert G. Athearn, *William Tecumseh Sherman and the Settlement of the West* (Norman: University of Oklahoma Press, 1956), 331; James M. Merrill, *William Tecumseh Sherman* (Chicago: Rand McNally & Company, 1971), 365.

57. U.S. Army, OQMG, "Consolidated Report of Horses and Mules Purchased, Sold, and on Hand, 1877–1884," QMCCF, Entry 1324, RG 92, NA.

58. Risch, *Quartermaster Support*, 535–37; Cruse, *Apache Days*, 255–56; Fairfax Downey, *Indian-Fighting Army* (reprint; 1941, Fort Collins CO: Old Army Press, 1971), 30.

59. "The Pack-Train in the Army," 490.

60. "The Pack-Train in the Army," 490.

61. "The Pack-Train in the Army," 490.

62. Edward M. Coffman, *The Old Army: A Portrait of the American Army in Peacetime, 1784–1898* (New York: Oxford University Press, 1986), 353–55.

6. ARMY MULES NEAR HOME AND ABROAD, 1898–1917

1. Risch, *Quartermaster Support*, 535–37; Cruse, *Apache Days*, 261.

2. Risch, *Quartermaster Support*, 535–37.

3. Cruse, *Apache Days*, 265.

4. Cruse, *Apache Days*, 264.

5. Cruse, *Apache Days*, 264–67; Risch, *Quartermaster Support*, 536–39.

6. Risch, *Quartermaster Support*, 536–39; Huston, *The Sinews of War*, 283.

7. Frank B. Freidel, *The Splendid Little War* (Boston: Little, Brown, 1958), 59, 60–64.

8. Freidel, *The Splendid Little War*, 60–64; Huston, *The Sinews of War*, 280–85; William Harding Carter, *The Life of Lieutenant General Chaffee* (Chicago: University of Chicago Press, 1917), 134–36; Matloff, *American Military History*, 328–32.

9. Risch, *Quartermaster Support*, 537; Essin, "Army Mule," 41; Huston, *The Sinews of War*, 286; Virgil Carrington Jones, *Roosevelt's Rough Riders*, 148, 151, 153, 162.

10. Huston, *The Sinews of War*, 284–85; Matloff, *American Military History*, 334; Robert Wooster, *Nelson A. Miles and the Twilight of the Frontier Army* (Lincoln: University of Nebraska Press, 1993), 214–31.

11. Huston, *The Sinews of War*, 287; Risch, *Quartermaster Support*, 537; Essin, "Army Mule," 41; Matloff, *American Military History*, 334–37.

12. Daly, *Manual of Instruction*, 23–24, 29–32; Lawton, *Instructions*, 1–18;

Report from Thomas Moore, March 16, 1878, Correspondence, 1871–90, Special Subjects File, CCF, RG 92, NA; "Pullman Pack Outfit and How to Use it," *Journal of the U.S. Cavalry Association* 17 (April 1907): 57–75.

13. Daly, *Manual of Instruction,* 125–30.
14. Albert R. Ginsburgh, "The Rise and Fall of the Two Nine Five," *Field Artillery Journal* 22 (1, 1932): 461–65; Daly, *Manual of Instruction,* 231–35, 125–30; "Recommendation That All Mules for Artillery Be Pack Mules," Entry 359270, CCF, RG 92, NA; Michael F. Parrino, *An Introduction to Pack Transportation and Pack Artillery* (New York: Queensland, 1956), 63.
15. Frank E. Vandiver, *Black Jack: The Life and Times of John J. Pershing* (College Station: Texas A & M University Press, 1977), 1:420–21.
16. U.S. Army, OQMG, Telegram to Quartermaster General from General Superintendent Long, Entry 127958, "Horses and Mules," Box 2139, CCF, RG 92, NA.
17. Cruse, *Apache Days,* 280.
18. Telegram to QMG from Long, and Miller Cable, Entry 127958, "Horses and Mules," Box 2139, CCF, RG 92, NA.
19. Cruse, *Apache Days,* 278–83; "Extract from the Report of an Inspection of the Horse Ship 'LEELANAW,'" Entry 127958, "Mules and Horses," Box 2139, CCF, RG 92, NA.
20. Monro MacCloskey, *Reilly's Battery: A Story of the Boxer Rebellion* (New York: Richards Rosen, 1969), 35.
21. MacCloskey, *Reilly's Battery,* 35.
22. Daly, *Manual of Instruction,* 146–47; H. L. Scott, "The Skilled Packer," *Journal of the U.S. Cavalry Association* 17 (61): 516–17.
23. Cruse, *Apache Days,* 288; Risch, *Quartermaster Support,* 567; Huston, *The Sinews of War,* 302–3.
24. MacCloskey, *Reilly's Battery,* 130, 132–33, 134.
25. MacCloskey, *Reilly's Battery,* 134.
26. MacCloskey, *Reilly's Battery,* 134.
27. MacCloskey, *Reilly's Battery,* 134–35.
28. MacCloskey, *Reilly's Battery,* 134–35.
29. MacCloskey, *Reilly's Battery,* 135–37.
30. U.S. Army, OFMG, "Mules and Horses in the Philippines," Entry 202749, Box 4338, CCF, RG 92, NA.
31. "Letter from Adjutant General F. C. Ainsworth to Commanding General, Philippines Division," Entry 26761, CCF, RG 92, NA; U.S. Army, OQMG, "Horses and Mules for the Philippines," Entry 26796, Box 4338, CCF, RG 92, NA
32. Essin, "Army Mule," 42.

33. U.S. Army, OQMG, "Mule Prices, 1910," Entry 261695, CCF, RG 92, NA.
34. Melvin Bradley, *The Missouri Mule: His Origin and Times*, (Columbia: University of Missouri Press, 1993), 1:186–88; Lamb, *The Mule in Southern Agriculture*, 42–44.
35. U.S. Army, OQMG, "American Mules for German Army Remounts in German-China," Entry 342385, CCF, RG 92, NA.
36. Risch, *Quartermaster Support*, 564–65; Daly, *Manual of Instruction*, iii–iv; Daly, *Manual of Pack Transportation*, 5–8.
37. Matloff, *American Military History*, 352–53.
38. Matloff, *American Military History*, 354–55; Huston, *The Sinews of War*, 303–5.
39. Clarence C. Clendenen, *Blood on the Border: The United States Army and the Mexican Irregulars* (New York: Macmillan, 1969), 158–62, 163.
40. Jack London, "Mexico's Army and Ours," *Colliers Magazine* 43 (30 May 1914): 5–6; Clendenen, *Blood on the Border*, 167, 169–74.
41. Frank Tompkins, *Chasing Villa: The Story Behind the Story of Pershing's Expedition into Mexico* (Harrisburg PA: Military Service Publishing Co., 1934), 75, 78, 125; Clendenen, *Blood on the Border*, 254–55, 266.
42. Alexander G. Fraser, "Draft Mules in the Field in Mexico," *American Veterinary Medical Association* 50 (December 1917): 357; Tompkins, *Chasing Villa*, 75.
43. Risch, *Quartermaster Support*, 595–97.
44. Risch, *Quartermaster Support*, 595–97.
45. Essin, "Army Mule," 43; Tompkins, *Chasing Villa*, 248, 250–52.
46. Tompkins, *Chasing Villa*, 121–23.
47. Tompkins, *Chasing Villa*, 235.
48. Tompkins, *Chasing Villa*, 137–46.
49. Tompkins, *Chasing Villa*, 38.

7. ARMY MULES FROM WORLD WAR I TO WORLD WAR II

1. Gen. Lucian K. Truscott Jr., *The Twilight of the U.S. Cavalry: Life in the Old Army, 1917–1942*, ed. Lucian K. Truscott III (Lawrence: University Press of Kansas, 1989), 7.
2. Bradley, *The Missouri Mule*, 1:188–89.
3. "Tennessee Mules for Use in British Army," *Nashville Tennessean and Nashville American*, 13 September 1915, 7.
4. L. J. Blenkinsop and J. W. Rainey, eds., *History of the Great War Based on Official Documents: Veterinary Services* (London: His Majesty's Stationery Office, 1925), 469, 472.

5. Blenkinsop and Rainey, *History of the Great War: Veterinary Services*, 461.

6. Blenkinsop and Rainey, *History of the Great War: Veterinary Services*, 476, 490.

7. "Army Mule on European Battlefields," *Johnson City (Tennessee) Staff*, 3 February 1917, 6.

8. Risch, *Quartermaster Support*, 681–82; "Though Awarded No D. S. C. the Mule Has a Fine War Record," *The Literary Digest* 61 (17 May 1919), 59.

9. U.S. Army, OQMG, Quartermaster Generals Document File, Nos. 114623 and 127958, CCF, RG 92, NA.

10. Weigley, *History of the United States Army*, 362–63; Matloff, *American Military History*, 376.

11. J. Clabby, *The History of the Royal Army Veterinary Corps: 1919–1961* (London: J. A. Allen, 1963), 18; Blenkinsop and Rainey, *History of the Great War: Veterinary Services*, 80.

12. Blenkinsop and Rainey, *History of the Great War: Veterinary Services*, 681–83.

13. Blenkinsop and Rainey, *History of the Great War: Veterinary Services*, 681–83; John J. Pershing, *My Experiences in the World War* (New York: Frederick A. Stokes, 1931), 1:147; Risch, *Quartermaster Support*, 681–82; Ginsberg, "Taps for the Army Mule," 50.

14. "Army Mule a Help in Time of Trouble," *The Literary Digest* 65 (19 June 1920): 75.

15. Pershing, *My Experiences in the World War*, 2:130–32.

16. Bradley, *The Missouri Mule*, 2:365; Clabby, *Royal Army Veterinary Corps*, 17; Huston, *The Sinews of War*, 376–77; Risch, *Quartermaster Support*, 686.

17. Bradley, *The Missouri Mule*, 2:365; Clabby, *Royal Army Veterinary Corps*, 17; Huston, *The Sinews of War*, 399.

18. Pershing, *My Experiences in the World War*, 2:193; Risch, *Quartermaster Support*, 681.

19. Huston, *The Sinews of War*, 378, 384, 389.

20. Huston, *The Sinews of War*, 682; Vandiver, *Black Jack*, 2:954; Donald Smythe, *Pershing: General of the Armies* (Bloomington: Indiana University Press, 1986), 207.

21. Ginsberg, "Taps for the Army Mule," 52.

22. Huston, *The Sinews of War*, 385–87.

23. "Mule Has a Fine War Record," 59–60.

24. Erna Risch and Chester L. Kieffer, *United States Army in World War II*,

The Quartermaster Corps: Organization, Supply, and Services (Washington DC: Office of the Chief of Military History, 1955), 2:315; Waller, *Horses and Mules*, 10.

25. "Memo from Col. Albert E. Phillips to F. Lt. Richard McMaster, May 23, 1932"; "Memo from Captain R. L. Allen, 4th F. A. to 1st Lt. Richard K̇. McMaster, F. A."; and R. K. McMaster, "Aparejo vs. Phillip Pack," all from the Collection of Swett Library, Field Artillery School, Fort Sill, Oklahoma, #UCU 421 091932 #59.

26. U.S. Army, OQMG, *Basic Field Manual: Animal Transport* (Washington DC: Government Printing Office, 1939), 187–92; U.S. Army, OQMG, *Basic Field Manual: Transport* (Washington DC: Government Printing Office, 1929), 225–46; Parrino, *An Introduction to Pack Transportation*, 49–52; McMaster, "Aparejo vs. Phillip Pack."

8. MULES IN WORLD WAR II

1. Risch and Kieffer, *United States Army in World War II*, 2:319, 322; Waller, *Horses and Mules*, 24.

2. Bradley, *The Missouri Mule*, 2:370.

3. Bradley, *The Missouri Mule*, 2:369–70; transcription of an interview of Frank Graham by Melvin Bradley, 28 September 1982.

4. Bradley, *The Missouri Mule*, 2:368.

5. Bradley, *The Missouri Mule*, 2:382, 384; William F. Ross and Charles F. Romanus, *United States Army in World War II, The Quartermaster Corps: Operations in the War against Germany* (Washington DC: Office of the Chief of Military History, 1965), 236–37; Waller, *Horses and Mules*, 23–24.

6. Ross and Romanus, *Operations in the War against Germany*, 238.

7. Clabby, *Royal Army Veterinary Corps*, 58.

8. Clabby, *Royal Army Veterinary Corps*, 63; Ross and Romanus, *Operations in the War against Germany*, 238.

9. Bradley, *The Missouri Mule*, 2:391.

10. Waller, *Horses and Mules*, 22.

11. Waller, *Horses and Mules*, 22.

12. Omar N. Bradley, *A Soldier's Story* (New York: Henry Holt, 1951), 157–59, 162–64; Carlo D'Este, *Patton: A Genius for War* (New York: Harper Collins, 1995), 530.

13. Ross and Romanus, *Operations in the War against Germany*, 238; Bradley, *The Missouri Mule*, 2:387; Albert E. Phillips, "From Jeeps to Packs," *The Cavalry Journal* 43 (September–October 1944): 26–28.

14. Albert N. Garland and Howard McGaw Smyth, *United States Army in*

World War II, The Mediterranean Theater of Operations: Sicily and the Surrender of Italy (Washington DC: Office of the Chief of Military History, 1965), 348–49.

15. Robert Geake, "Beyond the Jeep-Line in Italy," *The Cavalry Journal* 53 (January–February, 1944): 3; Bradley, *The Missouri Mule*, 2:390.

16. Telephone interview with Donald J. Willems, 27 May 1995.

17. Geake, "Beyond the Jeep-Line in Italy," 4–5.

18. Ross and Romanus, *Operations in the War against Germany*, 239; Bradley, *The Missouri Mule*, 2:387–88; Edora Ramsay Richardson and Sherman Allan, *Quartermaster Supply in the Fifth Army in World War II* (Fort Lee VA: The Quartermaster School, 1950), 18.

19. Risch and Kieffer, *United States Army in World War II*, 2:322; Ross and Romanus, *Operations in the War against Germany*, 240.

20. Donald J. Willems, "Papers and Accounts of the Italian Campaign and Need for Mule Pack Slings," Fort Carson Records, 1945–50, Archives, Fort Carson, Colorado.

21. Willems, "Accounts of the Italian Campaign"; Clabby, *Royal Army Veterinary Corps*, 66; Ross and Romanus, *Operations in the War against Germany*, 240; Richardson and Allan, *Quartermaster Supply*, 55.

22. Willems, "Accounts of the Italian Campaign"; Telephone interview with Donald J. Willems, 27 May 1995; Ross and Romanus, *Operations in the War against Germany*, 240.

23. Willems, "Accounts of the Italian Campaign"; Ross and Romanus, *Operations in the War against Germany*, 241; Richardson and Allan, *Quartermaster Supply*, 54–55; 75.

24. Bradley, *The Missouri Mule*, 2:391–92.

25. David Nichols, ed., *Ernie's War: The Best of Ernie Pyle's World War II Dispatches* (New York, Random House, 1986), 189–91, 195.

26. Willems, "Accounts of the Italian Campaign"; Matloff, *American Military History*, 480–82.

27. Transcription of an interview of Donald J. Willems by Melvin Bradley, 4 August 1985.

28. Ross and Romanus, *Operations in the War against Germany*, 242–43.

29. Phil Livingston, "All the Try of an Army Mule," *Crossed Sabres: A Journal of the U.S. Horse Cavalry Association* 14 (December 1990): 6–7.

30. Henry Demuth, "A Pack Artillery Battalion in the Pacific," *The Field Artillery Journal* 34 (February 1944): 93; Bradley, *The Missouri Mule*, 2:394.

31. Bradley, *The Missouri Mule*, 2:394.

32. Bradley, *The Missouri Mule*, 2:394–95; John Miller Jr., *The United States Army in World War II, Guadalcanal: The First Offensive* (Wash-

ington DC: Department of the Army, 1949), 314; "Pack Operations on Guadalcanal," *The Cavalry Journal* (November–December, 1945): 45–47.

33. David Haley, *With Wingate in Burma* (London: William Hodge, 1945); Leonard Mosley, *Gideon Goes to War* (New York: Charles Scribner's, 1955); Pat Carmichael, *Mountain Battery*, (Bournemouth, England: Devin Books, 1983), 4; Bernard Fergusson, *Beyond the Chindwin* (London: Collins, 1945), 52–53.

34. Fergusson, *Beyond the Chindwin*, 145, 146.

35. Charles J. Rolo, *Wingate's Raiders* (New York: Viking, 1944), 163–64.

36. Rolo, *Wingate's Raiders*, 164–65.

37. Clabby, *Royal Army Veterinary Corps*, 122.

38. U.S. Army, OQMG, "Mules by Air," Fort Carson, Colorado, Records, 1945–50; Ralph W. Mori, "Flying Mules over the Burma Hump," *The Cavalry Journal* 49 (September–October 1945): 42–52; John Masters, *The Road Past Mandalay* (New York: Harper, 1961), 136; Rolo, *Wingate's Raiders*, 204–9.

39. Masters, *The Road Past Mandalay*, 169–70.

40. "Mules by Air"; Mori, "Flying Mules."

41. Masters, *The Road Past Mandalay*, 194.

42. Clabby, *Royal Army Veterinary Corps*, 124–25; Terence O'Brien, *Out of the Blue: A Pilot with the Chindits* (1984; reprint, London: Arrow, 1989), 16.

43. Charlton Ogburn Jr., *The Marauders* (New York: Harper, 1959), 9.

44. Ogburn, *Marauders*, 9–10; John Costello, *The Pacific War: 1941–1945* (New York: Quill, 1982), 177; U.S. Army, Center of Military History, *Merrill's Marauders* (Washington DC: Historical Division, War Department, 1945), 1, 7–8; Bradley, *The Missouri Mule* 2:363.

45. Charles N. Hunter, *Galahad* (San Antonio: Naylor, 1963), 7.

46. Ogburn, *Marauders*, 66–67.

47. Bradley, *The Missouri Mule*, 2:401; John Randolph, *Marsmen in Burma* (Houston: Gulf, 1946), 27; Dan L. Thrapp, "The Mules of Mars, Part I," *Armored Cavalry Journal* 55 (November–December 1946): 57.

48. Dave Richardson, "Notes from a Burma Diary," in *The Best of Yank, the Army Weekly* (New York: E. P. Dutton, 1945), 176.

49. Bradley, *The Missouri Mule*, 2:401, 403.

50. Transcription of an interview of Maurice Ryan by Melvin Bradley, 6 May 1988.

51. Transcription of an interview of William Bennett "Woody" Woodruff Jr. by Melvin Bradley, 29 December 1988.

52. Transcription of an interview of William Bennett "Woody" Woodruff Jr. by Melvin Bradley, 29 December 1988.

53. Bradley, *The Missouri Mule*, 2:410.

54. Bradley, *The Missouri Mule*, 2:408–9; Thrapp, "The Mules of Mars, Part I," 55.

55. Thrapp, "The Mules of Mars, Part I," 57.

56. Dan L. Thrapp, "The Mules of Mars, Part II," *Armored Cavalry Journal* 56 (January–February 1947): 30.

57. Randolph, *Marsmen*, 153; Thrapp, "The Mules of Mars, Part II," 31.

58. Thrapp, "The Mules of Mars, Part I," 57.

59. Shelford Bidwell, *The Chindit War, Stilwell, Wingate, and the Campaign in Burma: 1944* (New York: Macmillan, 1979), 54; Bradley-Ryan Interview, 6 May 1988; Masters, *The Road Past Mandalay*, 182–83; Rolo, *Wingate's Raiders*, 51; Ogburn, *Marauders*, 67; Fergusson, *Beyond the Chindwin*, 68; John A. Rand, "Nine Hundred Mules," *The New Yorker* 30 (24 November 1954): 169.

60. Bradley, *The Missouri Mule*, 2:395.

61. Thrapp, "The Mules of Mars, Part I," 55; Rolo, *Wingate's Raiders*, 100.

62. Masters, *The Road Past Mandalay*, 164; Bradley-Ryan Interview, 6 May 1988; Bradley, *The Missouri Mule*, 2:428.

63. Rand, "Nine Hundred Mules," 168–81, 170.

64. Bradley, *The Missouri Mule*, 2:430–32; Rand, "Nine Hundred Mules," 180; William E. Jennings, "Veterinary Activities in World War II," *U.S. Armored Cavalry Journal* (November–December 1946): 45; Transcription of an interview of Melvin Bradley with Douglas F. Watson, 12 April 1990; transcription of an interview of Melvin Bradley with Delbert E. Long, 11 May 1990.

65. Rand, "Nine Hundred Mules," 180; Jennings, "Veterinary Activities," 44.

66. Bradley, *The Missouri Mule*, 2:340, 431.

9. CONCLUSION: THE UNWANTED ARMY MULES

1. Willems, "Accounts of an Italian Campaign"; Willems-Bradley interview, 4 August 1985.

2. Willems-Bradley interview, 4 August 1985.

3. U.S. Army, Army Ground Forces Board No. 1, Fort Bragg, North Carolina, *Report of the Study of Project No. AB-3246 Air Transport of Animals and Equipment*, 23 May 1947.

4. *Air Transport of Animals and Equipment*, 1–3.

5. *Air Transport of Animals and Equipment*, 13–15; U.S. Army, Army

Ground Forces Board No. 2, Fort Knox, Kentucky, Memo from Col. H. L. Flynn, Cavalry to President on "Informal Supplementary Report on Project for Air Transport of Animals and Equipment." Fort Carson Archives.

6. *Air Transport of Animals and Equipment*, 3–4, 6–11, 12.

7. Bradley, *The Missouri Mule*, 2:421–22; Telephone interview with Melvin Bradley, 5 May 1995; "Mules by Air," *Air Transport of Animals and Equipment*, 13–18.

8. J. C. Murray, "The Anti-Bandit War," *The Marine Gazette* 48 (May 1954): 53–59.

9. Woodruff-Bradley interview, 29 December 1988.

10. Waller, *Horses and Mules*, 31.

11. Interview with Col. Richard F. Krueger, 24 February 1968; Essin, "Mules, Packs, and Packtrains," 63; M. V. Motola, et al., *Final Draft Study: U.S. Army Requirements for Pack Animals* (Fort Bragg NC: United States Army Combat Developments Command, Special Warfare Agency, 1965), 43.

12. Motola, *Final Draft Study: Pack Animals*, 35–40, 91–108.

13. Motola, *Final Draft Study: Pack Animals*, 7.

14. Motola, *Final Draft Study: Pack Animals*, 14–15.

15. Motola, *Final Draft Study: Pack Animals*, appendix 2, "Pack Animals of the World," 29–32.

16. Department of the Army, United States Army John F. Kennedy Special Warfare Center, Fort Bragg, North Carolina, Memorandum through Chief, Concepts and Studies Division Director, Combat Developments Deputy Commander, "Pack Transportation in Support of SOF Operations," from Eve Iversen, 1st Lt., TC, Project Officer; Department of the Army, Office of the Deputy Chief of Staff for Operations and Plans, Memorandum to John Wickham from John O. Marsh, 4 January 1985.

17. Department of the Army, Office of the Deputy Chief of Staff for Operations and Plans, Memorandum through the Deputy Chief of Staff for Operations and Plans to the Chief of Staff, for the Secretary of the Army from Maj. Gen. John W. Woodmansee Jr. and Wayne Knudson, brigadier general, director of Force Requirements and army aviation officer.

18. Department of the Army, Office of the Deputy Chief of Staff for Operations and Planning, Memorandum from Johnny J. Johnston, major general, GS Director of Training to John J. Yeosock, deputy chief of staff for operations, U.S. Army Forces Command, Ft. McPherson, Georgia, "Mule Training in the 10th Mountain Division (Lt Inf)."

19. Department of the Army, Office of the Deputy Chief of Staff for Operations and Planning, Briefing Draft, "Utilization of Pack Animals,"

TRADOC, 4 September 1985; Tom Wicker, "Gee-Haw for the Army," *New York Times*, 12 April 1985, sec. 1, p. 27.

20. Wicker, "Gee-Haw for the Army," 27.
21. U.S. Army, Office of the Deputy Chief of Staff for Operations and Planning, "Fact Sheet," Subject: "Pack Transportation," by Louis V. Hightower III, colonel, GS, director, Unit Training; Telefax, "Pack Animals Operations in Support of Light Infantry," 4 September 1985; Iversen, "Pack Transportation in Support of SOF Operations."
22. Telephone interview with Eve Iversen, 9 June 1995; Iversen, "Operations Plan for Animal-Based Transportation Field Study."
23. "Army Drops the Idea of Re-enlisting Mules," *New York Times*, 26 July 1986, sec. 1, p. 10.

Bibliographical Essay

The army mule has, unfortunately, gone the way of the horse cavalry as a vital part of the U.S. Army. Nevertheless, the achievements and exploits of thousands of these marvelous animals have been preserved for posterity along with the records of other veterans of America's many conflicts in various archives of the United States. Essential to this study of army mules were the voluminous records of the army's Office of the Quartermaster General files, Record Group 92, at the National Archives, Washington DC. Other consequential primary source materials and government regulations and documents were found at Carlisle Barracks, Carlisle, Pennsylvania, in the U.S. Army Military History Institute. Archival materials at Fort Bragg, North Carolina, that came from Fort Carson, Colorado, were extremely useful in the concluding two chapters of the book.

Also extremely helpful were the personal papers of Lt. Eve Iversen, a member of the mule task force that looked into the possibility of reestablishing pack mules for the army. I was fortunate to have interviewed Iversen in December 1985, and again in 1995, for her materials have given me a perspective that would otherwise have been impossible.

Printed U.S. government documents were also essential. U.S. Congressional Records in the U.S. Serial Set were used in most of the chapters, and several of the 128 volumes of *The War of the Re-*

bellion: A Compilation of the Official Records of the Union and Confederate Armies are invaluable in chapter 3, "Mules and the Civil War."

Important to this study were several general military histories. Erna Risch, *Quartermaster Support for the Army: A History of the Corps, 1775–1939* (1962) was used extensively and was most informative concerning interpretation, besides the additional facts that were forthcoming; also important were two volumes from the Army Historical Series, James A. Huston, *The Sinews of War: Army Logistics, 1775–1953* (1966) and *Army Military History* (1969), Maurice Matloff, general editor. Russell F. Weigley, *History of the United States Army* (1967) and *The American Way of War: A History of United States Strategy and Policy* (1973) and Edward M. Coffman, *The Old Army: A Portrait of the American Army in Peacetime, 1784–1898* (1986) were useful, although not always cited in notes.

Extremely important for basic understanding, and in some cases specific mention or discussion of mule use, were some of the histories of various wars, conflicts, and particular eras. Especially helpful in this study were Robert M. Utley, *Frontiersmen in Blue: The United States Army and the Indian, 1848–1865* (1967) and *Frontier Regulars: The United States Army and the Indian, 1866–1890* (1973). Donald E. Worcester, *The Apaches: Eagles of the Southwest* (1979) is also worthwhile, for it not only narrates the story of U.S. Army Apache scouts and their use of packtrains but is one of the few contemporary volumes to discuss in an understandable manner the art of the Mexican method of packing. Also significant were John K. Mahon, *History of the Second Seminole War, 1835–1842* (1967), K. Jack Bauer, *The Mexican War, 1846–1848* (1974), James M. McCaffrey, *Army of Manifest Destiny: The American Soldier in the Mexican War, 1846–1848* (1992), Leo E. Oliva, *Soldier on the Santa Fe Trail* (1967), William Y. Chalfant, *Dangerous Passage: The Santa Fe Trail and the Mexican War* (1994), and Clarence C. Clendenen, *Blood on the Border: The United States Army and the Mexican Irregulars* (1969).

Not surprisingly, specific references to army mules were found in a bewildering variety of articles. Few military historians and authors took time to examine the matter of mule logistics in any detail. Therefore, in many primary and secondary narratives and articles where mule facts should be found, few, if any, references to mules appeared. In other works, where one would expect only a mention of the subject, material relating to mules, or at least meaningful leads to other sources, were found in abundance, making this writer appreciate those authors who were curious about the cantankerous but dependable mule.

In the introduction, the most important source for the desirable attributes sought in army mules was found in H. W. Daly, *Manual of Pack Transportation* (1917). Chief packmaster Daly had served as a civilian packer with the army for thirty years and recorded a wealth of material on mules and packing. This volume and *Manual of Instruction in Pack Transportation*, published in 1901 for West Point cadets, were essential to an understanding of the packing fraternity's concise demands for excellent mules and packs. Daly's manuals contributed to most of the chapters. Anna M. Waller's pamphlet *Horses and Mules and National Defense* also contained valuable resource material.

Several other publications in understanding and appreciating the attributes of mules were important as well. Among them were Robert Bryon Lamb, *The Mule in Southern Agriculture* (1963), James W. Steele's chapter "Army Mules" in *Frontier Army Sketches* (1883), W. B. Tegetmier and C. L. Sutherland's informative *Horses, Asses, Zebras, Mules, and Mule Breeding* (1895), and the classic but repetitious treatise *The Mule* by Harvey Wiley. The best contemporary accounts are Lorraine Travis, *The Mule* (1990) and Theodore H. Savory, *The Mule: A Historic Hybrid* (1979). I also relied on three of my earlier studies, "Army Mule" in *Montana* (1994), "mule" in *The Readers' Encyclopedia of the American West* (1977), and although not cited in footnotes in this chapter, "Mules, Packs, and Packtrains," *Southwestern Historical Quarterly* (1970).

In chapter 1, "Army Mule Power in Florida and Mexico," significant primary material was used. *The Personal Memoirs of U. S. Grant*, volume 1 (1885); *Chronicles of the Gringos: The U.S. Army in the Mexican War, 1846–1848, Accounts of Eyewitnesses and Combatants* (1968), edited by George Winston Smith and Charles Judah; Philip Syng Physick Conner, *The Home Squadron under Commodore Conner in the War with Mexico, Being a Synopsis of*

Its Services (With an Addendum Containing Admiral Temple's Memoir of the Landing of Our Army at Vera Cruz in 1847) (1896); volume 2 of *The Diary of James K. Polk During His Presidency* (1910), edited by Milo Milton Quaife; and Samuel E. Chamberlain, *My Confession* (1956) all contained valuable mule logistical information and instructive accounts of the use of mules.

Several other works were useful. Lloyd Lewis' biography of U. S. Grant before the Civil War, *Captain Sam Grant* (1950) provided valuable insights into Grant's understanding of animals, while Dwight L. Clarke's *Stephen Watts Kearny: Soldier of the West* provided a glimpse of the Army of the West's use of mules. A significant article by Floyd F. Ewing Jr., "The Mule as a Factor in the Development of the Southwest," in *Arizona and the West* (1963) provided resource materials for this and other chapters.

In "Mule Power in the Army 1848–1861," I relied on an additional number of meaningful primary and secondary resources. Percival G. Lowe, *Five Years a Dragoon ('49 to '54) and Other Adventures on the Great Plains* (1965), described wagon and packtrains as only an actual participant on expeditions could have. William Y. Chalfant, *Cheyennes and Horse Soldiers: The 1857 Expedition and Battle of Solomon's Fork* (1989), and Odie B. Faulk, *The U.S. Camel Corps: An Army Experiment* (1976) not only had excellent accounts of specific subjects but also much primary source material. Also helpful was *Uncle Sam's Camels: The Journals of May Humphreys Stacey Supplemented by the Report of Edward Fitzgerald Beale (1857–1858)* (1929), edited by Lewis Burt Lesley. *General George Crook: His Autobiography,* edited by Martin F. Schmitt was indispensable for this chapter as well as chapters on the Civil War and on pack and wagon mules in the West.

By far the best accounts of the Mormon expedition were found in Norman E. Furness, *The Mormon Conflict: 1850–1859* (1960), and Howard Roberts Lamar, *The Far Southwest, 1846–1912: A Territorial History* (1966). Significant information came from William G. Hartley, *My Best for the Kingdom: History and Autobiography of John Lowe Butler, a Mormon Frontiersman* (1993); Thomas G. Alexander and Leonard J. Arrington, "Camp in the Sagebrush: Camp Floyd, Utah 1858–1861," *Utah Historical Quarterly* (winter 1966); Eugene Bandel, *Frontier Life in the Army, 1854–1861,* edited by

Ralph P. Bieber (1932); Averam B. Bender, *The March of Empire: Frontier Defense in the Southwest, 1848–1860* (1952); and LeRoy R. Hafen and Ann W. Hafen, eds., *The Utah Expedition, 1857–1858* (1982).

In addition to the Official Records and archival material, a number of books were used as resources in the chapter, "Mules and the Civil War." By far the most comprehensive volume was the well written account by Edward Hagerman, *The American Civil War and the Origins of Modern Warfare: Ideas, Organization, and Field Command* (1988). Hagerman's understanding of logistical support is extraordinary and his research flawless. Also helpful were Russell F. Weigley's *Quartermaster General of the Army: A Biography of M. C. Meigs* (1959) and *The Atlas of the Civil War* (1994), edited by James M. McPherson. Charles Leib, *Nine Months in the Quartermaster's Department, or the Chances of Making a Million* (1862) and John D. Billings, *Hard Tack and Coffee, or the Unwritten Story of Army Life* (1887) contained worthwhile information as well.

In addition to the materials already mentioned, other works for the chapter, "Mules in the West and Efficient Pack Mules for the Army," were valuable. It would be difficult to write about mules and George Crook without using John G. Bourke, *On The Border with Crook* (1891) and *The Conquest of Apacheria* (1967) by Dan L. Thrapp, who had served as a mule packer during World War II and used his pack knowledge wisely. Equally important was Thomas Cruse's *Apache Days and After* (1941). Cruse's almost intimate contact with mules throughout his army career made the contents for this book important in this chapter as well as chapter 6. Anton Mazzanovich's accounts in *Trailing Geronimo* (1931) were important since he served both as a trooper and a packer. H. W. Lawton, *Instructions for Using Moore's Improved Pack Saddle* (1881) and Thomas Moore, *Instructions for Using the Aparejo or Spanish Pack Saddle* (1878) were essential for understanding portions of Daly's 1917 manual.

Although there are many references to Custer's Little Bighorn battle, the most important source for this study was the excellent article "Packs, Packers, and Pack Details: Logistics and Custer's Pack Train" by Richard G. Hardorff in *Custer and His Times: Book Three* (1987), edited by J. W. Urwin. Hardorff's analysis was essential for an understanding of how pack mules were mistreated and misused. Another useful article was John Gray, "The Pack Train on George A. Custer's Last Campaign," *Nebraska History* (1976). Also significant were the following volumes: John F. Finerty, *War–Path and Bivouac: The Big Horn and Yellowstone Expedition, or the Conquest of the Sioux* (1890); Kenneth Hammer, *Custer in '76: Walter Camp's Notes on the Custer Fight* (1976); Robert M. Utley, *Cavalier in Buckskin: George Armstrong Custer and the Western Military Frontier* (1988); *The Custer Reader* (1992), edited by Paul Hutton; W. A. Graham, *The Custer Myth: A Source Book of Custeriana* (1953), and *The Benteen-Golden Letters on Custer and His Last Battle* (1974), edited by John M. Carroll.

For chapter 6, "Army Mules near Home and Abroad, 1898–1917," significant material was found in a number of books and articles not already mentioned. For the Spanish-American War Frank B. Freidel, *The Splendid Little War* (1958); Virgil Carrington Jones, *Roosevelt's Rough Riders* (1971); and Robert Wooster, *Nelson A. Miles and the Twilight of the Frontier Army* (1993) were noteworthy. Interesting sources for use of mules in the Philippines were found in A. R. Ginsburgh, "The Rise and Fall of the Two Nine Five," *Field Artillery Journal* (1932); Michael F. Parrino, *An Introduction to Pack Transportation and Pack Artillery* (1956); and Frank E. Vandiver, *Black Jack: The Life and Times of John J. Pershing* (1977). For use of mules in the Philippines as well as in China, Monro MacCloskey, *Reilly's Battery: A Story of the Boxer Rebellion* (1969), was a splendid source containing valuable materials from MacCloskey's father, Gen. Manus McCloskey, who had begun his distinguished career in Reilly's Battery during the rebellion in China. An entertaining and informative volume on the U. S. Army's presence in Mexico was Frank Tompkins, *Chasing Villa: The Story behind the Story of Pershing's Expedition into Mexico* (1934). Tomkins had been one of the first troopers entering Mexico to chase Francisco Villa. Volume one of Melvin Bradley *The Missouri Mule: His Origins and Times* (1993) was a necessary source for the international mule trade and as a reference for army mules in World War I.

Significant sources for chapter 7, "Army Mules from World War I to World War II," came from several books and articles. Informative newspaper and magazine articles specifically about mules were

"Tennessee Mules for Use in British Army," *Nashville Tennessean and Nashville American* (13 September 1915); the widely circulated "Army Mule on European Battlefields," (3 March 1917); "Though Awarded No D. S. C. the Mule Has a Fine War Record," *The Literary Digest* (17 May 1919); and "Army Mule a Help in Time of Trouble," *The Literary Digest* (19 June 1920). Other helpful volumes included Lucien K. Truscott Jr., *The Twilight of the U.S. Cavalry: Life in the Old Army, 1917–1942* (1989); *History of the Great War Based on Official Documents: Veterinary Services* (1925), edited by L. J. Blenkinsop and J. W. Rainey; J. Clabby, *The History of the Royal Army Veterinary Corps, 1916–1961* (1963), and John J. Pershing's two-volume work *My Experiences in the World War* (1931).

Most valuable for "Mules in World War II," chapter 8, were interviews with various participants in theaters of war where mules were used. Many of these interviews were included in Melvin Bradley, *The Missouri Mule: His Origin and Times*, volume 2. Emeritus professor of animal husbandry at the University of Missouri, Bradley spent years interviewing men about their mules. He also provided me with manuscripts of interviews of men who served in the army during the war. I have also personally interviewed a number of the same participants. Bradley's second volume was invaluable for insights on the use and care of mules.

Also important were some of the volumes of the official U.S. Army in World War II series. The ones I used were: Erna Risch and Chester L. Kieffer, *The Quartermaster Corps: Organization, Supply, and Services*, volume 2 (1955); William F. Ross and Charles F. Romanus, *The Quartermaster Corps: Operations in the War against Germany* (1965); Albert N. Garland, *The Mediterranean Theater of Operations: Sicily and the Surrender of Italy* (1965); and John E. Miller Jr., *Guadalcanal: The First Offensive* (1949). Several other books were also helpful. Edora Ramsay Richardson and Sherman Allan, *Quartermaster Supply in the Fifth Army in World War II* (1950); and *Ernie's War: The Best of Ernie Pyle's World War II Dispatches* (1986), edited by David Nichols, both contained excellent accounts of mules in service. Meaningful accounts with significant mule materials in the CBI theater were found in the following books: David Haley, *With Wingate in Burma* (1945); Leonard Mosley, *Gideon Goes to War* (1955); Bernard Fergusson, *Beyond the*

Chindwin (1945); Charles J. Rolo, *Wingate's Raiders* (1944); John Masters, *The Road Past Mandalay* (1961); Terence O'Brien, *Out of the Blue: A Pilot with the Chindits* (1989); Charlton Ogburn, *The Marauders* (1959); Anonymous, *Merrill's Marauders* (1945); John Randolph, *Marsmen in Burma* (1946); Charles N. Hunter, *Galahad* (1963); and Shelford Bidwell, *The Chindit War, Stilwell, Wingate, and the Campaign in Burma: 1944* (1979). Three especially useful articles were Ralph W. Mori, "Flying Mules over the Burma Hump," *The Cavalry Journal* 49 (1945); a three-part series by Dan L. Thrapp, "The Mules from Mars," *Armored Cavalry Journal* (1 November 1945–47), and John A. Rand, "Nine Hundred Mules," *The New Yorker* (24 November 1954).

Index